Dedicated to Liam E. Robinson
1968-2003

CONTENTS

Preface

The title of the book came from a magazine article written several years ago which described our Village as being in a "Time Warp" and continued ..."Whilst the world has undergone momentous changes in the last 100 years the casual visitor will be hard pressed to notice them in the village of Tockholes as its shape and character have changed remarkably little during the century. It is a village of grand Elizabethan farmhouses and Victorian properties, often tucked away in the most surprising places, with many hidden architectural gems. The Village has always seemed slightly detached from the rest of the world. Indeed it is sometimes physically cut off in winter by snow drifts. But its raw beauty and unspoilt moors continue to exert a strong pulling power as thousands of people come every year to walk round the area. As for the villagers themselves they like the place just the way it is - even though they may lack the odd modern convenience like gas, but that is a small price to pay for living in such an idyllic rural retreat". And I have to agree with the writer on every point, although, of course, our predecessors would marvel at the 'unseen' advantages of modern living such as piped water, sewage disposal, central heating, kitchens and bathrooms - not to mention the luxury of being able to afford such conveniences.

In November 1978 an Exhibition of photographs, maps, news cuttings and documents relating to the Village was displayed in the Village Hall. The day turned out to be one of the wildest and wettest I can remember, with rain lashing against the building all day, and it was a battle against the wind just stay on one's feet, but that did not deter people from turning out to visit the Exhibition. As I recollect almost everyone in the Village called in at some time - so great was the interest. Many old photographs came to light and as a result it was decided a record should be kept and many of them were copied. So began the "Village Archives"! This sounds very grand but as there is nowhere to keep a permanent display the photographs are merely held in a folder and rarely seen. Now I hope everyone will have the opportunity to own a record of some of the images, colourfully descriptive newspaper reports, maps, plans and information collected over the years and so help preserve a little of the history of our Village.

And that is what this book is intended to be - merely a collection of information accumulated over the past 25 years. I have no doubt there is much more yet to be told, and who knows - there may be enough for another book! Many of the stories have been recounted previously but have been included to give an accurate account of what is known about our Village.

All the photographs in the book are from the Village Hall Collection, from the Blackburn and Darwen Public Libraries and from family albums of past and present villagers.

Finally, grateful thanks to the staff at Blackburn Library for their assistance with this project, United Utilities for allowing me access to their deeds of the area and permission to reproduce various maps from the deeds, and also to all those who have proof read and given further information and photographs relating to various properties.

Judith Jacklin
September 2003

Extract from Greenwood's Map of 1818

Extract from the Yates Map of 1786

TO TOCKHOLES

By

Mrs. Alice Cross

There is a place I love so well,
The Village of my birth,
I proudly boast this is my toast
"Dear Tockholes on the Moor".

So think a while and let us turn
Pages of history.
How fate decreed a Spartan Creed
At Tockholes on the Moor.

In Morris Brow, so we are told,
A preaching Cross once stood,
And pilgrims trod to worship God
At Tockholes on the Moor.

Long centuries a Mother Church
The faithful here has served.
The journey made for spiritual aid
To Tockholes on the Moor.

And some there were would not conform
In Charles the Second's reign
To Clarendon pact and Five Mile Act
At Tockholes on the Moor

The Chapel stands this fact to prove
In Sixteen Sixty Two
They won the fight to think aright
At Tockholes on the Moor

In cottages we know today
The hand loom weaver toiled.
His craft he plied and trade supplied
To Tockholes on the Moor

In Manor house and homestead proud
The yeoman farmer dwelt.
His works still live and place names give
To Tockholes on the Moor.

Look back with pride, look on with faith,
The future's bright and clear.
And never rest, give of your best
To Tockholes on the Moor.

Alice Cross was married to Jack Cross, owner of the Garage for many years, and was the daughter of Harry Crompton, sexton at St. Stephen's for over 36 years. The poem was written for a Women's Institute competition.

CHAPTER 1

LISTED FARMHOUSES & MONUMENTS

Tockholes covers about 2000 acres and is made up of a series of hamlets. The majority of these hamlets contain a farmhouse with outbuildings, nearby cottages at least 200 years old and, in most cases, a 17th century 'gentleman's residence/farm', all built from stone. It is possible the residences were built for younger sons of the gentry and modelled to a smaller scale on the family manor house, for example, Higher Whitehalgh Farm, built by the Liveseys, of Livesey Old Hall, for a younger son, Thomas. Many of the original owners are known to have owned property in Tockholes long before the farms were built and it is thought that old, wooden houses were replaced by the more permanent stone buildings we see today. The residents were probably men of independent means or had other occupations, as it is difficult to believe they would have made a living from farming alone, the land being considered too poor for profitable agriculture. Some, like Ralph Richardson of Silk Hall, are known to have styled themselves as manufacturers of silk or cotton and rented out their land, farms and cottages to tenant farmers.

Other smaller farms in the area were built with attached shippons, barns and outhouses, but possessed only a small acreage of land and the occupants usually supplemented their earnings by weaving, quarrying, coal mining, joinery or some other craft. A few cottages became alehouses and some became shops selling provisions for both human and animal consumption.

Many buildings in the Village have been listed as being of "Special Architectural or Historic Interest" by the Secretary of State for the Environment. Originally there were three categories:-

1. Grade I – these are buildings of exceptional interest

2. Grade II – buildings of special interest which warrant every effort being made to preserve them (those of particular importance in this category being listed as Grade II*)

3. Grade III – This did not form part of the Statutory List.

In 1984 the Department of the Environment revised its listings and many of the Grade III Listed buildings either qualified for selection if they possessed group value or they lost their listing altogether. The Grade II* are Higher Hill Farmhouse, The Old 'Manor' House Lower Hill, Ryal Farm and also Higher Whitehalgh, which has recently been incorporated into the Parish of Tockholes.

The remaining properties listed Grade II are the Lych Gate at St. Stephens Church; the Old School with external pulpit in the church yard; the nearby Sun Dial; Chapels Farmhouse; a barn near the farmhouse (now divided into two dwellings Chapels Barn Farm and Barndene); Lodge Farmhouse and integral barn; Lower Crow Trees Farmhouse; a barn near Lower Crow Trees (now a dwellinghouse); Higher Crow Trees Farmhouse; a barn near Higher Crow Trees; Higher Hill barns, north and west of the house; Manor House; two barns near Lower Hill farmhouse (now dwellings); Higher Red Lee farmhouse; a barn nearby; Red Lee farmhouse and adjoining shippons; Ryal Farm and barn; Silk Hall Manse and Farmhouse; Fine Peter's farmhouse and the Wishing Well in the corner of the former Hollinshead Hall grounds.

CHAPELS FARMHOUSE: is 17th Century. The chimney on the ridge in the centre is over what was originally the left gable. There are also two further chimneys at each end of the property. The left hand extension is thought to have been added at the end in 18th Century.

A modern porch now covers the front door and to the right are 2 chamfered mullioned windows on each floor to the right of the door. At the rear is a 2 storey late 18th Century extension, once used as a dairy. The interior has been extensively altered and now incorporates the dairy as living accommodation.

CHAPELS BARN: Early 18th Century. There is a later lean-to addition at the front of the property. The front wagon entrance is still visible and the right return wall has an owl hole with perching stone in the apex of the gable (now filled in). Converted to two dwellings in 1986, Barndene and Chapels Farm Barn.

Chapels Farm c 1978

Chapels Farm 2002

Chapels Barn c. 1985

Chapels Barn & Barndene 2002

Lodge Farm c. 1978

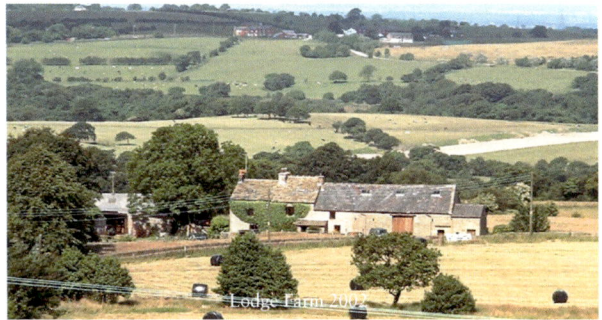
Lodge Farm 2002

LODGE FARMHOUSE has an integral barn and is C17th with C18th and C19th additions to the living accommodation at the left hand side of the row. The roof is on 3 slightly different levels and is of slate and stone slate, with 3 chimney stacks. There is now a modern lean-to porch covering the original doorway and window. The barn continues to the right hand side and has small breather openings. At the right end of the barn is a doorway with very large jambstones and lintel and a straight dripstone above. In the rear wall of the barn is an opposed similar doorway to the wagon entrance at the front of the building. There is also a lower building attached to the barn. It is now listed as a rare example of a very simple type of laithe house.

Many of the original oak roof trusses remain in the barn and massive oak supports/stall dividers (boskins) in the shippon. The interior of the house was almost totally reconstructed during the C20th, but several original beams and one lath and plaster wall remain in the central section. The ceiling of the section built inside the barn is made with split oak pieces laid across beams and infilled with plaster. The blocked wagon door at the front of the building was re-opened in 2002.

Lower Crow Trees c 1978

LOWER CROW TREES FARMHOUSE is a C17th building with slate roof and chimneys at each gable. The plan is L-shaped with projecting gabled wing to the front. All windows in the front wall have chamfered surrounds and hollow-moulded mullions. Left, right and rear walls have various altered openings. The Interior has been greatly altered.

Folklore states it was an old Coaching House on the main road to Preston. This road ran in front of the house and forked a few yards below the building, one branch leading to Red Lee and one branch to Stockclough Lane via Higher Whitehalgh, another

Lower Crow Trees 2003

7

known Coaching Inn. Yates map of 1786 suggests the latter branch was the more important. From Stockclough Lane the route continued over the River Roddlesworth at Feniscowles Bridge on to Preston Old Road. Remains of the road to Higher Whitehalgh can still be seen in the wooded area just below Lower Crow Trees, where there is track of large flat, grooved stones, the grooves probably having been made by coach wheels. A third route, now a footpath, led from Lower Crow Trees to Shaws Farm, Bradleys Farm and then to Stanworth, and would have been the most direct route to Preston, but the river crossing looks as though it would have been impossible for wheeled vehicles, bearing in mind the Roddlesworth Reservoirs now contain much of the water that would previously have flowed quickly along this course.

The interior of the house was extensively altered in the 1970's. Prior to that time it is understood the whole of the upstairs was one large room and downstairs there were three rooms, one of which contained a huge stone oven and a copper for boiling water. The land above the house was used as a vegetable garden and an orchard and the outside toilets were situated below the house. The water supply for the house and the barns opposite was piped from a well in the cellar of Higher Crow Trees, behind the barns and into the stone trough in the farmyard. The house has recently been renovated again and many interior features restored.

Lower Crow Trees Barn 2003

Higher Crow Trees Barn 2003

LOWER CROW TREES BARN was converted to a dwelling in 1990. It is situated 50 metres South of Lower Crow Trees Farmhouse and is dated 1671. The wagon entrance has now been utilised as a porch over the front door. The date stone in moulded surrounded and lettered in relief is inscribed "W.M. 1671". Adjoining this property is the barn belonging to Higher Crow Trees Farmhouse.

HIGHER CROW TREES BARN is situated 30 metres west of Higher Crow Trees Farmhouse and is late C17th with stone slate roof.

HIGHER CROW TREES FARMHOUSE is a C17th building with a slate roof (slightly higher at the left end), and gable chimneys. The left hand section, which projects slightly, is said to have been a shippon and has the large lintel of the former doorway and modern windows. The right hand side has been reduced to a single story lean-to and has an old chamfered doorway with hoodmould, a round-headed lancet window and to the right of this is lettered "I" "M" . There is also an inserted window above the door. The interior has been altered.

Higher Crow Trees c. 1978

The 1851 Census shows this property as being two houses, one of which was uninhabited. The oldest section of the present house is the right hand side of the building and in the downstairs right hand side room was an imposing ornate doorway (now plastered over) which would have led into another living area, the foundations of which are under the present yard area. The house is believed to have been a Toll House. Inside what is now the lounge is a wooden, sliding door at window height. This door must have fitted when the wall was built as the wooden panel actually slides in the cavity of the wall and is therefore of the same age. this could have been the toll booth.

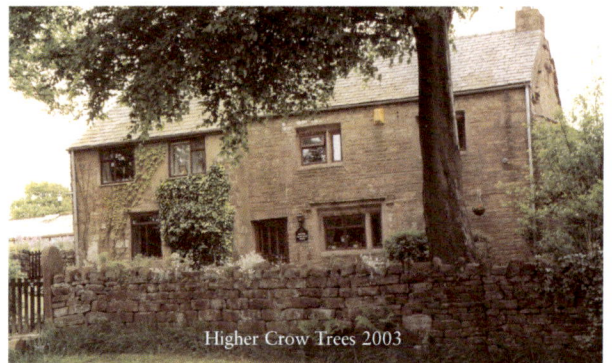

Higher Crow Trees 2003

8

Ryal Barn c. 1970

Plaque in Bedroom

RYAL FARMHOUSE: This has been a house of some importance judging from the imposing architecture and being in the style of a manor house. It is a large 17th Century farmhouse with some additions probably in the late C18th. The roof is tiled and has gable copings and kneelers, one main double chimney stack and a smaller one behind the ridge. On the North East elevation there is a projecting two and a half storey porch with kneelers and a moulded round-headed doorway enclosed by a hood-mould. On the second floor of the porch is a recessed mullioned window of three rounded-headed lights and a hoodmould and above this is a one light window, with arched head, now filled in. All walls have original double-chamfered stone mullion windows with hoodmoulds, and all are mostly unaltered. There is also an outshut to the left of the porch which has the remains of flush-mullioned multiple lights and may have been a loomshop.

The Interior has large chamfered beams with tongue stops and over a former doorway in the West wall of the living room is a moulded plaster plaque lettered I^{W}E 1676. The plaque is thought to commemorate the marriage of John and Elizabeth Walmsley. In the parlour is a stone fireplace with moulded Tudor-arched surround; and off the parlour, enclosed by timber framing, is a stone staircase which has 1/4 turns to left and right. In the chamber over the parlour is a stone fireplace with an elaborate but crudely moulded plaster chimney piece depicting two reclining figures, thought to depict two angels or two mermaids and containing the letter 'W' in a central scroll.

One interesting theory regarding the origin of the name 'Ryal' was given by George C. Millar in a Blackburn Times article. He suggested that "Ryal probably dated from the accession of James I, 1603, the Scottish Monarch who first introduced into this Country a gold coin called a Ryal. It is fascinating to speculate how the coin and the farm came to be associated, probably the farmer was included in the Deed of Tenure, but the fact will always be a mystery."

The Ryal estate was bought by William Walmsley, father of John, in 1660, and the house closely resembles Higher Hill Farmhouse, the home of John's brother Ralph. The Walmsley family who built this house is a branch of the Walmsley family who built the Dunkenhalgh near Accrington. The bricked up windows could have been closed due to the window tax of 1689.

Adjoining the farm on the West side is a small cottage, long since used as a dwelling, but which still contains the remains of a fireplace in the bedroom. A further C17th. building stands to the south of the farmhouse and is known as Ryal Cottage.

All the buildings in this area, including mid 19th Century Hollinshead Terrace, Ryal's Cottages and Garstang Terrace, are constructed of local stone from nearby quarries.

The **Barn** to the West of Ryal Farmhouse is dated 1771. and has a corrugated sheet roof, with kneelers to former gable copings which are now missing. There is a wagon entrance to the centre and left of this are 3 windows at ground floor. To the right is a doorway with a large lintel above and over the lintel is a date stone with incised lettering J & S 1771. The left end wall has 3 doorways, all altered.

Ryal Barn 2003

9

Higher Hill Farm c. 1915

Higher Hill Farm and Barns c. 1915

HIGHER HILL FARMHOUSE: is C17th with some C19th alterations. It has a stone slate roof with gable copings and kneelers, one chimney on the right, a smaller chimney behind the ridge, and a third one at the front left corner. There is a projecting wing to the front of the house and a projecting porch also at the front. There is a two storey outshut to rear.

Some windows have been replaced with C19th sashes, but there are original windows, mostly with hollow-moulded mullions, chamfered surrounds, and hoodmoulds, in all walls. In the rear wall is a king-mullioned window. The princi-pal external features of interest are a complete garderobe at 1st floor level on the left hand return wall, and a stone at 1st floor level of the right gablewall lettered "RW" (= Ralph Walmsley).

Garderobe

Higher Hill c. 1975

Inside the parlour is a Tudor stone fireplace with chamfered surround, and in the adjoining room is a stone staircase which has ¼ turns to left and to right, the left turn passing the restored single-seat garderobe.

This was the home of the Walmsleys, yeomen, who bought the Ryal estate in 1660. The house is very similar to Ryal Farmhouse.

FIRST BARN at Higher Hill is about 20 metres north of the Farmhouse. It is probably C17th, subsequently extended, with a stone slate roof and gable copings. There is a lofted addition at the left end and breathers in 2 levels. The original doorway had a large rectangular lintel, now blocked, and opposed wagon entrances with canopies. The addition at the left end has a doorway, with a horizontal rectangular window to the left of it and a square opening above. The roof is a collar-truss construction.

SECOND BARN is about 20 metres west of the Farmhouse and is probably late C17th with some later additions to the front. The roof is stone slated with gable coping. The building has a wagon entrance and an altered doorway at the left hand end.

Wedding party outside Higher Hill Farm circa 1899 Front row left to right Phoebe Mares, Ellen Mares holding baby Richard Mares, Groom William Leigh, Bride Lilly Mares; Unknown lady; William's Brother; Mr. Mares Snr.; Jane Hannah Mares; Elizabeth Mares; Richard Mares 2nd row left Mary Mares married Mr. Moss who is standing behind her. 5th left Lucy Mares, 6th left Jane Mares (nee Ainsworth) wife of Richard Mares. (Richard Mares was a Parish Councillor for 17 years and he and his wife Jane appear on the inset below right)

Mr & Mrs Mares
parents of Richard Mares

Richard & Jane Mares

To be Sold by Auction

(pursuant to certain deeds executed by Walmsley Richardson, of Tockholes in the county of Lancaster for the payment of his Debts).

At the house of Mr. James Barlow, the sign of the Dun Horse, in Blackburn on Monday the 20th day of August, 1770, at Four o'clock in the afternoon, according to terms to be produced at the Time of Sale.

ALL that Freehold Messuage and Tenement, with the Appurtenances called the Hill House, in Tockholes, and the Closes of Land thereunto belonging, containing by estimate 47 acres of land of the measure there used, being lately the inheritance of the said Walmsley Richardson, and in the possession as well of him, the said Walmsley Richardson, as of Adam Richardson his Father or their Tenants.

N.B. There is a Rookery upon the Premises, and the Buildings are extraordinarily good. And a Quantity of old and young Timber growing upon the said Estate.

Also to be sold, at the same Time and Place, the Life Estate, late of the said Walmsley Richardson, of and in all that other Messuage and Tenement with the Appurtenances, called the Lower Hill House, or the Lower House Lands, in Tockholes, and the closes of Land thereunto belonging containing by estimation fifty two Acres of land of the measure there used, in the possession of the said Walmsley Richardson and his Tenants. Upon which said Estate there is a very good Tan Yard lately fixed with all proper conveniences, and now occupied as such by the said Walmsley Richardson.

The said Adam Richardson and Walmsley Richardson will shew the premises, and further particulars may be had of Mr. Banister Pickup, of Livesey, and of Mr. Peter Nevill, of Blackburn, the Trustees named and appointed in the said Deeds executed by the said Walmsley Richardson.

And the said Banister Pickup and Peter Nevill do hereby and in the Pursuance of the said deeds give notice to such of the Creditors of the said Walmsley Richardson whose Debts have not yet been ascertained and made out to them, that if the same be not respectively done within the space of three Months now next coming, they will be excluded any benefit by virtue of the said deeds.

And all persons indebted to the Estate of the said Walmsley Richardson are desired to pay their respective Debts to the said Banister Pickup and Peter Nevill, or one of them, otherwise they will be sued for the same without further Notice.

The Manchester Mercury July 24th 1770

RALPH WALMSLEY'S BIBLE, PRINTED IN 1631

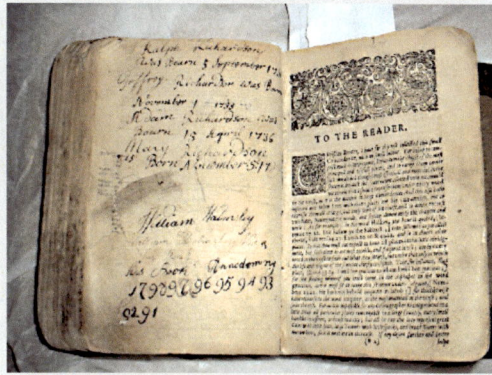

A short time ago "The Blackburn Times" published an article dealing with the centenary of the present St. Stephen's Church, Tockholes, which was opened in 1833, and mention was made of a Ralph Walmsley, who provided the first endowment towards the support of the first resident minister at "Tockholes Chapel" in 1642. There was occasional celebration of divine service in the old pre 1833 edifice – which was supposed to date from the time of Henry VIII, as a Chapel-of-Ease – by the Vicar of Blackburn and his curates, but there was no regular ministry before the setting up of the Presbytery in Lancashire during the Commonwealth era. The deed of conveyance is dated December 28 1649 and consisted of a parcel of land in Tockholes "upon a certaine place called Chappell Greene," along with "one messuage, cottage or dwelling-house thereupon erected," and was conveyed in trust "to the use and behoof of such a Preachinge Minister or Ministers as shall be resident at Tockholes Chappell from tyme to tyme."

The Walmsleys were staunch Presbyterians and were influential yeomen in Livesey and Tockholes, the family residence being at the fine old Manor House at The Hill, Tockholes, now owned by the Liverpool Corporation.

Today, through the kindness of J. Critchley, of Tithebarn Cottage, Livesey, we are able to give a photograph and historical data of the family Bible of the Ralph Walmsley above named, which bears his signature, and also that of other members of his family, one of whom, Ralph Walmsley, was a Governor of Blackburn Grammar School in 1675. The original owner of the book died in 1665 – a centenarian – and a slab in the burial ground of the Blackburn Cathedral reads: "Here lyeth the body of Ralph Walmsley, who died the [20] day of November 16[65] circiter centum."

The Bible, which has never been out of Tockholes Church parish, came into the possession of the Richardson family, through marriage, nearly 200 years ago, and has been in the family ever since, the present owner being Mrs. James Critchley, who is the only child of the late William Worsley Richardson, of Tockholes and Livesey. The Richardsons have been landowners in the district for over 300 years, and at one time their farms extended from the present Silk Hall property to the township of Withnell at Red Lea. Adam Richardson was a trustee of the Old Independent Chape in 1735, and one of his sons, Ralph, was a prominent silk manufacturer and built the present Silk Hall property, Tockholes, in 1764.

The Bible is in a good state of preservation, and was printed in London in 1631 by Robert Barker. Christopher Barker, father of Robert Barker, lived in St. Paul's Churchyard, London, and was printer to Queen Elizabeth. The "Bishops" and "Genevan" Bibles bear the insigne of Christopher and his son Robert. Robert lived in the reigns of James I and Charles I and paid £3,500 for the correction and translation of the Bible. He printed the first edition of our Authorised Version in 1611.

Mrs. Critchley is the possessor of another old family Bible which belonged to the Andertons of Walton-le-Dale and Brindle, and bears the printed date 1608.

Blackburn Times 5th August 1933.

Lower Hill (Manor House) c. 1920

MANOR HOUSE, LOWER HILL

This is a large farmhouse, probably early C17th, now divided into several dwellings. The roof is of stone slate and slate with gable copings and kneelers. There is a projecting porch at the middle of the main range and a crosswing at the right end, added to which is a recent extension. The house is a two storey building but the wing and porch are 2½ storeys. All original windows are recessed with chamfered surrounds and chamfered mullions, those at the front having hoodmoulds. There is a king-mullioned window at first floor level to the right of the porch. At the left end is a later workshop addition. The gabled porch has a large doorway offset to the right with moulded surround, large lintel and hoodmould, and a small window to the left of it, and a window to each of the first and second floors. The rear is now mostly concealed by a later lean-to out-shut which is built around a very large chimney stack and some original windows still remain. Inside in the main living room is a very large stone arched inglenook fireplace and two quarter-round moulded beams. There are two stone staircases and stone-flagged upper floors.

Lower Hill Barns 2003

Locally known as The Manor House, this property appears on the old maps as Lower Hill House and, after Higher Whitehalgh, is the oldest in the area. The earliest deed to the property is dated 1635. It was once the home of the de Richardson family, prominent land owners in this area, and subsequent generations of Richardsons are known to have had connections with various other properties in Tockholes and are mentioned

on several occasions throughout this book. A legend connected with this house claims that a lighted candle used to be placed in one of the back windows as a signal to the inhabitants of Hoghton Tower that a priest had arrived. During the 16th and 17th centuries Catholic priests travelled the Country administering communion and acts of worship in secret in private houses, always living in fear of the severe penal laws should they be discovered conducting such ceremonies.

BARNS near Manor House, Lower Hill have similar descriptions to those at Higher Hill. All but one are now converted to dwellings.

HIGHER RED LEE FARMHOUSE, now a residence only, has a stone slate roof with gable copings and kneelers and a chimney on the ridge. It is a 2½ storey house with a full height gabled porch, a lean-to out-shut to the rear and an offset doorway to the front right with moulded surround and moulded hoodmould. Above the front door is a square date stone lettered 'RAE 1674' (Richard and Elizabeth or Ellen Aspden). Inside the porch is a stone side bench, an inner doorway with a heavily studded door and a flight of dog-leg stone stairs to the upper floor. The interior contains an inglenook and the remains of an old wattle-and-daub smoke hood are visible in a cupboard. There is also a small firewindow and a recess for a saltcupboard. The fireplace is a chamfered stone parlour fireplace.

Higher Red Lee c. 1978

A R E 1674

In 1877 the house and lands were the property of Col. Feilden of Witton Park, and in 1886 were occupied by Isaac and Sarah Smith. *Nightingale* described the house as *"very remarkable. The entrance door is studded with pieces of iron, as are also some of the inner doors. On the outside, over the porch, is the inscription A.R.E. 1674 = Richard and Elizabeth Aspden. And on the wall inside is R.A. 1675 E.A., the latter being probably the time when it was finished. This house also has its ghost stories. The last tenant used to say that "boggarts" were often heard in the garrets. A small flag in the centre of the house is also pointed out on which it is said no one can ever churn, because it is bewitched. The true reason is much more likely to be the one given by the present tenants - that it is too narrow for any churn to stand upon."*

Abram's research of the Aspden family shows that a Robert Aspden of Red Lee was witness to a deed dated 1620 and that Richard Aspden of Tockholes, yeoman, was taxed to a Subsidy for lands in Tockholes in 1663. Richard also occurs as a Trustee in a deed of gift to Tockholes Chapel in 1670 and it was he who re-built the homestead in 1674. He married Elizabeth or Ellen Aspden and died in April 1679.

RED LEE BARNS: similar in description to previously mentioned barns with 3 bays and wagon entrance. The stable set back at the right end has a chamfered doorway at the inner angle and a window to the right of it. It is

Barns & Red Lee Farmhouse 2003

lofted. There is a continuous lean-to cowshed at a lower level to the rear. Both this barn and the shippon connected to Red Lee Farmhouse are currently in the course of renovation to dwellinghouses.

RED LEE FARMHOUSE is currently undergoing extensive renovation work and the following description relates to the house prior to commencement of the work:- The Farmhouse is probably early C17th. and has a stone slated roof with gable chimneys. It is a two storey dwelling and has a projecting first bay with the roof carried down over it. There is a plain doorway and two square windows. In the second bay is a four light double chamfered stone mullion window which was originally a five light window and over this is an unusually large hollow-moulded hoodmould. A similar five light window, without hoodmould, is at first floor level and also a small chamfered window above the doorway. To the right the lean-to shippon projects like the first bay and has remains of an old window (perhaps four or five lights) and an inserted door: perhaps formerly a right wing. The rear has an out-shut like a stair turret with the roof carried down over it and the remains of a two-light window to the left. Inside is a very large stone arched fireplace, now blocked and covered.

It is assumed that in view of the Aspden connections to Higher Red Lee that this Farmhouse must be the one once owned by the Hoghton family. Abram conjectures in his research of the Hoghton's of Red Lee that this is a family of lesser gentry, being a branch of the Hoghtons of Hoghton Tower. Richard Hoghton of Tockholes, gentleman, is thought to be the son of Gilbert Hoghton named in the military levy of 1574, who in turn was probably the Gilbert Hoghton mentioned in the Hoghton genealogy as being the natural son of Sir Richard Hoghton, Knt. who died in 1558.

In 1622 Richard Hoghton of Red Leigh, Gentleman, was entered as a foreign burgess on the Preston Guild Roll along with his sons Gilbert, William and Edward. Richard, Gilbert and William were also recorded on the Roll of 1602 but the address given at that time was simply 'Tockholes'. Branches of this family resided in Tockholes until the early part of the 19th Century.

SILK HALL: The house is now three dwellings. The front faces Long Lane to the south and the projecting porch is on this elevation. There are three storeys, the top floor originally being a warehouse/workshop, and later, meeting rooms, with an external entry in the gable wall at the rear.

The porch is also three-storeys and is gabled with gable coping and kneelers. It has a plain doorway with massive dressed jambs and lintel, the latter with a moulded panel inscribed RRS 1764. Most of the windows have been altered. The rear wall is rendered and has a round-headed stairlight. Outside, at the left gable, is a flight of stone steps giving access to the top floor. Inside, the Manse has the original staircase, original doors with fielded panels and the top floor workshop, originally entirely open, is now partitioned with the addition of a later staircase into it from the 1st floor of the house. The property was built by Ralph (and Susannah) Richardson[1] "for a residence and for the purpose of his business as a chapman in silks". In 1772 it was acquired by the Trustees of Tockholes Chapel and used as a Manse.

The Richardson family had long resided in Tockholes and were extensive landowners and manufacturers of silk. An Adam Richardson appears as a trustee of the Chapel in 1735 and his third son, also Adam, owned a carding engine at Shaw Brook. It was his second son, Ralph, who built the three-storey property, Silk Hall, as a house and warehouse in 1764. The 1851 Census reveals that several silk weavers still lived in the Hall and connecting cottages almost 100 years later, and that two other silk weavers resided at Lodge Farm and Engine Bottoms, presumably employed at the Silk Hall premises. This suggests that silk was actually woven on the premises as well as stored in

Silk Hall, Cottages & Sunday School c. 1910

the warehouse, but by 1861 they were all listed as cotton weavers. A reason for the change in fibres could have been due to the fact that cheaper imports from France had been allowed into England causing the industry to become unviable. Near to Silk Hall is Rose Cottage, the old dye house connected with Ralph Richardson's silk business. It was probably built at the same time as Silk Hall.

[1] *(Abram A History of Blackburn Town & Parish pp 701-2)*

13

AN ANCIENT HALL.

FARM LANDS COME UNDER THE HAMMER.

SILK HALL, TOCKHOLES.

The forthcoming sale by auction of Silk Hall Farm, Tockholes, immediately reminds one of the history attached to Silk Hall, which is now the property of the Trustees of the Tockholes Congregational Chapel. A description of Silk Hall is given later, but it would not be out of place to deal with a little of the history of Congregationalism at Tockholes. Born in a dark and trying age, the outcome of religious bigotry and intolerance and afterwards fiercely and persistently assailed by persecution, Tockholes Independency has always proved itself to be sturdy and strong. For more than a couple of centuries the stalwarts of Tockholes Congregationalism have been intimately associated with the outlying district and their record finds its beginning in the dark days of oppression and commands the admiration of all who were acquainted with the privations and hardships steadfastly endured by the zealous pioneers in the great cause of religious freedom. The prospect of fines and imprisonment should they be detected by the representatives of the law had no fears to them, and they gathered in secluded spots until the penal laws in ecclesiastical matters were suspended in 1672. Licenses to preach were immediately taken out by the Lancashire Nonconformists and those of Tockholes were amongst the number. The following is a copy of the license relating to Tockholes:—

"License to John Harvie to be a Pr. (Presbyterian) Teacher in a meeting house in Tockley (Tockholes) erected for that purpose in the Parish of Blackburn, Lancaster. 1 May '72. The meeting-house in Tockley (Tockholes) in the Parish of Blackburn, in Lancashire. Pr. (Presbyterian) meeting. 8 May, '72."

This early meeting house was probably only a temporary structure, but in 1710 the old chapel was erected, and the deed conveying the site for the chapel was dated April 1st, 1710, and was made between James Garsden, yeoman and Jennet Garsden, widow, of the one part and James Marsden, Robert Eatough and James Walmesley, all of Tockholes, yeoman of the other part. The consideration was three pounds for twenty square yards of land. This chapel was used for public worship until the 15th February, 1880, on which day the Rev. Albert Lee preached in the building for the last time, and on Saturday afternoon of the 8th May, of the same year, two memorial stones of the new chapel were laid and was opened for worship on September 9th, 1880. The present pastor is the Rev. David Critchley, who has ministered to his flock in the village for thirty-two years.

SILK HALL.

Silk Hall consists of three cottages, a large lecture room, a farm house, a manse and another cottage detached from the other block of buildings formerly called "Dye House," now Rose Cottage. The amount of land belonging to the farm is about eleven acres. In 1791 the rate for land and farm houses was threepence in the £ and cottages twopence. The property formerly belonged to the Richardson family, at one time extensive landowners and important silk merchants in the village. Ralph Richardson, the son of Adam Richardson, who appears as a trustee of the chapel in 1735, built for himself "Silk Hall." Over the doorway facing Long lane is a stone containing the following inscription:—"R.S.R., 1764—Ralph and Susannah Richardson." It was on the 20th August,

1772, that Silk Hall became the property of the Chapel Trustees and to illustrate this fact in full we cull the following from the Rev. Dr. Nightingale's "The two centuries and a half of Nonconformity in Tockholes.

"A more important endowment was that of a small landed estate in Mellor, near Blackburn. The bequest was made early in the 18th century, by, it is generally thought, some member of the Hoghton family. This property was afterwards exchanged for an estate in Tockholes. Mr. Abram's account of the matter, which will be more interesting than anything I can say upon it, I here give in full: "By an indenture," says he, "dated August 20th, 1772, the trustees conveyed in exchange to Mr. Wm. Higginbotham, of Manchester, 'all the several parcels of land, meadow and pasture, with the Messuages, barn, and other buildings lately erected,' etc., being 'parcel of a tenement called Little Areleys, in the Manor of Mellor,' and consisting of plots called 'The Two Old Areleys, the Further Marsh, the Nearer Marsh, the Further Field, and the Little Field,' with dwelling-house, barn, etc., containing, 'by estimate eleven acres of land of the measure there used.' The property in Tockholes secured in lieu had belonged to the Richardsons. By deed, dated Jan. 2nd, 1769, Ralph Richardson and others mortgaged to Mr. T. Waldegrave (then minister of the chapel), for £650 and interest at £4 10s. per annum, certain houses and 'four closes called Wall Bank, Hoghton Close,' etc., in Tockholes. Revd. Thos. Waldegrave, the mortgagee, gave, by indenture of 3rd April 1772, a lease to Thomas Bennett, of Derby, Wm. Higginbotham, and others, for possession of the same estate, described to be 'the newly-erected Messuage or dwelling-house commonly called or known by the name of Silk Hall,' with 'a cottage or dwelling-house thereto adjoining; also the newly-erected dwelling-house standing near the same, and the

CLOSES OR PARCELS

of land known as the Over Wallbank, Lower Wallbank, the two Hoghton closes,' etc. In the deed of exchange above mentioned, by which the property passed to the Trustees of Tockholes Chapel, the description is: 'All that Messuage or dwelling-house, cottages, closes, pieces or parcels of land' comprising the 'dwelling-house known by the name of Silk Hall, and the cottage or dwelling-house thereto adjoining, and those two newly-erected cottages or dwelling houses standing near the same, and the parcels of land thereto belonging, in Tockholes, named Hoghton Close and the Edge Barn, the Over Wallbank, Lower Wallbank, the two Hoghton Closes, formerly one close only, called Hoghton Close; containing in the whole by estimation six acres of land of the measure there used (customary measure). With this land was paid a 'sum of £85 to make an equality in the said exchange.' The estate has been extended somewhat by the addition of a portion of a subsequent enclosure of waste land."

Since the trustees obtained possession of it Silk Hall has been the minister's house. It is large and commodious, is beautifully situated and at a convenient distance from the chapel; whilst standing upon rising ground it commands on a clear day magnificent views of Tockholes Valley, with its fine woods, Hoghton Tower, Preston and the Ribble. The room above, used as a silk warehouse formerly, has long served a variety of purposes. It was originally divided into three rooms, the first being used for handloom weaving, the middle one for religious purposes and the back room as a day and night school. A ragged school, which exercised a most beneficient influence over the village, was for years kept there, but Silk Hall must be associated with the week-night and Sunday evening prayer meeting.

Darwen News 26 April 1924

Darwen News 26th April 1924

14

Silk Hall 2002

An important endowment to the Independent Chapel of a small landed estate in Mellor, Blackburn, generally thought to have been bequested by a member of the Houghton family in the early 18th Century, was later exchanged for the Silk Hall Estate in Tockholes. In the deed of exchange dated August 20th 1772 the property passed to the Trustees of the Chapel under the following description 'All that messuage or dwelling-house known by the name of Silk Hall, and the cottage or dwelling-house thereto adjoining, and those two newly-erected cottages or dwelling-houses standing near the same, and the parcels of land thereto belonging, in Tockholes, named Hoghton Close and the Edge Barn, the Over Wallbank, Lower Wallbank, the two Hoghton Closes, formerly one close only, called Hoghton Close; containing in the whole by estimation 6 acres of land...'. With this land was paid a sum of £85 to make an equality in the said exchange[2] . In 1886 Nightingale describes the estate as consisting of 3 cottages, a large lecture-room, a farmhouse, a manse and another cottage detached from the other block of buildings, formerly called "Dye House", now Rose Cottage. The amount of land belonging to the farm was 11 acres.

Rose Cottage 1978

Once in the hands of the trustees of the Chapel Silk Hall became the minister's house, but the room above, formerly used for a silk warehouse, has been used for a variety of purposes. Originally it was divided into three rooms, the first being used for handloom weaving, the middle one for religious purposes and the back room as a ragged school. In later years it was used for week-night and Sunday evening prayer meetings. In 1870 the place was re-roofed and the floors were replaced. The three upper rooms were made into a large lecture-room, fitted with new furniture, and used for Sunday evening meetings, tea parties and public meetings generally, and a small anteroom was used for week-night meetings. The cottages and land were rented out and the income was used for chapel expenses and to supplement the minister's stipend.

In the early 1920's owing to the heavy costs of keeping the Farm Building and the Cottages in repair and in view of the likelihood of heavy financial demands being made in the near future, the Trustees decided to sell the properties and in March 1924 a Public Auction took place when the Farm fetched £631. Rose Cottage was sold later by private treaty for £171 and the other three

Rose Cottage 2003

cottages were sold for £255. The Lecture Room was still used by the Liberal Club up until 1931, and a couple of the Ministers also lived in the house after the sale, presumably as tenants, but the house has long since been privately owned.

FINE PETER'S FARMHOUSE and attached barn is dated 1757. There are two parallel ridged roofs of stone slates, with gable copings and kneelers to the barn. It is an L-shaped plan with a rear extension. There is an unusual semi-circular projecting porch with Tuscan doorcase and above is a date stone inscribed "PME 1757. The rear wall incorporates a misshapen segmented head to an old wagon entrance and has various C19th windows and doors.

This house is supposed to be haunted. Apparently white figures and a ten-legged table have been seen to move about and two swords drawn across each other, once kept over the doorway, have also been seen to move. That was a report from over 100 years ago and we are assured by the present owners that they have never seen or heard anything remotely unusual!

Another legend attached to this house is that one occupant used to forge bank notes in the loft, which was at that time flagged. He was arrested in Preston in the act of passing a counterfeit note and only escaped the death penalty through the devotion of his brother, who,

Fine Peters 2002

[2] P.64 & 65 Two Centuries & a Half of Nonconformity in Tockholes by B. Nightingale

15

on hearing of the arrest made off with all haste to Tockholes to destroy the evidence. The story goes he ran his horse so hard that when he reached the Rock Inn he found he could outgo his horse! He therefore set off on foot to Fine Peters and disposed of the copper-plate engravings and printing machinery before the arrival of the parish constable, and so saved his brother from the hangman – but not from penal servitude.

A newspaper article of more recent times, by a local historian, takes the story further. He writes – "By accident I stumbled upon some confirmation of the local legend, when, in the Manchester Mercury for February 8th 1774 I found the following item:- A few days ago was committed to the House of Correction at Wakefield, Thomas Harrison and James Harrison, two sharpers, who pretended to be dealers in cotton manufactory at Blackburn. Thomas Harrison had on a dark coloured coat with metal buttons, a shabby surtout (i.e. frock coat) of a brick colour and said he came on the 7th January last from London and that he brought certain forged bills to his brother James Harrison, late of Tockholes near Blackburn. I think this lends credence to the legend and it is hardly likely that Tockholes would house two such sets of rogues."

The Barker family outside Higher Whitehalgh c. 1880

HIGHER WHITEHALGH farmhouse is early C17th. It has a projecting two-storey gabled porch with a finial at the apex and has a chamfered doorway offset to the left and a similar inner doorway. There is a small blocked opening to the right, above, a two-light first floor window with a hoodmould, and above this a date stone with moulded surround, lettered in relief 1616 T.L. G.M.R.S. The roof is of graded slate at the front and stone slate at the rear. There is a chimney on the ridge and one at the right gable. The left return wall has a blocked first floor doorway and the right return wall has a blocked first floor window, said to have been used for preaching. At the rear the principal features of interest are a garderobe chute and an original but altered single storey dairy. The property was a known 'Coaching Inn' on the main route to Preston. The large barns in this complex have high entrance doors which would allow access for coaches, and stabling.

A recent owner, who had lived there since childhood, recalled a flight of stone steps on the outside gable, leading to a pulpit, which his father eventually removed for safety reasons, the steps having become dangerous, but only the outline of a blocked window now remains. The house has also been known as "White Hough" and "White Oake". The word 'halgh' is the Anglo Saxon word meaning 'saint' or 'shrine' – hence 'White Saint' or 'White Shrine', so could this place have been used for religious purposes?

A branch of the Liveseys (of Livesey Hall) had a freehold at Whitehalgh in Livesey. Over the porch is a date stone inscribed 1616 and the initials T.L. and G.M.R.S., the first initials standing for 'Thomas Livesey', the other initials to some unknown connection of the builder of the house. Several generations of Liveseys lived at the house thereafter. A James Livesey of Whitehalgh died there in May 1658. His son Richard had a son, another James, who was baptised there on 14th September 1659 and also a son Thomas, and a daughter Christabel who died in 1689. A further Thomas Livesey of Whitehalgh had his son, Lawrence, baptised on 27th April 1794.[3]

OLD SCHOOL with external pulpit is built on land adjoining St. Stephen's Churchyard. The School, dated 1834 on the plaque beside door, is a very simple rectangular single-storey structure with a plain doorway offset to the left and one two-light window to the left of the door. At the right the only opening in an otherwise long, blind wall is an arched, raised doorway enclosed at the base by a stone pulpit on a pedestal. Above and to the right of the entrance is a square plaque inscribed "St. Stephen's School, Tockholes, was erected A.D. 1834 upon the Glebe Land by voluntary subscription, aided with a Grant of £150 from the National Society, London. Gilmour Robinson, Int."

Old School c. 1910

3 From Abram's History of Blackburn Town & Parish

The present building is what remains of a once much larger school. On the 1894 OS Map the school is shown as being over twice the size of that remaining today. The old photograph of the school (*below*) shows that the front wall is built several inches above the edge of the roof tiles, like a parapet. This is probably the capped-off remains of the demolished section. The outside pulpit was built from mullion windows rescued by the Rev. Ashley T. Corfield from the demolition of Gerstain Hall and replaced an old wooden pulpit, purchased from Mellor Church, which originally stood to the left of the door. The door into the present pulpit was once a window and is accessed from inside the building via a couple of stone steps. The structure was opened with due ceremony at the Anniversary Service on the 3rd July 1910 by the Bishop of Manchester and was dedicated to the late Mr. John Pickop.

In 1926 the building was re-roofed in order to preserve it and in 1978 renovation work was carried out again, this time to enable the building to be used as a Youth Club and Sunday School. The inside dividing wall was taken down to make one large room and a large, old square fire place with a copper dish set in the top was removed from the front right hand corner to give more space. A concrete floor was laid and an internal breeze block wall built to create a cavity wall. Bottled gas heating was installed, electricity laid on and the building was re-roofed, but sadly it was still dark and dank and is now only used for storage purposes.

SUNDIAL is 10 metres west of the Old School. It has an octagonal base with short spear-headed railings surrounding the pedestal of 4 clustered colonnettes supporting a circular table, but the plate and gnomon are missing.

The base is lettered "G. Thornber sculpt."

The Sundial was the gift of Rev. Gilmour Robinson, Vicar of this Parish from 1830 – 1856. The missing brass plaque was engraved by Richard Dugdale of Blackburn and read:-

> *"Contemplate when the sun declines,*
> *Thy death with due reflection;*
> *And when again his rising shines,*
> *Thy day of resurrection."*

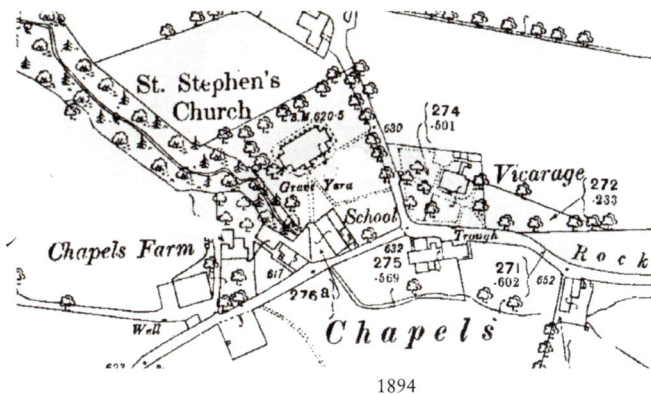

1894

Sun Dial 2002

Open Air Service outside the Old School 1906

THE LYCH GATE was erected in 1906 in memory of John Pickop J.P. a native of Tockholes, who rose to prosperity and became Mayor of Blackburn. Both his father and grandfather before him had been staunch supporters of the church. He had left the village as a young boy to make his living in Blackburn and had become one of the richest men in the town, one of the most respected magistrates, a leading lawyer, and Mayor in 1873-4. Whilst becoming a great benefactor to religious and philanthropic institutions throughout the district, he never forgot the place of his birth and was an eminent benefactor to Tockholes. *(His full obituary is included in Chapter 9)*

School House, Church and Lych Gate c. 1906

The Gateway was designed and erected by Mr. Walter Stirrup of Blackburn and was built to be in keeping with the porch of the Church. The stone for the building was obtained from the ruins of the old Hollinshead Mill and the cost of £260 was donated almost exclusively by Tockholes people. The original inscription read *"This gateway was erected to the Glory of God and in grateful memory of John Pickop, Esq., J.P. Born at Tockholes 1832. Died at Blackburn 1903. He was a generous benefactor of his native place"*. The present inscription reads *"In Memory of John Pickop Esq. J.P. died 1903"*. The Front of the arch is lettered "I Am The Resurrection And The Life". At the rear gable is a plaque with the names of the Vicar and Churchwardens, dated 1906. A more recent addition has been the plaque on the inside erected in 1987 to the memory of Mr. John (Jack) Coar, Church Warden and Treasurer for many years.

The opening ceremony was on Saturday the 1st August 1906 and was performed by Mrs. Thornton, wife of the Bishop. A procession of children and scholars from the School, headed by the Darwen Borough Band, led the way to the Gateway, where several speeches were delivered to numerous visitors. The procession then re-formed and proceeded to a field where a gala was held.

The following extracts from a newspaper report of 5th August 1906 described the much more impressive military parade and unveiling ceremony which took place the next day:

"The following Sunday's ceremony was of far greater grandeur than that of the previous day. Everything was idyllic. Overhead there was a cloudless blue sky and the sun shot forth his rays with quite unaccustomed radiance. The landscape was picturesque. And what a vast concourse there was! Seldom – if ever – has the pretty little village of Tockholes been so largely invaded. There would be quite 5000 people present, all drawn together to witness the unveiling and dedication of the lych-gateway with all those solemn and sacred rites which are attached in a combined ceremonial of the English Church and the military. The men of the 1st V.B.E.I. Regiment turned out in large numbers for the ceremony. The Blackburn men, under the commander, Col.

Johnston, V.D., came with the men by the Livesey route. The other officers present were Captains T. Robinson, Dixon, Bailey and Elliott, and Adjutant Ackroyd. The Darwen men journeyed by way of Earnsdale and Sunnyhurst Wood and were under the command of Captain C. St. John Broadbent. The two sections joined arms at the head of Rock Lane. Here they were met by

Col. H. J. Robinson, V.D., late commander of the Battalion, and the Vicar (Chaplain the Rev. A. T. Corfield) and a large procession was formed. The past and present scholars of Tockholes Schools, to the number of 150, headed the march and following them came the Vicar and Church officers, the wardens, Mr. John Coar and Mr. George Barker carrying their halberde. Then came the regimental band playing a martial air, with Lt. Norwood wielding the baton at their head. Behind were the Volunteers with their Colonel, mounted, leading them onwards.

No more suitable spot could have been chosen for an al-fresco service, for it had been wisely decided to have the whole of the service in the open air. The gateway, the central object, nestled in the hollow, and whilst large numbers kept to the churchyard behind, the most impressive scene lay in front. Across the road the field rose up like the half of an amphitheatre. Here were the sons of Mars drawn up. What a pretty scene it was! Hosts of dainty ladies, all tastefully attired in light summery costumes, commingled with the scarlet tunics of the volunteers to make a perfect spectacle. And as the band, in perfect harmony, and with that sweetness peculiar to a military band, struck up an overture, no one present could but be impressed by the solemnity of the occasion. Quietness, save for the strains of music – even in that vast crowd, reigned supreme. A volume of sound poured forth a moment later, however, when the majestic old time favourite the "Old Hundredth" was rendered. Prayers were afterwards said by the Vicar and following on another hymn the chief ceremony of the afternoon took place.

During the ceremony Colonel Johnson removed a large white ensign which had been covering the dedication to Mr. Pickop and a trumpeter played the "Last Post". Col. Johnson then made a valiant and successful effort to be heard by all when addressing the assembly. He paid tribute to Mr. Pickop's excellent service and generosity to the Volunteers. His name had been the sixth on the roll of volunteers when the company was originally formed in Blackburn, and during the Boer War he defrayed certain heavy expenses of the two active-service contingents who went out to South Africa from the East Lancashire Regiment. Colonel Robinson V.D., the veteran commander, on behalf of the subscribers formally handed the gateway over the charge of the Vicar and Church officers. The Vicar brought the ceremony to a close and the congregation sang "Onward Christian Soldiers". Refresh-ments were served to the men in a field near the school and the officers were entertained at the Vicarage by the Chaplain and Mrs. Corfield. The return march was commenced shortly after 6 p.m."

THE WISHING WELL is a building enclosing a well or spring, probably C18th. The open forecourt is protected by high walls which have stone side benches and, at the outer ends, the chamfered piers had ball finials, which have 'disappeared'. There is a heavy chamfered doorway, with a heavy board door, flanked by single-light chamfered unglazed windows, each fitted with iron bars. In the gable is a large oval opening.

Inside is a vaulted roof with a pendent ball in the centre, stone side benches, diamond-paved floor with a central gutter draining from the well at the centre of the rear wall. A small sunken stone tank with a reredos of Ionic colonnettes frames an alcove containing a crudely carved lion's head and paws, above which is a moulded rectangular surround to a plaque *(now missing)*. To each side of this structure is a rectangular recess enclosing a rectangular pool both linked to that in the centre, and a rectangular recess in each of the side walls. Described by Abram in 1877 as *"an antique well enclosing a spring of water of curative properties to which, of yore, the name of 'Holy Well' was given"*.

Wishing Well c. 1975

Local history records that a holy well stood on this site from medieval times and in the early 1970's a hoard of medieval coins was found nearby which would seem to substantiate this theory. During construction of the car park at Slipper Lowe a spearhead dated between 1400-1200 B.C. was also discovered.

"Here no less than five different springs of water, after uniting together and passing through a very old carved stone representing a lion's head, flow into a well. To this Well pilgrimages were formerly made and the water which is of a peculiar quality, is remarkable as an efficacious remedy for ophthalmic complaints." – anonymous quote mentioned in *Nightingale's* History of Tockholes. The water collects in a large stone trough at the rear of the Well, or 'Holy Well', and overflows down a channel into the Well house and out through the carved lion's head, the lion allegedly representing the "Lion of Judah",

Wishing Well interior 2003

i.e. Christ, from whose mouth poured forth plenty. Originally, water issued from a cleft in the rock and made a pool on the ground. Then during the C17th the present stone roofed building was erected with stained glass windows, the latter suggesting the building may have been consecrated.

Rear view of Well House showing the collection tank c. 1975

It is believed the spring has been in use for centuries and could have been a resting place for pilgrims from the South on their journey to Whalley Abbey. It has also been suggested that the trough was a 'dipping well', or baptistery, as it is similar in design to other known baptisteries in Lancashire. Total immersion was a custom widely practised by the Baptists, and even earlier by the Anglo Saxons, but as the Lancashire and Cheshire Baptists make no mention of any of the wells in this area having been used by that denomination, then this oral tradition could date back to Saxon times. Even this theory is improbable as the present trough is not of Saxon origin and neither are there any steps down into the deep water. It is probably a springhouse, a structure built over a natural source of water for the storage of dairy products and other foods that needed to be kept fresh.

In 1861 Liverpool Corporation purchased land at Roddlesworth as a catchment area to supply the reservoirs and so began an elaborate scheme to catch water and reserve it in reservoirs linked by a water course system. By 1903 the scheme was so advanced that the Corporation bought all the Roddlesworth Valley and the moorland above so as to preserve their water rights. They cleared the tenants and demolished their rented properties because of the risk of pollution to the watershed. One of these casualties was Gerstaine Hall, or Garstangs. Footings of the building can still be seen on the land opposite the Royal Arms. This ancient manor house was believed to have been built in the 14th century and a deed dated 1367 refers to a William de Gerston quitting his claim and all his right to "the hamlet in Tockholes" in favour of his son John de Gerston and another. The porch of the house was famed for its architectural beauty and was surmounted by tiers of windows, each smaller than the one it preceded.

Only known likeness of
Gerstain Hall

It was from this building that the Vicar at the time of the demolition, Rev. Ashley Corfield, rescued the Well now in Rock Lane and the mullion windows which he used to build the outside pulpit in the church yard (*See Chapter 3*). There was also a house known as Lower Garstangs containing several coats-of-arms of the Walmsley family. *Nightingale* tells us that in 1886 the then tenant was John Brindle and that over the door was the inscription "J.P. 1748" = James Pickop.

Another casualty was Halliwell Fold Farm. In 1883 a road was built from the nearby Halliwell Fold Bridge to Hollinshead Mill for the purpose of transporting coal from Withnell railway station to the Mill and this farm supplied a chain horse for extra power to assist the horse and cart up the final long, steep slope to the mill. This coal was to augment coal from the local mines which was not of sufficient quality to power the mill engine. Hollinshead Mill, now a car park and the site of the Roddlesworth Information Centre, was also demolished and finally Hollinshead Hall and Farm House suffered similarly in 1911/2. The stone from these buildings was then used to build the present boundary walls around the Hollinshead woodlands. The above mentioned Holy Well is in these grounds close to the foundations of the Hall and Farm. A more detailed account of Hollins-head Hall and the Well is to be found in Chapter 7.

Part of the ruins of Gerstain Hall (Higher Garstang) 2003

CHAPTER 2

COTTAGES & FARMS

LOWER LOWE AREA

The Village also possesses a wealth of history in other cottages and farms not included in the 'Protected' list. Many of these are 200+ years old and have been extensively, but tastefully, modernised.

The spinning and weaving of textiles was for many years carried out as a domestic trade. The wife and children would spin the yarn and the husband would weave it into cloth. The cloth was then sold and the income would help feed and clothe the family and purchase new raw materials. **Shirley Gardens** (once called Crook Row), **Victoria Terrace** on Old School Lane (previously Bethesda Row) and **Ivy Terrace** (Well Head) are all examples of weavers' cottages. When home weaving was the main industry in Tockholes, there were inner connecting doorways between each of the cottages on Shirley Gardens and Victoria Terrace, which enabled the Cloth Merchant to go from cottage to cottage collecting the 'pieces'. These doorways have long since been locked and the cottages renovated. The first house in

Shirley Gardens (now number 5) was built in 1798 and the row was completed about 1800.

At each end of Shirley Gardens there has been a shop, one for groceries and the other for animal feed-stuffs. Margaret Tapley, author of "A Tockholes Child in the First World War" described the sweet shop at Number 1 as being "small, where plump, kindly Mrs. Smalley sold sherbet and aniseed balls along with tea, soap and bran for the hens. She also doubled up as village midwife and layer-out."! Mrs. Tapley spent the war years with her grandparents who lived at No. 5 Victoria Terrace, the cottage having once been a dame-school which her grandmother had attended as a child. For many years Mr. & Mrs. Percy Green lived at 1 Shirley Gardens and had a sweet shop in their house. They also owned a long, wooden shed in the field at the opposite end of the Row where they sold teas, sandwiches, crisps and 'pop' to the many folks who came to visit "Green's Swings" at the side of the shed. This was a very popular destination for a walk from Darwen or Livesey, especially for those with children to entertain at weekends and holidays.

Ivy Cottages 1978

Ivy Cottages 2002

Shirley Gardens 1978

Easter 1949

Shirley Gardens 2003

VICTORIA TERRACE: In July 1807 Ralph Richardson (Yeomen) sold to John Cocker (Cotton Manufacturer) a plot of land 12 yards x 33 yards and known as Lower Loe, *(Low)* upon which the said John Cocker had 'lately erected' at his own expense three cottages "contiguous to the School" for an annual ground rent of £1.13.0d. (This is probably how Old School Lane got its name). As previously mentioned, the Richardson family were prominent land owners in Tockholes during the 18th Century, and through marriage had become connected to the even more prominent Walmsley family of "The Hill" (now Higher Hill). Amongst their holdings was the Lower Hill estate, part of which included the land upon which Victoria Terrace is built.

Victora Terrace 1978

The Cocker family were prominent non-conformists and had at least one grave in the Bethesda graveyard, mentioned by *Nightingale* as 'a family vault'. Many of their descendants are buried in that vault and also many more in the present Chapel graveyard. Bradley's Farm, Stockclough Lane, was once known as Cocker Fold, so called because James Cocker resided there, followed by his son, James Jnr. The John Cocker mentioned in the deed above was a son of James Cocker Snr., who for a time lived at Top o' th' Low. He and his wife, Alice, had nine children, one of whom, Esther, married Banister Pickop and they in turn were the parents of John Pickop Esq., JP., the well known benefactor of various developments in Tockholes who is mentioned on many occasions in this book and whose obituary appears in Chapter 9.

The Deed of 1807 describes the site in Old School Lane as "part of a certain close of land there called the Lower Loe and containing in length 33 yards and in breadth 12 yards and containing in the whole 396 superficial square yards or thereabouts ... which said plot of land adjoins on the south side thereof to an occupation road, on the West side thereof to the old highway leading to Tockholes Chapels and on the North and South sides thereof to the other part of the said close called the Lower Loe", together with rights and privileges of passage on foot or on horseback and with horses, carts, carriages and cattle over the Occupation Road and also the right to fetch water from the springs or riverlets of water in the said close at the back of the school contiguous thereto and to lay and spread clothes in the said close to air and dry. Also further liberty and privilege to erect and build a bog-house or house of ease and to lay ashes up to the same on some convenient part of the Loe at the back of the school for the use and convenience of the owners and occupiers.

The Deed clearly states that three cottages were built on the site, but today there are five. At some stage it is thought the school was converted into two further cottages and it would seem reasonable to assume that these are the two at the east end of the terrace in view of Margaret Tapley's account of her grandmother's cottage. The area of 12 x 33 yards is just enough to enclose the five cottages, before the modern extensions were added, and there were no back yards at this time.

Victoria Terrace 2002

It has been suggested that the original cottages had no back doors because the earliest occupants had no right of access to the land at the back, but the deed states that they did have the right to fetch water and dry clothes on the '*Close at the back of the School contiguous thereto*'. This land was eventually acquired in the early 1930's and each cottage then had its own garden.

In the 19th century most occupants of Bethesda/Victoria Terrace were listed as handloom weavers, and later cotton mill workers, but other occupations were mentioned such as shoemaker, shopkeeper, housekeeper, police constable, washerwoman and general labourer. In 1844 John Cocker died and was buried in the family vault at Bethesda Chapel. In 1851 his heirs sold the five cottages to Joseph Bradshaw, a Glazier of Darwen, who in turn sold them ten years later to James Shorrock, a Darwen Engineer. Nine years later they became the property of the more famous members of the Shorrock Family, Eccles Shorrock (of India Mill fame) and Ralph Shorrock Ashton, Darwen Cotton Manufacturers. In 1871 they were sold to Roger Townley, a Darwen Mechanic, who mortgaged them to Withnell Paper Company. Townley sold them in 1883 to Walmsley Halliwell, Innkeeper of the Infirmary Hotel, Blackburn and on his death the properties passed to Thomas and Margaret Halliwell who sold them to Caleb Kennelly, Licensed Victualler of Blackburn for £55. Kennelly was a Parish Councillor in Tockholes for many years and lived at No. 4. On his death in 1916 all five cottages passed to his daughter, Ada Selina Frances Graham, who returned from India to live at No.4 when she was widowed. In 1920 she purchased Lower Hill Farm and all its land, including that around Victoria Terrace, for £450, but twelve months later sold Lower Hill Farm for £460 and kept the land surrounding Victoria Terrace.

Ada Graham died in 1928 without issue and a Caleb Kennelly Counsell, Publican of the Waterfall Hotel, Glenmeay, Isle of Man, inherited the properties, selling them in 1930 for £775 to Sarah Jane Bulcock, wife of George Bulcock, Cloth Looker of Blackburn. She moved into Number 5 and in 1932 sold No. 1 plus 1000 square yards of land to George & Harriet Duckworth, Poultry Farmer, for £210, and in 1943 sold her own property, No. 5, to Robert Sowerbutts, Retired General Dealer of Darwen. Sarah Bulcock died in 1945 leaving Numbers 2, 3 and 4 to her son, Edward Bulcock, Coal Merchant, and by the 1950's each house had become individually owned, as is the case today.

Thanks to Alex Heede for the above information relating to Victoria Terrace

ENGINE BROW

The properties in Engine Brow were weavers' cottages similar in style to Shirley Gardens and Victoria Terrace and probably of a similar age. The O.S. Map of 1848 referred to this area as Moorgate. As is apparent from the photographs, extensive restoration work has taken place over the years. Originally, the cottages comprised of four small living rooms position centrally in the front of the row with a long, narrow loomshop running from the front to back at each end and two more loomshops across the back of the two central cottages. The eighteen windows to the loomshop can still clearly be seen across the back of the row. The hoist doorway to the storage area above one of the end loomshops was still visible in 1978.

Engine Brow 1964

Engine Brow 1978

Engine Brow 2003

Engine Brow 2003

The two cottages at the north end of Engine Brow came into the possession of a Charitable Trust on the 20th August 1841 and the rents from the properties were used by the Trust to augment the Schoolmaster's salary. They eventually became derelict and for over fifty years were unable to be sold as the original title deeds could not be found and there were no Trustees alive. In 1989 the legal position was clarified and the houses were sold. The money was invested in a new Educational Trust, which also owns the old school in the churchyard and the land upon which the present day school stands, and the interest on the investment is now used to benefit the school.

Engine Brow 1978

ENGINE BOTTOMS, DAM COTTAGE AND SHAW BROOK

Nightingale recorded that Engine Bottoms, was once the site of a Carding Engine or Mill, owned by an Adam Richardson. Adam resided at Crow Trees and also owned Shaw Brook *'near to which he had his carding engine'*. The name "Engine Bottoms" given to this area is no doubt a relic of this time. The mill was later later converted to a dwelling known as Dam Cottage, probably taking its name from the dam connected with the nearby water supply.

Further information taken from an old Survey Book and also quoted in *Nightingale* relating to the carding Engine is as follows:-

Augt. 18th 1791.

Memorandum of Mr. Adam Richardson's

Carding Engine or Mill.

Dam Cottage 1978

	£	s.	d.
Supposed to earn in a year by our calculation Cona.	90.	0.	0.
Supposed for Horses	16.	0.	0.
Attendance for 50 weeks at 16s. per week	40.	0.	0.
Wear & Tear & all support	20.	0.	0.
Losses and Disappointments by stoppages etc.	6.	0.	0.
Leaves	82.	0.	0.
	8.	0.	0.
Reduced as Land (5/8 of value) Addressed as Cottages (2d. in £)	4.	16.	0.

Dam Cottage 2003

The total amount of Mr. Richardson's rate would therefore be about 9½d.

SHAW BROOK COTTAGE is now a single dwelling made from two cottages, but at one time this was a terrace of six dwellings. Foundations for a cottage to the right of the present building were discovered whilst preparing the garden area. In front of the cottages was a dam, the overflow of which crossed the road just below the cottages, thereby creating a ford. It then flowed to the mill (Dam Cottage) to power the water-wheel sited on the south wall. The dam no longer exists and the stream now flows under the road through the culvert.

Thanks to John Hebden for Shaw Brook Cottage information.

Shaw Brook Cottage 1978

Shaw Brook Cottage 2003

24

SHAW BROOK FARM. The date of construction of this property is unknown. The O.S. Map of 1848 shows a long building at this location, possibly farmhouse and shippon, and another building opposite. The Census Returns for 1841 and 1851 show four families resident in these properties. In each of these decades only one person was listed as a farmer, the remainder were mainly employed in the cotton industry as weavers, winders etc. and there was one shopkeeper and one coal miner. By 1861 only two properties were occupied, again, one resident being a farmer of 1 acre and the other resident being the Schoolmaster, Mr. Thomas Nightingale. The Nightingale family appeared in the 1871 and 1881 Returns, but by then had no neighbours and no-one was farming. In 1891 the property was occupied by Thomas Nowell, a farmer aged 71 and the 1894 map shows the buildings were still much the same layout. The current farmhouse is only a portion of the original buildings and it is not known when the outbuildings were demolished. The house was restored in the late 1980's.

Shaw Brook Farm 2003

1848 O.S. Map

25

LEIGH COTTAGE is thought to have been a Smithy. By 1851 it was listed on the Census as two cottages, one of which was empty. During renovation in the late 1960's, a huge beam in the north gable end, was discovered, which would have been the barn door entrance into the Smithy, and after taking the sand and lime plaster off the internal walls another beam of comparable size was found in the dividing wall between the two cottages, suggesting that at one time the building might have been capable of housing horses and carts. There was also much evidence of calcium, possibly from hoof clippings, but no evidence of burning which one would expect in a smithy. This evidence could have been destroyed at the time the building was converted into cottages. On the South gable were three walled-up openings, the lower two were windows, and the third was mid-way between the floors, suggesting a workshop rather than living accommodation.

Leigh Cottage 1978

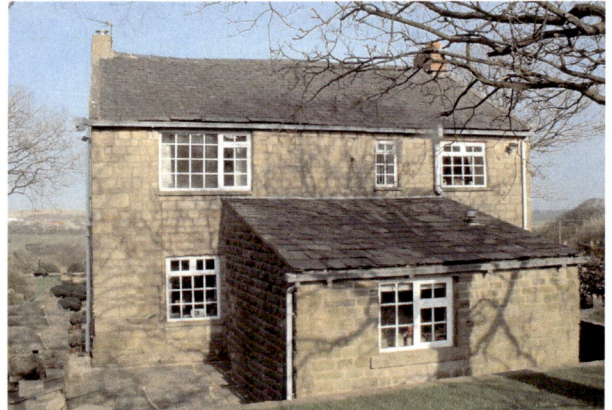

Leigh Cottage rear view 2003

ROCK LANE AREA

THE OLD SCHOOL HOUSE was built in 1882 for the use of the headmaster of Tockholes C of E School. It was built on the site of two old cottages shown on the map taken from a deed dated 1881. The original intention had been to restore the old cottages, but after much discussion it was decided they were beyond repair and deemed unfit for human habitation.

Chapels House (left) and the Old School House

CHAPELS HOUSE was built in 1995 on the site of the ruins.

According to this map the road is marked "Rock Lane" but there is some confusion as to whether it is in fact Chapels Lane at this point. Today Rock Lane is designated as running from The Rock Inn to the road leading to Pickering Fold.

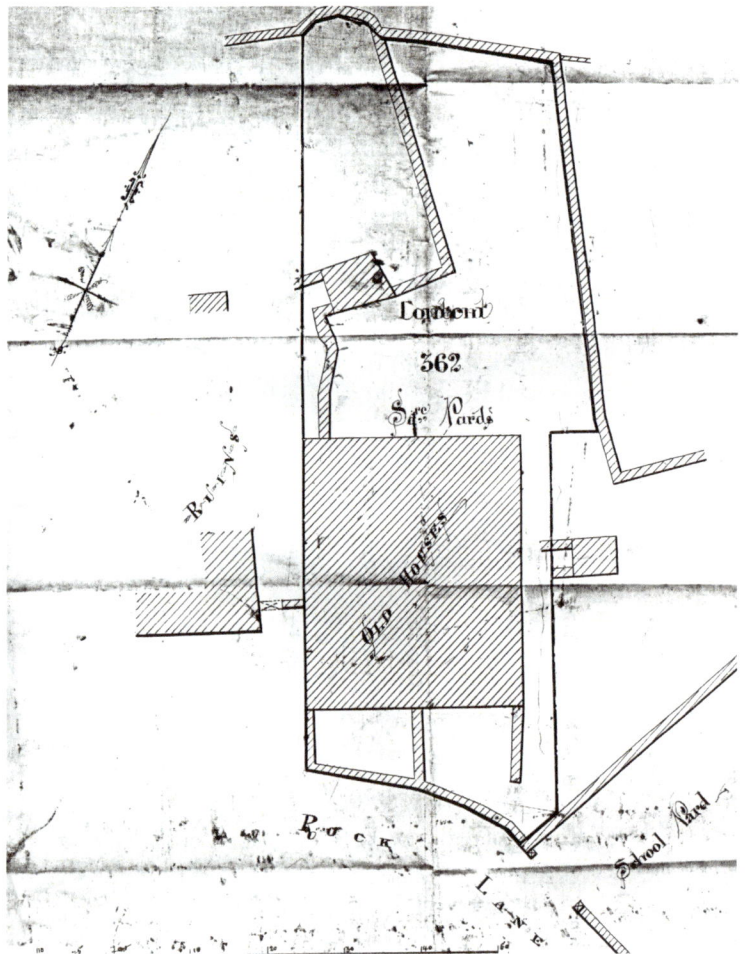

Map from deed of 1881 showing old cottages, ruins and School Yard entrance now the site of Chapels House, Old School House and Lych Gate

26

THE OLD VICARAGE. In 1649 a house was given by the local gentry for the use of a Curate at Tockholes. This house stood in what is now part of the graveyard, but by 1855 it had decayed to such an extent as to become 'perfectly uninhabitable' and fund raising was started to replace it. By 1860 parishioners and friends had raised £400 and a landowner donated the site for a new vicarage. The church commissioners made a grant of £600 and the new building began in May 1861. This building, now known as The Old Vicarage, served as a vicarage until 1980 when its maintenance became unsustainable for this small parish and the parish was united with that of St. Cuthbert, Darwen, under the leadership of the Rev. William Fielding. A Curate was subsequently appointed to the united benefice to work at both churches, and he became 'Curate-in-Charge' of Tockholes and resided at the Old School House. This arrangement lasted for just over 20 years, when the parish was finally joined with that of St. Cuthbert. Outwardly, the building remains much the same today, but modernisation has taken place inside.

The Old Vicarage 2003

Gorse Barn, Gorse Cottage and Gorse Farm 2003

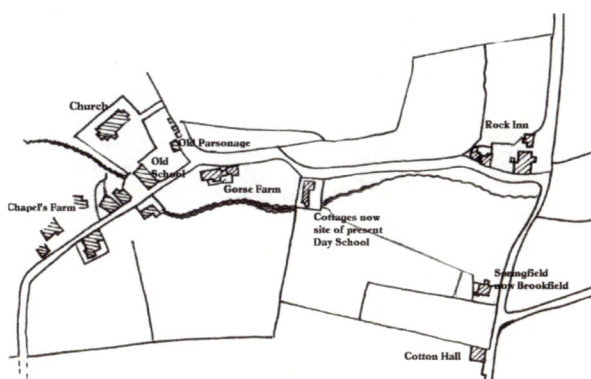

Map c. 1850

GORSE FARM/COTTAGE/BARN. In the Registers for St. Mary's Church, Blackburn (now the Cathedral) is an entry of marriage between Omphrey Gorse of Wigan and Priscilla Jolly of Tockholes in 1651. It is possible therefore that this building was built for the Gorses or perhaps it already existed and was the home of the Jollys, later becoming known as Gorses, Gorsts and subsequently Gorse Farm.

Renovations carried out in 1981 showed that the original farmhouse was the central portion only, the right hand side and the barn to the left being later additions. The removal of old plaster in the Cottage showed that the roof level was once 18" lower than at present and that there were once two connecting doors between the Cottage and the Farm House, one on either side of what is now the fireplace. One led into Farmhouse itself and the other into the dairy. In the cottage bedroom adjoining the barn was a wide doorway about 4 feet in height and now blocked off, which led onto the hayloft of the barn. In the roof are some interesting beams, one having an obvious fork where the branches were left on to make it long enough to reach between the walls and another one which curves like the meandering of a river

.

Gorse Barn & Gorse Cottage 1973

The ground floor level dairy at Gorse Farm is built on to the back of the house and is now a bathroom. Under the dairy is a cellar, accessed by a trap door and a flight of stone steps. In the centre a stone table is fixed into the flagged floor. There are also several niches around the walls, possibly for the storage of cheese and butter. During restoration a wattle and daub wall was uncovered in one of the bedrooms. The floors in both the farm and the cottage are solid and were once flagged, with the exception of the right hand room of the farm and this has a wooden floor with a 2 foot space below and traces of steps leading down to a lower level earth floor. Could this additional room have been used to house a loom perhaps, or maybe it was used for animals? The middle window to the Farmhouse was originally a door and inside there is a recess to the left of this opening, which could have been a window, but the pebble-dashing obscures the evidence from the outside.

The Gorse Barn conversion was completed 1975. This building was a later addition to the Farm and Cottage as the walls are not keyed in. The barn had one room at the front right hand corner, created with stone walls, and one step down from the main barn area. A small outside front door also gave access to the room and there were two small windows, one at the front and the second at a higher level on the gable. Fixed to the walls of this room were iron rings for tethering animals. The central main barn door was retained and is now the main entrance. Another small door gave access to the shippon at the front top corner and led through to a lean-to attached to the back of the building, once used for storing farm implements. In the yard at the back was a pig-sty and there are still two water troughs set into the garden wall. To the side of the troughs are three stones built into the wall creating steps to the higher land above where hen cabins were once situated.

PICKERING FOLD is a small hamlet consisting of four properties, Pickering Fold Farmhouse, Bridge Barn, Middle Barn and Squirrels Run – the two latter properties being created as detached properties by the removal of the central cottage. Prior to renovation it had been a farmhouse, large detached barn and a row of cottages which had been uninhabited for many years, with a further barn attached at the North end of the row.

In 1831 the premises and several other properties and land in the vicinity were owned by William Pickering, a wealthy farmer, who gave a plot of land attached to the grounds of St. Michael's Church as the site for a new Church and graveyard extension. A deed dated 20th May 1831 gave his address as simply "Tockholes" but a newspaper announcement regarding the sale of Pickering's Estate shortly after his death in 1838 refers to the property as Chrichlows. By 1851 the Census Returns described it as "Yew Fold" and listed four families as living there, presumably one family in the farm house and the rest in the cottages. A plan drawn at the time William Pickering gifted the land upon which the new Church was to be built quite clearly shows the layout of both St. Michael's Church, Pickering Fold Farmhouse and the row of cottages, and if the plan is to scale then the Farmhouse was a similar size to the ancient Church of St. Michael. This plan does not define the number of cottages, but a further Map of 1930 clearly shows the row of cottages and attached barn. The large detached barn to the East is also shown on this map. About 1907 the Farmhouse was rebuilt and externally remains much the same today. The inside was re-arranged during renovation of the site in 1989.

Pickering Fold Farmhouse 2003

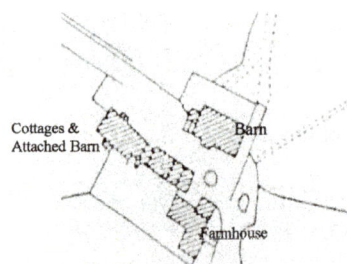

Cottages & Attached Barn
Barn
Farmhouse

Map circa 1930

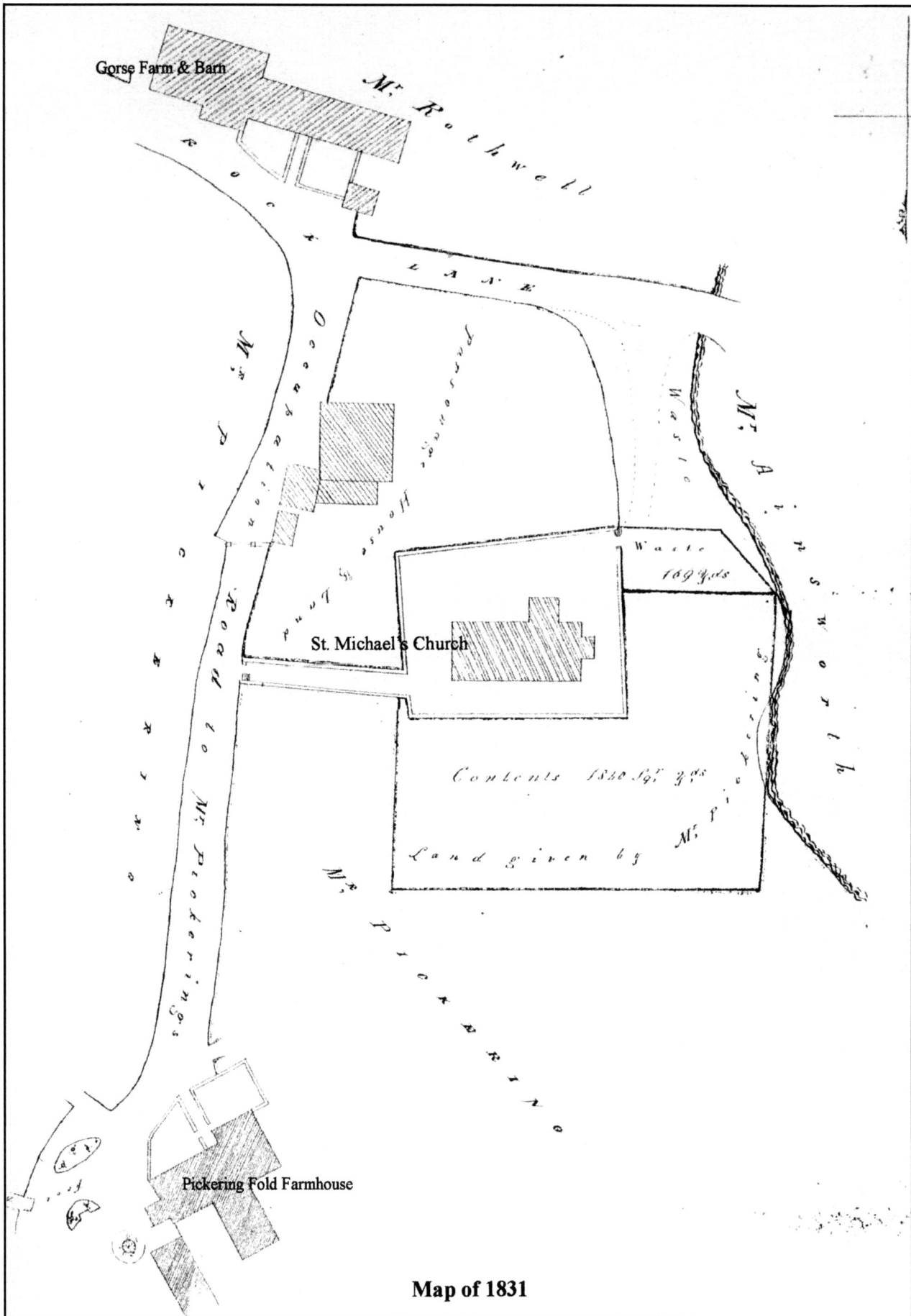

Gorse Farm & Barn

Mr. Rothwell

Rock Lane

St. Michael's Church

Waste
169 Yds

Contents 1320 Sq. Yds.

Land given by Mr. P.

Mr. Ainsworth

Mr. Pickering

Pickering Fold Farmhouse

Map of 1831

William Pickering died on the 21st October 1837 aged 85 years. Several months later his Estate was advertised for Auction showing not only his ownership of Pickering Fold but also of "Spring Fields", "Worsleys", "Higher Garsdens" and "Lower Garsdens", all situated in Tockholes, along with other properties in Darwen and Blackburn.

In the centre of the farmyard, between the farmhouse and the detached barn, stood an ancient oak tree, the trunk of which was surrounded by a low stone wall. A news report of 1903 surmised it to be at least 600 years old and described it as "a little giant" because in height it was disappointing, though what it lacked in that respect was more than counterbalanced by its girth. Four men could only just span it. The trunk was hollow and, like most oak trees in England, has been reported as a one time hiding place for soldiers on the run from Cromwell's army! This cannot be confirmed, but it was once the home of a dog and its young family, all having mysteriously disappeared from the nearby farmhouse and found several days later happily ensconced in the hollow. In 1961 the tree had to be removed to ease the access for modern farm machinery.

Middle Barn & Squirrels Run 2003

Pickering Fold Cottages and attached Barn 1989
now Middle Barn & Squirrels Run

The detached Barn at Pickering Fold in 1989 - now Bridge Barn

Bridge Barn 2003

Rear view of the derelict cottages at Pickering Fold
and the annexe to the farmhouse - 1989

The Famous Oak Tree felled in 1961

30

VALUABLE FREEHOLD FARMS AND PREMISES.

To be Sold by Auction,

BY MR. WM. SALISBURY,

(By order of the Trustees for Sale, named in the Will of William Pickering, Esq., deceased.)

At the House of Mr. BLOMLEY, the *Old Bull Inn*, in Blackburn, in the County of Lancaster, on THURSDAY, the 5th of JULY, 1838, Sale to commence at Two o'clock in the Afternoon, subject to such Conditions of Sale as shall be then and there produced;

LOT I.

THE Inheritance in Fee-Simple of and in all that Large, Compact, and TITHE-FREE ESTATE, called *"Holden's, or Pastures,"* situate and being in the Township of *Edgeworth*, in the said County, consisting of a Farm-House, Barns, Out-buildings, and the several Closes or Parcels of Land thereunto belonging and therewith occupied, containing, altogether, 83A. 2R. 25P., of the large Cheshire Measure, and now in the occupation of *Lawrence Whittaker*, as Tenant at Will.

This Estate is capable of great improvement, and contains Stone suitable for Draining and Building purposes. A valuable vein of Coal is also supposed to lie under the same.

LOT II.—All that FREEHOLD MESSUAGE, TENEMENT, FARM, and PREMISES, called *'Pickering's Farm,'* situate and being in *Edgeworth* aforesaid, consisting of a good Farm-House, Barn, and suitable Out-buildings, and the several Closes or Parcels of Land thereunto belonging and occupied therewith, containing, altogether, 14A. 3R. 30P., of the Measure aforesaid, now in the occupation of *James Entwistle*, as Tenant at Will.

This Farm, which is Tithe-Free, was formerly an Allotment from the Commons of Edgeworth, and was awarded to Mr. Pickering in right of Pastures Estate. The Buildings are nearly new, and are in good order and repair.

LOT III.—All those MESSUAGES or DWELLING-HOUSES, BARNS, Out-buildings, and Premises, called *'Pickering Fold,'* or *'Chrichlows,'* situate and being in *Tockholes*, in the said County, and the several Closes and Parcels of Land, thereunto belonging and occupied therewith, containing, altogether, in Customary Measure of seven yards to the Rod, 42A. 0R. 11P., now in the occupation of *James Heald, John Haworth,* and *James Catterall.* Along with this Lot will be sold two PEWS in Tockholes Church.

The above admeasurement includes a Small Croft, called *"Wheat Croft,"* occupied by James Catterall, along with Spring Fields Estate. The Timber growing upon this Lot will be sold with it.

LOT IV.—All that Small ESTATE of LAND, called *"Spring Fields,"* situate in *Tockholes* aforesaid, heretofore part of Chrichlows, comprising a Farm-House, three Cottages, Barn, Out-buildings, and the several Closes or Parcels of Land thereunto belonging and occupied therewith, containing, altogether, 5A. 3R. 5P., (exclusive of Wheat Croft,) of the Customary Measure of seven yards to the Rod, now in the several occupations of *James Catterall, Richard Gregory, Mary Gregory,* and *George Snape.*

The Farm Buildings on this Estate are nearly new and in good repair.

LOT V.—All that other Small ESTATE OF LAND, called *"Worsley's,"* situate in Tockholes aforesaid, also heretofore part of Chrichlows, consisting of a Farm-House, Barn, and suitable Out-buildings, and the several Fields or Closes of Land belonging thereto and occupied therewith, containing, altogether, 6A. 3R. 32P., of the Customary Measure of seven yards to the Rod, now in the occupation of *Joseph Edge.*

The Buildings on this Estate are in good order, having been recently erected by the late Mr. Pickering.

LOT 6.—All that MESSUAGE, TENEMENT, FARM, and PREMISES, called *'Hindley House,'* or *'Higher Garsdens,'* situate in *Tockholes* aforesaid, comprising the Farm-House, Barn, and other Out-buildings, and the several Closes of Land belonging thereto and occupied therewith, formerly part of the Hindley House and Ryle Estates, containing, together, 9A. 1R. 6P., of the Customary Measure of seven yards to the Rod, now in the occupation of *William Smith.* Together with such right of getting Turf on Baron Pasture, as is mentioned in a certain Lease granted for that purpose, the particulars of which will be given at the time of Sale.

LOT VII.—All that MESSUAGE, FARM, and PREMISES, called *"Lower Garsdens,"* situate in *Tockholes* aforesaid, formerly part of the Hindley House and Ryle Estates, consisting of the Farm-House, Barn, and other Out-buildings, and the several Fields or Closes of Land belonging thereto and occupied therewith, containing, together, 14A. 0R. 19P., of the Customary Measure of seven yards to the Rod, now in the occupation of *James Hargreaves.* Together with such right of getting Turf on Baron Pasture, as is mentioned in a certain Lease granted for that purpose, the particulars of which will be given at the time of Sale.

The Five last-mentioned Estates are of Freehold Tenure, and are Tithe-Free.

LOT VIII.—The Fee-Simple and Inheritance of and in all those THREE MESSUAGES or DWELLING-HOUSES, now occupied as Four Dwellings, situate and being in the village of *Lower Darwen*, in the said County, and fronting the highway there, with the Gardens and Appurtenances thereto belonging, now in the several occupations of *Joseph Holden, John Fielding, Richard Holden* and *Matthew Shaw.*

These Premises contain 295 superficial Square Yards or thereabouts, and are free from the payment of any Ground Rent.

LOT IX.—All that FREEHOLD MESSUAGE or DWELLING-HOUSE, situate and being at *Bottom Gate*, in Blackburn aforesaid, with the Garden and Appurtenances thereto belonging, now in the possession of *Christopher Grimshaw.*

These Premises occupy a site of 33½ superficial Square Yards or thereabouts, and are free from the payment of any Ground Rent.

The respective Tenants will show the Premises, and further Particulars may be known on application at the Office of Mr. WILKINSON, Solicitor, Blackburn, with whom Plans of the different Estates and Property are left for inspection.

Blackburn, June 2nd, 1838.

News report relating to the Auction of Pickering Fold in 1838

Pickup Brow 2003

PICKOP BROW, OLD WIFE HEY, & MANOR HOUSE (Once MOUNT PLEASANT)

PICKOP BROW is another row of handloom weavers' cottages. Two of them had ground floor loomshops at one side which were fitted with triple windows. In each case, the outermost windows have been filled in and the central ones deepened[4]. During renovation work in the 1980's when a kitchen extension was added at the back of Number 1, window openings were uncovered with iron bars still set into the frames. What was once the old back door is now the doorway into the kitchen extention.

OLD WIFE'S HEY

This property was a farmhouse with attached barn. Its age is uncertain. Since the early 17th century the Pickops had held a freehold estate on the border of Livesey and Tockholes, anciently called Green-Tockholes. In 1641 a 'James Piccop purchased from Thomas Witton, gent. a messuage and 8 customary acres of land in Green-Tockholes for the sum of £50' and thereafter various branches of the Pickop family retained property in this area for over 200 years. It is likely this is the farmhouse James Pickop purchased and after whom the area is named. The house was much altered in the 1970's when the barn was lowered and incorporated into the living accommodation.

Today all this area is referred to as Pickop Brow. In 1920 land was purchased in the vicinity of Pickop Brow Cottages and Old Wife's Hey and ribbon development took place when several bungalows and a pair of semi-detached houses were built at intervals from that date.

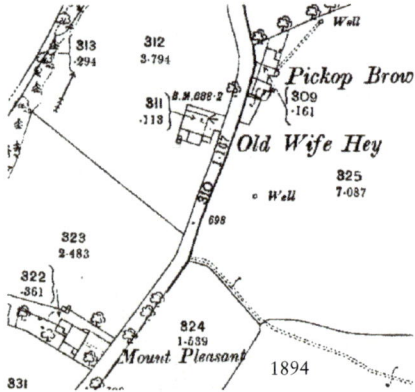

Old Wife's Hay 1964

Old Wife's Hey 2003

Mount Pleasant/Manor House, 2003

MOUNT PLEASANT or Manor House is the ancestral home of the branch of the Pickop family who were ancestors of John Pickop, J.P., the well-known late 19th Century benefactor of this Village who is commemorated on the Church Lych Gate.

GREENTHORN FARM

The 1841 Census refers to the area as Well House, and makes no mentioned of the farm, but lists 9 separate families living around there. Two further dwelling-houses were listed at 'Tockholes Fold'. Today it is these two buildings which are known as Tockholes Fold Farm. The 1894 O.S. map, however, lists Greenthorn as Tockholes Fold Farm and shows it along side a row of cottages called Well House Cottages.

The Barn attached to Greenthorn Farm is now a dwelling known as Swallows Barn, and outwardly this row appears much the same today as in the photographs. The farmhouse has two front doors and two porches and was probably two dwellings at one time, but not within living memory. Forty eight people were listed as living in this area on the 1841 census of which six heads of household were weavers, one a Grocer and two were farmers. The Well House properties no longer exist. In 1908 Greenthorn Farm was on the market to let, along with 17 acres of land, as the farmer, Mr. Lofthouse, was 'finishing farming'.

Greenthorn Farm c. 1910

[4]*"Handloom Weavers' Cottages in Central Lancashire By J. G. Timmins 1977)*

The photograph with the gramophone was taken outside Greenthorn Farm between 1908 & 1912 and shows the Ainsworth family entertaining three elderly guests. The Ainsworths were the maternal grandparents of Mr. Jack Ainsworth Grimshaw, Clerk to the Tockholes Parish Council for many years during the 1960's and 70's. He and his wife, Edna, lived at No. 5 Victoria Terrace. His grandmother, Elizabeth Ainsworth Snr. seated on the left of the picture was born in 1853 and died at 21 Gregory Street, Darwen 9th December 1922 aged 69. Edwin Ainsworth, Jack's grandfather, standing centre, was born in 1856 and died 13th November 1912 at Greenthorn Farm aged 56. He was the proprietor of Boro Mews, Church Bank Street, Darwen, Funeral Undertaker & Coach Proprietor. Elizabeth Grimshaw (née Ainsworth) their daughter and Jack's mother, is shown standing on the right of the picture. She was born 11th June 1887 and died 12th January 1961 aged 74. Her sister, Sarah, is seated centre. Jack was born 6th January 1915.

Thanks to Jack for the above information

TOCKHOLES FOLD to the south of Greenthorn still remains and the large square barn is still a barn. Whilst the barn bears a C19th date the age of the house is unknown, but is thought to be at least 250 years old. It was once in the occupation of a branch of the Hoghton family of Hoghton Tower. Thomas Hoghton married firstly Mary Marsden and their first son, William, was baptised 12th November 1759. Their address registered at that time was Tockholes Fold. Thomas married twice more, one of his wives being Jane Peel, aunt of Sir Robert Peel, the first baronet.

This house, too, was once two dwellings. In 1841 a young farmer, James Mellody, aged 30, resided there with his wife, five children and an Ellen Mellody, aged 16. In the other house lived Henry Hollinshead, aged 20, a man of independent means, and three other people.

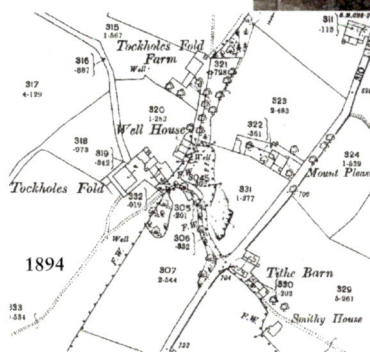

Tockholes Fold Farm 2003

VINE HOUSE, TYTHEBARN & SMITHY HOUSE

This group of buildings consists of a detached house, Vine House, and two cottages known as 1 & 2 Tythebarn. However, in 1841 seven separate households were listed for this area. James Horsefield, Agricultural Labourer, and his wife, Isabella, both aged 30, and their four children; John Ramsbottom, 38, Weaver, his wife Catherine, 41 and five children; Thomas Townley, 45, Weaver and his wife Alice, 41 and five children; William Pickop, 44, Weaver, his wife Ann and six children; Robert Campbell, 19, Weaver and his wife Alice, also 19; James Margerison, 58, Weaver, his wife Lydia, 55 and five children and in the Smithy House, Edward Cotrell, 55, Farmer, his wife Betty, 55 and six children. A total of 45 people living in this small area. The Smithy House was opposite Tythebarn and no longer exists.

Vine House & Tythebarn 2003

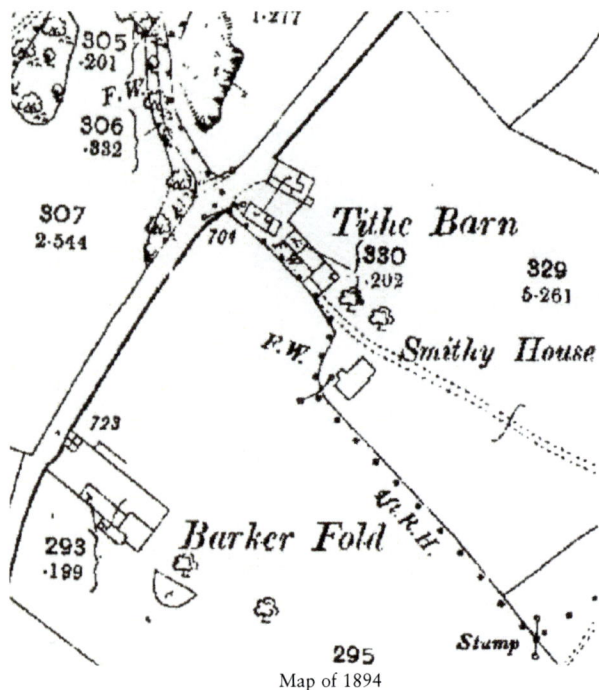
Map of 1894

BARKER FOLD: To date no recorded history of the farm being built has come to light and one can only suppose that "barkers" who stripped bark from trees to tan leather gave this area its name. A deed in the County Records Office at Preston shows that in 1663 James Brown paid William Walmsley a rent of 5 shillings for land called "Barkers Lands" and a Will shows that in 1671 William Walmsley left "Barkers Lands" to his son, John. From 1691 the farm, along with others, belonged to the Manor of Tockholes. In 1838 Eccles Shorrock, the Darwen Cotton Merchant, bought Barker Fold, along with other properties, as part of the manor holding. The Shorrock family held Barker Fold until 1921 when it was sold, with other properties in Tockholes, Lower Darwen and Darwen, to pay for the care of Eccles Shorrock III in a Brighton Hospital where he eventually died.

In 1964 the Ward family bought the property and an elderly neighbour told them of a cellar in which she used to cure bacon. After investigation the cellar was located and found to contain ceiling hooks and an 8' x 4' stone table resting on two stone pillars. The cellar also has an arched and cobbled ceiling.

The original layout of the property seems to have been two central dwellings with a barn attached at the East end and shippon to the West. The barn and cottages eventually became one dwelling. It was in continual use as a farm until 1963 when it became residential only, the land being let to a local farmer. In 1977 the unused shippon and 1/3rd acre of land was sold for conversion to a house, now Foxes Barn.

Barker Fold (left) and Foxes Barn 2003

CROSSLANDS FARM. The farmhouse was uninhabited for many years at the end the 20th century although the land was still farmed. The house was restored in 2000 and is now occupied. The age of the property is unknown, but a building is marked on this site on Yates Map of 1786. During renovation work in 2000 a mullion window was discovered under some plaster work on what had been an outside wall, but at some later date had been in-filled and covered by an extension. At the rear is evidence of several other in-filled mullion windows and inside the house are two ancient fireplaces with huge lintels suggestive of the Tudor period.

Rear view of the restored Crosslands Farm 2001

Thanks to Alice Cookson for the Barker Fold information and to Beryl Rhodes for the information on Crosslands Farm.

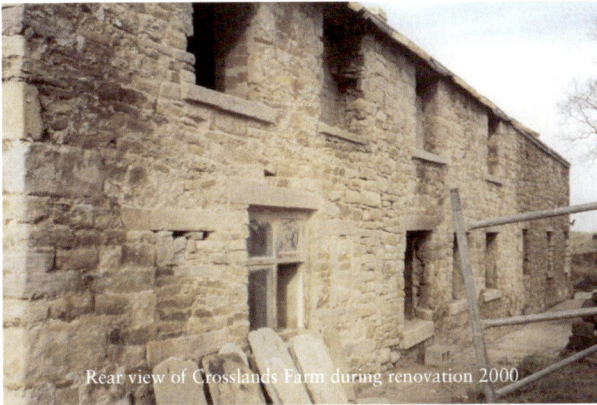
Rear view of Crosslands Farm during renovation 2000

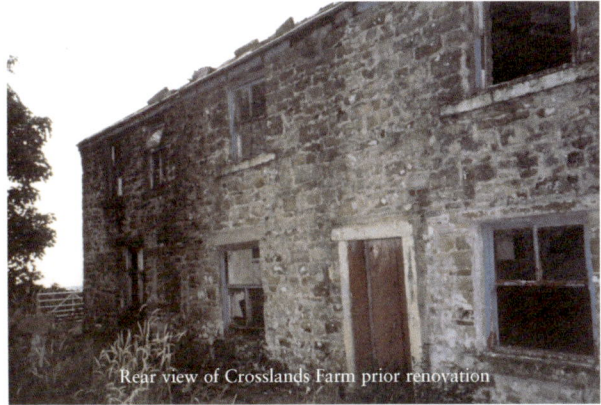
Rear view of Crosslands Farm prior renovation

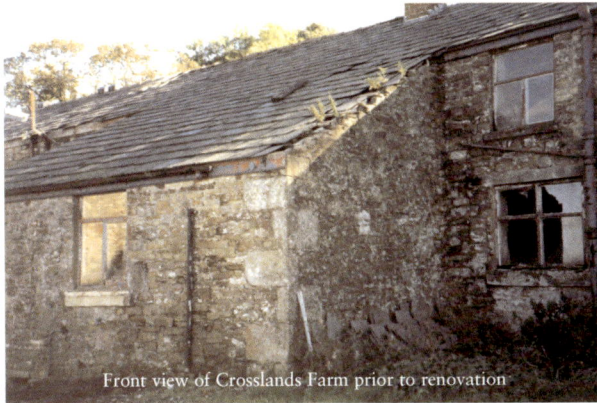
Front view of Crosslands Farm prior to renovation

Crosslands Farm 2003

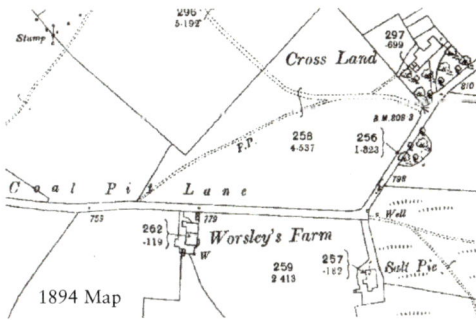
1894 Map

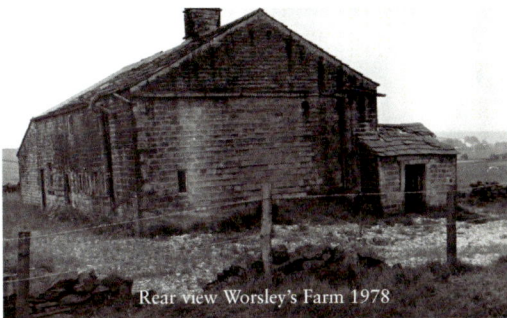
Rear view Worsley's Farm 1978

Close up detail of the loomshop windows and doorway
at Worsley's Farm 1977

Front view of Worsley's Farm 2003

WORSLEYS FARM[5] is one the few remaining examples of a ground floor loomshop equipped with a long row of windows as opposed to separate or triple windows. The loomshop was at the back of the farmhouse and had a series of windows running almost the entire length of one of the longer walls. The window openings were almost a yard deep and were divided irregularly by stone mullions varying in width between $7^1/_2$ and 10 inches. At one end part of a sill was removed to form a doorway, presumably previous access to the loomshop being gained through the house. These premises were part of the Rothwell Estate, but were disposed of, along with the remainder of the Estate, in 1950. At that time they were advertised as "a stone-built farm dwellinghouse containing Porch, Kitchen, Scullery, Pantry and two Bedrooms. The stone-built Farm buildings comprised Shippon for eight, Shippon for four and Barn." The property stood in a derelict state for many years and was eventually refurbished about 1980. Several years later, the adjoining barn was adapted as extra living accommodation.

[5] Information and detail photograph of loomshop windows courtesy of J. G. Timmins - "Handloom Weavers' Cottages in Central Lancashire" 1977)

Brookfield (Springfield) c. 1910

BROOKFIELD (Formerly Springfield)

The 1841 Census records **Brookfield** as one dwelling, but it appears as two on the 1851 and 1861 Returns. By 1871 one part was empty and from then onwards it reverts to one dwelling again. The doors to the cottages were in the gable ends and the back of the building was a barn with hayloft above. Access to the hayloft was via a ladder and also through the window-like opening in the gable to the side of and above the porch, shown on the old photograph. Auction particulars dated 1950 describe the farm as "a stone-built farm dwelling-house containing, porch, two living rooms, kitchen, three bedrooms, attic and large cellar. The stone-built farm buildings comprise shippon for three with loft over, and detached stable for two."

Brookfield c. 1978

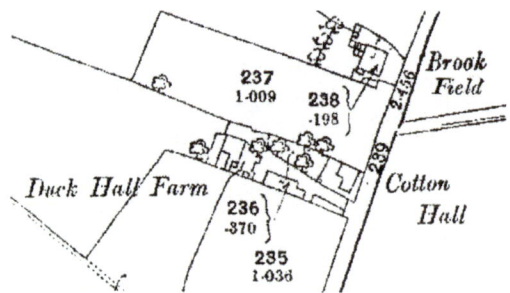

1894 Map

COTTON HALL
(Formerly Top Lane)

The date stone on **Cotton Hall** is 1812 and in 1841 it was listed as a Beer Shop, but like Duck Hall, was thought also to have been a warehouse for cotton fabric. Both properties are on the one time main route from Bolton to Blackburn and would therefore have been easy collection points for merchants travelling to the markets.

Cotton Hall c. 1910

Cotton Hall 2003

Cotton Hall c. 1975

36

DUCK HALL is now one dwelling and has been listed on the Census Returns as such since 1871, but in 1841 four dwellings stood on this site, one occupied by a Farmer, the rest by Weavers. In 1851 one cottage was unoccupied, and by 1861 two cottages were empty.

At some time one building was used to store 'duck' – a strong un-twilled linen or cotton fabric used for small sails and as outer clothing, especially for sailors – hence the name 'Duck Hall'. It has also been known as Walshes.

In the mid 1940's a previous owner of this property was known to have all his teeth extracted whilst lying on a trestle table in the Car Park at the Rock Inn. Apparently the light was better out there than in the house!

Duck Hall 2003

Thought to be Close Farm c. 1900

CLOSE FARM

The age of this property is unknown, but it appears on the Census Return of 1841 as **Old Close**. The original building of farmhouse with barn attached was extended on the North gable in the 1930's by the addition of extra living accommodation and bedroom. There has also been an extension at the front of the barn that partly covers the old high, arched wagon entrance and in more recent days a porch has been added over the front door to the house. A date stone of 1884 once sited on the barn has been removed and placed in the new porch. A nearby farmhouse, Tottering Temple, last appeared on the Census of 1881 and it is recorded that stone was taken from this property and used to build a barn at Close Farm, but the date this occurred is not recorded.

Close Farm 2003

WEASEL FARM was built in 1891 and replaced the original old farmhouse situated behind the present building. At that time Mr. Horsfield Horsfield and family occupied the old property and it was he who carted the stone from a derelict cottage opposite the Church Lych Gate to build the present Farmhouse. He intended living in the new house, but instead moved to Pickering Fold Farm. For a short time the old house was known as Weazle in th' Wall and was a four bed-roomed property with attached stables and a further attached outhouse, once used as a pigsty.

Over the front door of the present building is a date stone inscribed R.R.R. 1891. The initials are those of Richard Rainshaw Rothwell, then owner of much of the land in this vicinity, including the above-mentioned derelict cottage in Rock Lane. The Census Return of 1851 lists the Farm as having two couples in residence each with 6 children. It is thought they shared the dwelling as there was no separate farm cottage to this property. The old farm eventually fell into disrepair and the final remains were demolished a few years ago. The large detached barn at the road edge has now been made into a dwelling and is known as Weasel Barn.

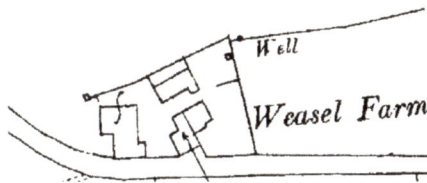

1894

Weasel Farm & Weasel Barn 2003

Thomas Edmondson and his sister, Betty, at the side of the current Farmhouse. The old house and stables are on the right

37

Bungalows - Top Road 2003

On the South side of Weasel Lane and along the ridge of the field between the Lane and Golden Soney, several wooden chalets were built in the 1920's and 30's for use as holiday accommodation. Due to the shortage of housing during the Second World War the chalets became permanent homes and over the last 20 years or so most of them have been replaced with modern bungalows.

Weasel Farm, Weasel Barn, High Bank, Glenholme, Fair View, Jankyns, Lynwood, Stonycroft, and inset Rock Mount – May 2003

TOP O' TH' LOW

The exact date of construction of many of the houses in this area is difficult determine, but several appear to be marked on the earliest maps, although no properties are named. It is recorded that in the mid 19th Century a few children received schooling from a Mr. Thomas Nightingale in his shop at Top o' th' Low, before the school moved to Silk Hall, presumably referring to the building we now know as the Old Post Office, and for a short time, one of the cottages in the area was used as a place of worship by a second breakaway group from the Chapel, the first breakaway group having built the Bethesda fifty years previously. The second group broke away because of a conflict of opinion concerning the appointment of a new minister in 1853.

GOLDEN SONEY
This row was a farm with a barn on the West side and a shippon to the East. It is now divided into four dwellings – The Gables, Vine Cottage, Golden Soney Farm and The Shippon. The age of the property is uncertain, but it appears on Greenwoods Map 1818 and is probably much older.

Top o'th' Low Tockholes c.1935

Front View Golden Soney 2003

Rear View Golden Soney c.1950

38

To be SOLD by AUCTION

On Wednesday the 5th Day of MARCH 1794, AT THE house of THOMAS SHARPLES, the Higher Sun in Blackburn in the County of Lancaster, between the Hours of SIX and EIGHT o'Clock in the Evening, according to such Conditions as shall be then and there produced.

ALL that ESTATE or TENEMENT, situate, lying and being in TOCKHOLES, in the said County, commonly called or known by the Name of **Top 'o th Law**, otherwise **the Lower Spring**, Consisting of Three DWELLING-HOUSES, with Cellars under the same, a Barn, and other suitable Out-Offices; together with a Close of MEADOW LAND thereunto belonging, containing half an Acre or thereabouts, and now in the several Possessions of Mr. John Cocker, Mr. John Townley, and Charles Gregory, at the yearly rent of 14L 7s.

The above Premises are held under and by Virtue of a Demise, for the Term of 999 years, nine of which, and no more, are expired, and will be sold for the Residue of such Term, subject to the Reservations and Covenants in the said Demise.

The said Mr. John Cocker will shew the Premises, and further Particulars may be had at the Office of BEARDSWORTH and Co. in Blackburn.

Blackburn Mail 12th February 1794. Page 1

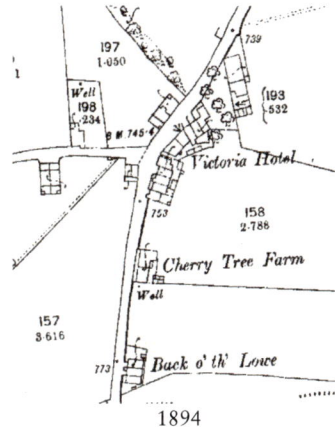

1894

Top o'th' Low c.1900

Hill Crest & View Cottage (top centre) Victoria Inn (left) Nook Cottage (right) 2003

Cranborne 1978

Post Office c. 1900

Post Office c. 2003

THE VICTORIA INN, THE OLD POST OFFICE ROW, WEAVER'S COTTAGE, CLOVER COTTAGE, HILL CREST, VIEW COTTAGE AND CRANBORNE all appear to be represented on Greenwoods Map of 1818, but again, the exact age of each property is unknown, with the exception of Clover Cottage dated 1812. The advertisement of 1794 is thought to relate to the Old Post Office Row and Barn. Also in this area is one new property, **Inglenook**, built in 1990, and a further property is in the course of construction.

Nook Cottage 2003

NOOK COTTAGE: Date unknown but would appear to be represented on Yates' Map of 1786 and is probably much older. The front bedroom window was once much lower, the lintel still being visible, indicating the upstairs was probably a stockroom where goods would have been winched up for storage. There was also a small window at the back of this area, now filled in. The ground floor is divided into two rooms, a sitting room and kitchen, and could have been a loom shop in a previous life. At the rear of the building is evidence of a doorway and on the gable further evidence of a previous attached building.

The cellar is accessed from the kitchen down a flight of stairs against the gable wall. On the opposite wall are the remains of a stone fireplace which reaches from floor to ceiling and almost fills that wall in width. A doorway once led from the cellar to the road and there are windows in both that wall and the gable wall, all now blocked off, showing the land must have been lower at one time. In one corner of the second cellar room are the remains of a low stone wall, the purpose of which is not clear, but it may have been used as a means of heating water in much the same way as the one which stood in the old School. At the beginning of the 20th Century the land at the side of Nook Cottage was acquired and a Grocery & Café built on as a semi detached dwelling. This is now known as **Old Victoria Stores.**

Old Victoria Stores May 2003

WEST VIEW TERRACE. The land on which this Terrace stands was acquired in 1922. Numbers 1 and 2 were built in 1924 as a pair of semi-detached houses for members of the Paley family who lived at Cherry Tree Farm and numbers 3, 4 and 5 were added shortly afterwards.

West View Terrace 2003

CHERRY TREE FARM & BARN. The date stone on this property is 1842. It appears on the map of 1848 but it does not appear on the Census Returns until 1861 under the name Cherry Hall Farm. In the mid 20th Century it was a well-known Tea Room used as a stop-over by cyclists. The barn has been converted to a dwelling now known as Glendale Farm.

Cherry Tree Farm & West View Terrace, 1978

BACK O' TH' LOW

Another row of handloom weavers' cottages, also known as Three Houses, these cottages appear on Yates Map of 1786 but are unnamed. The two bungalows, Heather Lea and Copper Beeches, between Back o'th' Low and Cherry Tree Farm, are 20th century dwellings.

Back o'th' Low 1978

Copper Beech, Heather Lea & Back o'th' Lowe, 2003

HIGHER HILL AREA

Left to right: High Barn, Quarryman's Farm, Cheetham Buildings, Other Cottages, Overgrown Packhorse Road

This is a hamlet of weavers' cottages, built near the previously mentioned Higher Hill Farm. On the approach to this area is a now defunct sandstone quarry and the Farm known as **Quarryman's Farm** was once a Beer House known as the Quarryman's Arms. For many years the Nelson Family ran a business known as "Nelson's Refreshment Rooms" in a cottage at the northern end of Cheetham Buildings and the photograph below shows this family outside their house, the "Refreshment Rooms" sign quite clearly visible. Two of the daughters at one time lived at 3 Shirley Gardens, Emily Maud Nelson and Mrs. Ivy Kay. Emily died in 1969 aged 78 and her sister, Ivy, died in 1991 aged 90 years. All family members are buried in the Churchyard.

High Barn, previously Quarryman's Barn, was converted to a dwelling in the 1980's and has magnificent views over the countryside towards the Fylde Coast. All the other properties in the area have also now been modernised.

Tea Rooms c.1910

Winter 1940 outside 1-3 Higher Hill Cottages

Cheetham Buildings 2002

Cottages at Higher Hill 2002

1 & 2/3 Higher Hill Cottages 2003

HIGHER WHITBANK

Winter 2002

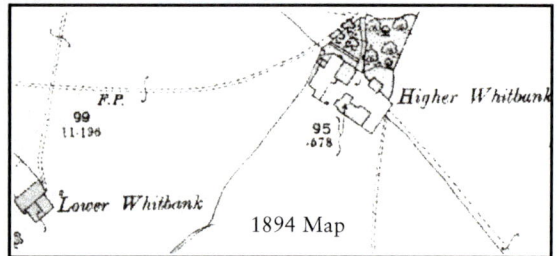

1894 Map

This is an early 18th Century farmhouse, for several years known as Towers Fold, due to the fact the Chapel Minister, the Rev. James Towers, lived there with his family from his appointment in 1722 until his death in 1749. He is buried beneath the pulpit in the Chapel. The 1851 Census reveals three families living at the address Towers Fold, which suggests that some of the buildings appearing on the 1848 map were probably cottages as well as outbuildings to the farm. One family is listed as both power and handloom weavers, another family as farmers and the third as cloggers and power loom weavers. The listing for 'Whitbank', probably Lower Whitbank, shows a family of handloom weavers, but only a pile of stones now remains indicating the position of Lower Whitbank. During the 20th century Higher Whitbank was known locally as 'Waterman's Cottage' because the Water Bailiff, employed by Liverpool Corporation to oversee the land and Reservoirs, lived there. The house is now in private ownership.

Higher Whitbank rear view 1978

Higher Whitbank front view 1978

Higher Whitbank front view 2003

UNKNOWN

During the late Spring of 2002 whilst Transco was building a high pressure gas pipeline through this area, diggers unearthed the foundations of a previously unknown building in Tockholes. It does not appear on any of the old maps so far examined, nor does it appear on any Census Return. It is situated in the field to the West of the main road between the turning for Higher Hill and the gateway to Higher Whitbank, about 10 yards in from the wall. It covered quite an extensive site and was a long, narrow building, similar in design to Lodge Farm and Gorse Farm, but with the addition of a 'porch' or small outbuilding at the front. What appears to have been a fireplace was set centrally against the back wall and room dividing walls could be clearly seen. The archaeologists were brought in but apparently found nothing of significance and the site has now been refilled.

It was probably just another farm complex, but in view of the fact the building was so close to what used to be the main road between Blackburn and Bolton it is possible that it was a hostelry catering for travellers on their way to the markets.

Overall view of the uncovered site

New Barn Farm 2003

NEW BARN FARM

Again, the age of the property is unknown. The present house is built on or near the site of an earlier dwelling and the barn, estimated to be at least 150 years old, is also thought to have replaced an older building, so giving rise to the name by which the farmstead is known. A plan made in 1877 shows both the house and barn being of a similar size at that date. It is understood the first house was once an Ale House in the days prior to the building of The Royal Arms, custom probably being drawn from the workers at the Sandstone Quarry and the Coal Mines on the land behind the farm.

BRADLEY FOLD FARM (Bradley's)

The property is thought to have been built by a descendant of the Marsden family who held estate in Tockholes as long ago as 1523, Hugh Marsden, being recorded as having paid the King's Subsidy tax in that year. Another Marsden, William, living at Ryal Fold, was noted as a Governor of Blackburn Grammar School in 1634.

On one of the bedroom walls in the farmhouse are the initials I.M.M. and a date of 1704. This refers to a James and Mary Marsden, James being a descendant from a branch of this long established family, but the significance of the date is unknown. James Marsden of Bradley in Tockholes, yeoman, is recorded as having married Ann Heaton of Samlesbury, in 1702, but *Abram* does not record a Mary around this time.

Bradley Fold Farm 2003

KILN BANK FARM

Kiln Bank Farm c. 1935

This property was situated in the fields to the east of Trash Lane, near Berry's Tenement. On the 1894 OS map the premises are shown as comprising a long narrow building on the road side and a further detached property in the field to the southwest of the house. The date of origin is unknown, but it is thought it could have been early 17th Century. On the Census of 1841 it is called Saddlestone and lists four families as living there, a total of 21 people. From a painting of 1920 and the above photograph of Darwen Moors, chimneys can be clearly seen on both properties, suggesting that both buildings were dwellings at one time or another, perhaps with two cottages in each building, housing the farm workers mentioned on the 1841 census. The smaller of the two buildings later become a barn.

Windmill - July 2002

In the early 1850's, along with Berry's Tenement and other farms in the area, the land was acquired by the Darwen Corporation Waterworks as a catchment area to feed Dean Reservoir (completed 1854), and thereafter the farms were worked by tenant farmers. A branch of the Croft family first appears at Kiln Bank on the 1871 Census and this family farmed there until 1941. William Croft and his wife Nancy are the first listed, along with

five children. Ten years later there were nine children, and ten years later again William is listed as a widower with eight children, one of whom, Daniel, eventually took over from his father. Lastly, one of Daniel's sons – another William (Bill) – worked the farm with his wife, Matilda (Tilly) and family, from the late 1920's until they left in 1941. Life was quite hard at Kiln Bank as all water had to be carried daily to the house from a well in the field to the east of the house. To lighten his wife's workload, Bill dug a trench from the barn to a point a few hundred yards lower down the hillside, in which he laid a water pipe, and built a windmill to power a water supply back up to a trough near the

Haymaking c. 1930

barn. Water was then channelled to the house from the trough. The windmill and water trough can still be seen today and presumably the pipe is still in the ground. The family moved to Higher Meadow Head Farm in 1941 as the Landlord had refused all requests to improve the

Trough uncovered 2002

44

farmhouse. The property eventually became ruinous and the stone was used for other purposes. Now there is no trace of the buildings. The Croft family were dedicated supporters of the Chapel and many family names can be found on the gravestones in the Chapel yard. They are still represented by Joyce Rothwell, daughter of Bill and Tilly, and her daughter Ann Swanton, who has recently moved back to the Village.

Kiln Bank Farmhouse Circa 1900

Three of the children of William & Nancy Croft.
The lady is thought to be Sarah Croft who died of 'flu on the 4th March 1925, aged 54, seven days after her brother Eli, also a 'flu victim

Kiln Bank Farm & Barn c. 1935

William & Matilda Croft
Last tenants of Kiln Bank Farm

20th CENTURY BUILDINGS

Whilst the majority of houses in the Village are over 200 years old and the Village is now washed over with 'Green Belt' status, as well as the renovation of most of the stone barns in the area, several new dwellings were erected during the 20th Century. As previously mentioned bungalows were built on Pickop Brow in the 1920's and several wooden holiday chalets appeared on Weasel Lane and the Top Road, most of which have now been demolished and the sites rebuilt with modern dwellings. The chalets most recently converted are **Rosemount**, between Golden Soney and The Victoria Inn and the chalet at the top of Weasel Lane now called **Ravenscroft.**

Two further bungalows , were erected in 1926 – "**Cumbria**", the only house in Long Lane, and "**The Paddock**" at Top o'th' Lowe behind Nook Cottage. The Paddock was modernised c.1970.

'**Clayton Bank**', Trash Lane, is another bungalow thought to have been built in the 1920's and extensively modernised 30 years ago.

Rosemount 2003

Ravenscroft, May 2003

Clayton Bank 2003

Cumbria' (foreground); The Paddock (top right) 2003
Golden Soney (top left)

Inglenook 2003

Cumbria 2003

House in course of construction May 2003

46

The several new properties classed as 'infill' are **Inglenook**, built in 1990; **Chapel House** 1995; "**Pickop Cottage**", Pickop Brow c. 1990; **Holly Brook Cottage**, Tockholes Fold, built in the late 1990's and one presently in the course of construction at the top of Old School Lane, opposite Cranborne

Holly Brook Cottage - May 2003

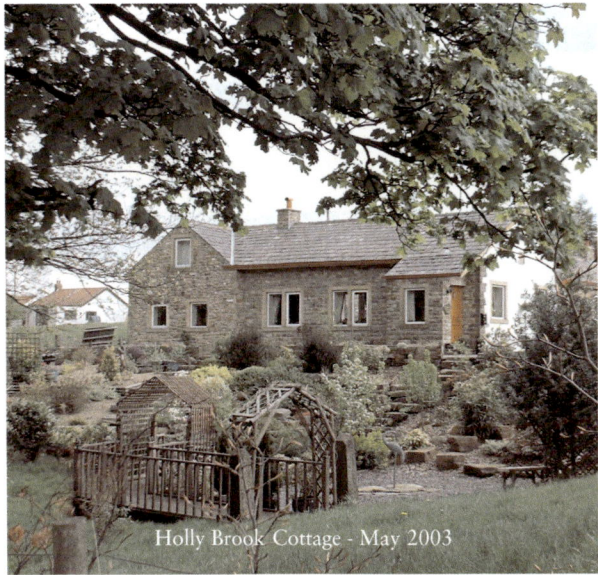
Pickop Cottage, Pickop Brow - May 2003

Ruins of Higher Pasture Barn Farm 2002

To conclude this Chapter:-

There are several properties on the periphery of Tockholes about which there is no information or photographs in the archives. These include Berry's Tenement, Houghtons, Carr Hall Cottages, Winter Hill Cottages and Higher and Lower Meadowhead Farms and Barns. Also Shaw's Farm, near Bradley Farm, which is a modern house built on the site of the ruins of the ancient 'Shaws Farm'.

Properties no longer in existence which have not been previously mentioned and which are not detailed due of lack of information include Treacle Row, Salt Pie, Lands End, Coal Pit House, Tottering Temple, Spring Side, Mount Pleasant, Lower and Higher Dean Farms, Howcroft, Green Hill, Moss Farm, and Higher Pasture Barn Farm on the Coal Pit Lane at the southern boundary of the Village leading to Lyons Colliery. The majority of these names appear on the 1849 map alongside.

CHAPTER 3

CHURCH & CHAPELS

Artist's impression of St. Michael's Church

CHURCH

A plaque erected in the 1833 Church building and later transferred to the porch of the 1965 building reads "Tockholes Church – Built A.D. 640; Rebuilt 1494; Restored 1620; Rebuilt 1833" and goes on to list the known Incumbents and Vicars from 1292, the earliest being Adam de Tockholes. Why the date of 640 was assumed is a mystery and is probably a myth, the date being extremely early in terms of the history of the Church in England.

Mention has been made at various times that a church existed on the present site as long ago as the 1450's but no evidence has been found to date. Further accounts state that a Chapel was built there in 1486, another states 1494, and another says it was built during the reign of Henry the VIII *(1509-1547)*. It is not named in the *Valor* of 1534 and has no pre-Reformation endowment. Little is known of its history but it was probably built as a Chapel of Ease by the Radcliffes, lords of the Manor of Tockholes. By 1610 it was served by a 'Reader', John Shawcross, who was paid by the inhabitants of the area.

In 1620 St. Michael's Church was either re-built or restored and the date 1620 appeared over the main door of the church and on some of the stained glass. It is thought that a bell tower was added at this time. The structure was a diminutive building, low in elevation, about 52 feet long by 22 feet wide. It seated 170 people.

Over the east window was a stone with the initials of Sir John Radcliffe, Knt. Some years after the 1620 rebuilding or restoration, presumably when funds permitted, a 20" bell was hung in the tower. It was inscribed Gloria In Excelsus Deo and dated 1633. It was from the foundry at Wellington, Shropshire, held from 1605–1642 by William Clibury. In 1833 the bell was moved from St. Michael's and hung in the south-west turret of St. Stephen's.

On 23rd February 1832 the foundation stone of the new Church was laid by Lawrence Brock-Hollinshead

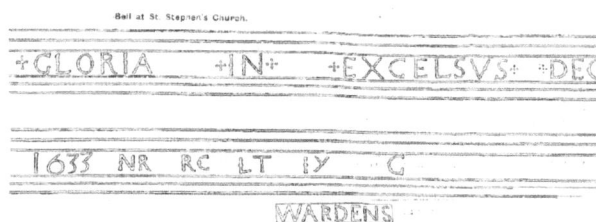

Esq., Lord of the Manor, and the building was completed the following year and consecrated by the Bishop of Chester on the 26th November. The new Church was dedicated to St. Stephen and was built on a new site just to the North of St. Michael's at a cost of £2400. This was defrayed by private subscription aided by a grant of £1200. St. Michael's Church was not demolished until the new building was completed.

Built in the early English style, St. Stephen's Church was about 74 feet long and 45 feet wide. Its plan consisted of a nave, chancel, porch on the south side, and a square projection at the west end in place of a tower,

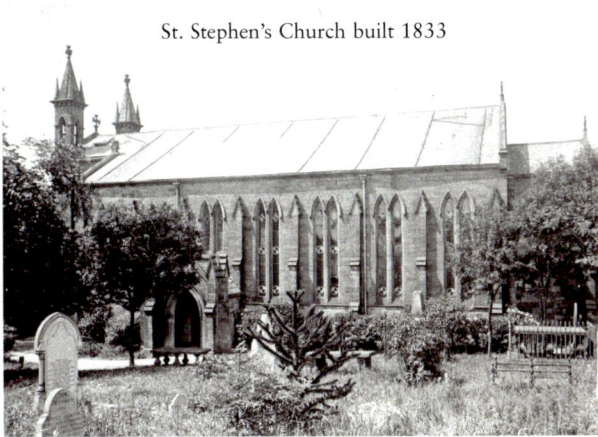

St. Stephen's Church built 1833

surmounted by angle turrets, each with four pinnacles, one of which contained the old bell. The windows were of lancet shape. The beautiful east window depicted the life of St. Stephen, and was erected by John Pickop Esq, J.P. in memory of his parents, Banister and Mary Pickop. A news report of July 1903 states that in the mid 1890's a Miss Kate Pickop bequeathed the sum of £100 for the re-decoration of the sacred edifice. The walls were treated in salmon pink, the roof painted white and the chancel walls were pale green, which enhanced the effect of the East Window. The two lancet windows in the chancel were the gift of L. B. Hollinshead Esq., and the two windows on each side of the body of the church nearest the chancel end were ornamented with escutcheons in stained glass of the arms of the Rev. Dr. Whittaker, the Rev. G Robinson, the Rev. R. Hornby, W. Pickering Esq., W. Feilden, Esq. M.P., Joseph Feilden Esq., L.B.Hollinshead Esq. and ? Ratcliffe Esq. Inside there was a gallery and sittings for 804 persons. Also in the Church was a pedestal upon which was placed a cannon ball. This was thought to have been fired at St. Michael's Church during the Civil War and had been discovered in the Churchyard many years later, probably whilst digging the foundations of the 1833 church.

A great deal of correspondence took place between Rev. Gilmour Robinson – Curate in Charge of Tockholes, the architect, Thomas Rickman, and the Rev. Dr. John Whittaker, Vicar of Blackburn, concerning the building of the new Church. Thomas Rickman was a Birmingham man with a considerable reputation in his field, but from the very outset there were problems, many of them apparently caused by the shortcomings of the builder, Thomas Walsh, according to Rickman. In March 1833 Rickman wrote to Dr. Whittaker *"I begin to wish I had never seen Walsh.....I wish thee could possibly impress him by any means with the mischief he is doing to his own character*

by his continual trifling with me … I do not know what to do but take the job entirely out of his hands, which would be incurring useless expense and endless trouble". Correspondence continued for several years both during and after completion of the building. Robinson's letters appear to have been considered petulant and a nuisance, and the tone of Whittaker's replies, though courteous, were often scathing in content.

Amongst the many letters written by Gilmour Robinson were complaints that the heating system proved to be faulty and on being used nearly burned the building down. On at least one occasion it was impossible to sit in the gallery because of the smoke seeping through the wood-work and masonry. Robinson also considered the roof to be inferior and the slates not suitable for the weather conditions experienced in Tockholes. Rain often penetrated through the roof in several places causing damage to carpets and decorations etc. and also through a window. The bell tower had been designed too small to allow the bell to swing or ring properly, but Rickman replied insisting that the bell be hung as *"there was no intention that the bell should be swung, but that the clapper must be pulled against it to produce the ringing"*! He finally lost patience in one of his letters and concluded angrily to Robinson *"Mind thee thy sermons and I will mind thy church"!*

Even the consecration ceremony brought difficulties. The Bishop of Chester, the Rt. Rev. John Sumner Bird

Interior of St. Stephen's Church c. 1933

(later Archbishop of Canterbury) had planned to attend in October 1833 but this proposal brought hasty letters from Rev. G. Robinson and Walsh to Dr. Whittaker saying that the church could not possibly be ready in time and so it was finally arranged that the Bishop should come in the November instead. It was respectfully pointed out that the roads to the Village were not suitable for the usual type of coach and ultimately the Bishop chose to ride on post-horses. He later sent a bill to the Vicar for the sum of £19.4s. 6d. to cover this cost!

Some 50 years after the opening, plans were underway to raise money to replace the floor 'so injured by dry rot', and also to re-arrange the aisles and remove the organ from its cold position in the west gallery to the body of the church. A new heating apparatus was also required. Gilmour Robinson was eventually proved right on all counts as the church had to be demolished in 1964 due to extensive rot in the roof, the roots of which rot had also penetrated into the rubble filling of the walls.

Thoughts from my Window Seat
(As I see the Demolition of Tockholes Church
April 1964)
By Alice Cross

"What is the Church?" We oft would intone
At our desks in the Village school.
"We are the bricks and faith holds us fast
And Christ is the Cornerstone"

What will be framed? Man cannot alone
Build a house fit for worship and prayer.
But he will succeed, and God's Glory reveal
If Christ be the Cornerstone

And what of ourselves? Shall we ever atone
For the Cross? And yet we must try
By thought, word and deed build a temple within
And let Christ be the Cornerstone.

St. Stephen's during demolition

The last remnants of the Church

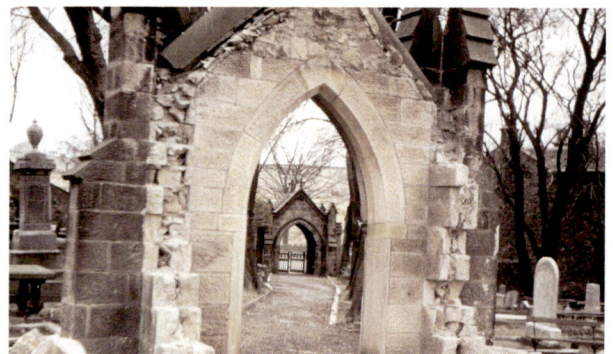
Remains of Porch now incorporated into present Church

St. Stephen's 1966

The present Church building was erected in 1965 and dedicated by the Bishop of Blackburn, Dr. C. R. Claxton on the 26th March 1966. The Church is a modern structure built partly in brick and partly in cedar wood. The porch from the 1833 Church was retained and incorpor-ated into the present building. The building was intended to be temporary and was only meant to last for 12 to 15 years, but apart from the addition of a metal 'barn' roof covering in the 1980's to cure a raining-in problem, it has lasted well and remains unaltered.

The area originally covered by the 1833 Church is still visible and some of the buttresses are incorporated into the present foundations. Many of the fittings from the old Church were lost or destroyed but amongst those preserved are the pulpit, the gift of the relatives of the Rev. & Mrs. Thomason, and dated July 1883, an old oak chest in which the church records were once kept, the Lectern Bible and the communion table acquired as a memorial to those church members who gave their lives in the First World War and inscribed at the base

"To the Glory of God and in Memory of the following who fell in the Great War 1914-1918 – Arthur Catterall, Charles Lloyd, Arthur Worthington (Sidesman), Henry Shaw, John Turner, William Kitchen, John Nelson, James Turner, George Yates. It was provided by general sub-scription and dedicated by the Venerable Archdeacon Allen on 12th September 1920.

Over the years, many people have willingly given their services to the church, one such man being Mr. Jack Coar. In 1968 he was honoured for his 25 years as Vicar's Warden and presented with a silver cigarette box to commemorate the event. Jack went on to serve for another 11 years and by then had also served for 27 years as treasurer. He died in 1987 and is commemorated by a plaque in the lych gate. His grandfather, John Coar, also served as Church Warden for 26 years and there was a plaque to this effect in the old church.

Mr. L. Ranson (Registrar) Jack Coar, (Left Vicar's Warden) Bishop of Blackburn Rt. Rev. C. R. Claxton; Canon P.A. Schofield, Bishop's Chaplain, Rev A. Livesey, Vicar, Ven. H. N. Hodd (Archdeacon of Blackburn) Mr. Milton Rossall (People's Warden)

Similarly, Milton Rossall, a member of an old established family in Tockholes, served along side Jack as People's Warden for 29 years and was also a School Manager. He was a good and faithful servant to Tockholes Church and School and served 7 Vicars. He played a major part in the effort to build the new Church and the extension to the School. Milton retired from his duties in May 1979.

Rev. Allan Livesey became Vicar of Tockholes in 1964 just after the decision had been made to demolish the 1833 Church and build the present one. The new plans had been drawn and demolition had just begun when he took up office. A couple of months later the Church minutes record his words of encouragement to the P.C.C. when he stated "I have stood among the ruins of the Church and I have felt very much like Nehemiah of old when he stood among the ruins of the Temple in the City of Jerusalem. Nevertheless by work and faith and prayer he saw it rise again". Mr. Livesey retired in 1974 and died in 1982 aged 72. He is buried in the Churchyard.

From the early 1950's the Parish Church was constantly under threat of closure due to falling church attendances and the decline in the number of clergy, but in 1980 a merger took place with St. Cuthbert's Church, Darwen, whereby the two churches became a joint benefice called St. Cuthbert with St. Stephen and the Curate of the newly formed amalgamation became Priest-In-Charge of Tockholes and resided in the Village. However, in 2001 the P.C.C. was persuaded that St. Stephen's should become a united benefice with the parish of St. Cuthbert and in October 2001 a Commission, appointed by the Bishop, finally recommended the closure of the Church at Tockholes and the renovation of St.

NEW CHURCH AT TOCKHOLES

The new church of St. Stephen's, Tockholes, which will be consecrated by the Bishop of Blackburn (Dr. C. R. Claxton) tomorrow may be described as a church that his literally risen out of the ashes of the past.

The church has been built on the site of the old church, which had become so decayed that much of the timber was burnt on the spot.

Some of the sorrow felt when the old building was demolished has now been offset by the erection of a splendid modern building. This keeps a link with the former church by the retention and inclusion of the archway.

The new church has large glass windows and is electrically heated. Seating capacity is 120.

PARISH'S PLEDGE
The decision to demolish the old church and rebuild was taken during the incumbancy of the Rev. P.G. Aspden. Demolition started in January 1964, at the same time as the present vicar, the Rev. Allan Livesey, took over.

Overall cost of the scheme is £11,000. The parish, by means of Christian Stewardship have raised a considerable amount towards this; the diocese have made a grant of £2,000 and a further interest free loan of £7,600.

The parish which was at one time described as having "died" has so come alive again that it has pledged itself to repay the diocese the sum of £500 per year off the interest free loan.

Further services, in addition to the consecration will be held on Sunday when the Bishop of Burnley (the Rt. Rev. G. Holderness) will be the first celebrant of Holy communion at 10 a.m.

The vicar will conduct a service of praise and thanksgiving at 3 p.m. to which the public are invited.

New furnishings at the church include: a brass alms dish, Altar cover and pulpit fall, flower vases, church wardens staves, prayer books and processional cross.

In addition the Mothers' Union has provided a new aisle and chancel carpet.

Evening Telegraph

Cuthbert's Church. At the time of writing services are still being held in St. Stephen's twice a month and it is hoped provision will be made for worship to continue elsewhere in the Village should the building be demolished.

If the earliest building had been renovated in 1833 instead of being rebuilt, it is understood the parish would have been saved because it would have had a building of historic importance. A sad end, therefore, to one of the oldest parishes in the district.

Rev. Gilmour Robinson
Gilmour Robinson was described as "a man of considerable medical skill, tall in stature and of military bearing; a Freemason, Constable, and one who had served his country in the Battle of Waterloo." He was born in January 1796 into a military family and educated at the Royal Military College at Marlow, which later became Sandhurst. He was gazetted to the 59th Regiment of

Foot in July 1813 as an Ensign, but by September 1814 had become a Lieutenant. He fought in the Peninsular Wars as well as at Waterloo and presumably learnt his medical skills in the army, skills he readily used to minister to his parishioners free of charge. In 1826 he became a curate at Kirkham and four years later was offered and accepted the position of Incumbent of Tockholes, a job he held until his death at the age of 61 in December 1856.

Only known likeness of Gilmour Robinson

After several bequests in his Will the residue of his estate was invested and the income divided and paid to "the deserving poor, resident in Tockholes, and members of the Church of England." This bequest became known as 'the Robinson Dole' and was paid out on the Feast of Saint John the Evangelist every year for almost 130 years. Eventually the dole was considered so small as to be insignificant and the money was simply added to the general funds of the Church.

Robinson was a Freemason and had risen to high rank in the movement. At the date of his death he held the office of D.G.M. for the district of West Lancashire and his funeral was attended by over 100 members of the movement from Lodges in Liverpool, Southport, Lancaster, Preston, Blackburn, Darwen, Accrington and many other towns in West Lancashire. He was buried with Masonic form and ceremony and the mourners were led by a parade of brethren in full Masonic costume. Several local dignitaries also attended, including Sir W. H. Feilden Bart., H. B. Hollinshead Esq., Thomas Dutton, Esq and Jonathan Morley Esq., as well as numerous friends and members of his congregation. He is buried in St. Stephen's churchyard.

Rev. Ashley T. Corfield

Mr. Corfield came to Tockholes in November 1889. He was formerly curate of St. James' Ashton under Lyne, 1884, and Balderstone from 1885 to 1889. In June 1889 he married Clara Mary Pughe, the second daughter of the Vicar of Mellor. He was educated at Trent College and at St. Catherine's College, Cambridge and was the 5th son of the Rev Frederick Corfield.

Rev. & Mrs A. T. Corfield

An athletic man, Corfield possessed cups for rowing and running during his time at Cambridge and is considered to be the 'father' of Darwen Golf Club, the Committee bestowing on him the honour of life membership in recognition of his services. He also served as Chairman of the Parish Council from its inception in 1894 until his removal in 1910 and held a seat on the Blackburn Board of Guardians. He was President of the Village Club, Chairman of the Tockholes Polling District of the Darwen Conservative Association and Chaplain of the 1st V.B. East Lancashire Regiment.

He appears to have been a very popular vicar, and gained great respect and loyalty from his parishioners. He was not averse to rolling up his sleeves and lending a helping hand, and indeed was responsible for building the present outside pulpit and toches stone. He also taught religion in the day school and helped out on many occasions when the school master was ill. On the last day of every term he was known to deliver sweets to each child in the school. He remained at Tockholes for 21 years, but in 1910 he accepted the living at Bamber Bridge. Twelve months later he moved to Heanor in Derbyshire, his father's old parish.

Corfield was a keen historian and was responsible for the preservation of several antiquities in the Village. Just before he moved to his new parish of Bamber Bridge, he rescued many stones from the demolition of Gerstain Hall and, as previously mentioned, used them to erect the present outside pulpit built against the old school in the churchyard,

Well in Rock Lane 1910

the Norman arch over the trough in Rock Lane and also the gateway, just above the well, leading to the old Vicarage.

The Public Well was built into the wall surrounding the Vicarage and fronting Rock Lane, and was opened with even greater ceremony than the pulpit. As Chaplain to the 1st V.B. East Lancashire Regiment, Rev. Corfield obviously used his influence and arranged for the Church parade of the 4th Battalion, under the command of Col. Johnston V.D. to attend at Tockholes for the Opening Ceremony. A long report of the event, and of the sermon preached, appeared in the Blackburn Gazette of the 10th August 1910 which also reported on the dreadful weather. The Darwen section of the Battalion started from the barracks in 'threatening' weather and shortly afterwards the rain 'poured down', but they were not deterred. The Blackburn section, however, started for Tockholes, marched a portion of the distance, and owing to the heavy downpour by which they were drenched, they were ordered to return, so that only the officers of the Darwen Section, together with Boy Scouts from Darwen and Withnell, were present at the Church. When they eventually reached their destination, Col. Johnston declared the well open: "Residents of Tockholes. It is my great pleasure to dedicate this well to the glory of God for the use of man and beast for now and evermore." The service, which had been planned as an open-air service using the new pulpit, then took place in Church due to the inclement weather.

TOCKHOLES ANTIQUITY

The Village of Tockholes is well-known for having many connections with the ancient past. Looking at its old houses, dating into remote times, the old Congregational Chapel, and the Church of St. Stephen's which have governed the two religious sects of the district for many generations, one cannot but realise the antiquity of the village.

Now comes information of the revival of history probably not known to many. In the old churchyard, and against the *relect (sic)* of the old St. Stephen's schoolroom, a pulpit has just recently been erected, the material of which dates back as far as the 15th century. The old well, which stood in the main roadway leading from the Rock Inn to the Church has also been rebuilt with stone which has been obtained from the same quarter as that used in the erection of the pulpit. About twelve months ago the Liverpool Corporation gave instructions to demolish the old hall which stood opposite the old weaving shed. The hall, which was a 15th century building, was the house of the De Gerstaines, the ancestors of the Lancashire Garstangs. Rather than allow these old stones to be destroyed, the Rev. A. T. Corfield obtained a number of them, which included the mullions and side stones of the windows, and with these, along with the assistance of Mr. John Lofthouse, of the Rock Inn, and Mr. John Paley, of Withnell, he has built the pulpit, which is for use on occasions when open-air services are being held. The pulpit is now complete with the exception of the door, and that will be made of oak. The well, which has been re-built by the same persons, boasts a fine old Norman arch, and gives an antique appearance to the roadway. It is now fed by water from the Vicarage. Over the doorway leading to the Vicarage, has been placed another stone from the same Hall, which bears the date of 1699, but which was evidently inscribed some time after the De Gerstaines took up residence in the village, inasmuch as the style of the figures is quite distinguishable from the style of the other initials which the stone bears.

We understand the pulpit will be formally opened on Sunday week, July 3, by the Bishop of Manchester, who will be present to preach the anniversary sermons.

Blackburn Times June 1910

The Rev. William Hodgkin, B.A.

Mr. Hodgkin was the longest serving vicar of this parish, being here for 40 years. Born in 1870 he was the son of Joseph Hodgkin, Vicar of Treales, and his wife, Hannah. He attended Kirkham Grammar School and later earned his B.A. degree at Keble College, Oxford. After Oxford he attended Edinburgh Theological College and later, in 1906, obtained his L.Mus. Mr. Hodgkin first came to Tockholes in 1911 after several short curacies in the Manchester area. He married Beatrice Blake and had two children, William Blake Hodgkin, who also became a Vicar, and a daughter, Meg. He was a much respected and well-liked man, parishioners still recalling him with fondness long after his death.

During his incumbency he saw his parishioners through the tremendous difficulties of the First World War and considered the effects as having revolutionised the entire structure and framework of society. He saw the introduction of the telephone, the development of the bus services from Darwen and Blackburn, (an event he thought had, to some extent, destroyed the sense of "ruralness") the installation of electricity in the Village and the Church and the change from hand-blowing the organ to electric blowing. He witnessed the surrender of episcopal jurisdiction by the See of Manchester to that of the new See of Blackburn and he struggled with falling congregations due to "an indifference to things religious which had swept over the Country (like a plague of locusts) since the Second World War". He retired in 1951 and died in 1955. He is buried in the churchyard alongside his wife.

Thanks to Mrs. W. Hodgkins Jnr. and her daughter for much of the above information.

Rev. Wm Hodgkin with his presents to mark his retirement in 1950

Centenary celebration 1933

1933 Centenary Celebration Photograph:-
Back Row Left to Right: Frank Entwistle; William Hodgkin Jnr.; Harry Crompton (Caretaker); Milton Rossall; Mrs. Polly Outhwaite; Miss. Annie Bailey; Miss Isobel Rossall; Molly Holdsworth; Miss Dorothy Crompton

2nd Row: Mrs. Lang; Miss Polly Turner; Mrs. Mary Holden; Miss Meg Hodgkin (Vicar's daughter); Miss Betty Rossall; Mrs. Alice Turner; Miss Mary Ellen Coar; Mrs. M. Rossall; Miss Mary Rossall (later Whittle); Jim Hutchinson; Harry Catterall (Organist); Jack Outhwaite

Front Row: Bob Myerscough; Richard Thistlethwaite; William Worthington, Rev. W. Hodgkin; Albert Lang; Jack Coar; Sam Roberts.

RECOLLECTIONS OF LIFE IN TOCKHOLES

By The Rev. Peter George Aspden
Vicar of Tockholes 1959 – 1964

Tockholes in 1959 was, in many respects, not much different to today. Many properties have been improved and some farms no longer exist as such.

In 1959 the vicarage was in use as a vicarage. There was no central heating. There was a Rayburn in the kitchen, which had a tendency to go out overnight if the wind changed direction. All rooms had fireplaces, including the old bathroom, which had been created from a bedroom. As newly married we only furnished the then dining room and two bedrooms, until Gareth's arrival when we used the bedroom over the kitchen for him. Fortunately, the dining/living room gained some heat from the Rayburn and with a good fire could be reasonably comfortable in an evening.

When we first toured the house and saw a large bath with shower attachment it did not occur to us that there might be a problem with the water supply and nobody cared to mention the fact. Only when workmen were working on the roof and ran out of water was the truth revealed – Tockholes had no mains water! The vicarage, in company with the farms had its own private supply. Water was piped from an old cattle trough below The Rock to a large tank in the field besides the vicarage. This held several thousand gallons and the water was fed by a stop cock to the filter beds in the yard and so into the pumping chamber. A float switch in the upstairs tank switched on the pump and all was well if you had remembered to keep the pumping chamber full. If not the pump made a horrible noise and had to be switched off and primed, which usually meant an involuntary shower and 'unparsonical' language! In the yard was a large tank in two parts which was the original water supply. You wondered how they coped. Our first experience of water problems came on a Monday in May 1959. The washing having been done it was a good idea to open the stop cock for the usual ten minutes. Nothing happened. Consultation took place with Colin who was decorating. Drain rods were borrowed from Alan Gibson at Pickering Fold Farm, but still no water. The truth was beginning to dawn on Colin (not the vicar) who suggested we took the inspection cover off the tank. The tank was virtually empty, the level of water having fallen below the outlet pipe. We put Colin's ladders down into the tank and went down in turn, just to say we had done it! As we put the lid back Colin suggested prayers for a thunderstorm as thunder was rumbling in the distance. The day got hotter and hotter. In the evening around 9 p.m. I was in the old study when there was a tremendous flash of lightening right over the church. Hurtling down the drive and into the churchyard I soon saw all was OK and heavy drops of rain sent me back home as quickly as I had gone down to the churchyard. Then the thunderstorm began and lasted until about three o'clock in the morning. By 9.30 a.m. the outbuildings across the yard were barely visible, so heavy was the rain. Next morning not only was the tank full but the yard was flooded as the old water tanks were fed from the overflow of the new and water was gushing out of the pipe. All one could do was open the main stop cock and let gallons upon gallons of precious water run through the filter beds and through the overflow into the septic tank, which certainly got flushed out! The reprieve did not last long and during that hot summer water had to be carried every evening from the horse trough behind Gorse Barn. Though the supply into the trough slowed down, it never stopped. As one can imagine, water was a constant topic of conversation in summer, the question "How's your water?" being normal to residents but not to people out for a walk. Of course the question was often asked for sheer devilment to see how strangers would react. They usually moved away at high speed!

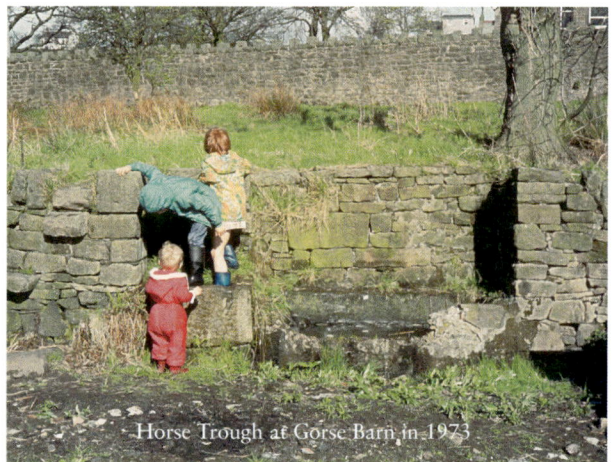
Horse Trough at Gorse Barn in 1973

As there was no mains water so there was no mains sewerage. The school had large buckets in the outside toilets, as had many houses. These were emptied once a week by the sewerage cart which came round the village. The stink was terrible in hot weather and it is almost unbelievable that even in 1959 conditions like that could exist. There were plenty of reservoirs around but the water authorities were very jealous regarding them and no way would they think of supplying Tockholes. An article in the local paper described the people of Tockholes as THE BUCKET BRIGADE. Despite the problems of water supply – most people having to carry water from the nearest spring (always called wells) you never saw a dirty child in school and houses in the village were generally spotless.

The church was large – it seated seven hundred with ease. Despite its size acoustics were no problem and speaking was effortless. There was a good organ and separate choirs for morning and afternoon. Communicants numbered twenty or so; Matins usually half a dozen, Evensong could be thirty or forty depending on the weather and time of year. The church had a lovely east window and in one window the de Radcliffe Coat of Arms, a remnant of medieval glass which sparkled with beauty in the way that modern glass so rarely does. There were two chalices dating from the C18th, which had been presented by a member of the Brock Hollinshead family, the Squire of Tockholes.

On an old harmonium there was a huge Bible. It was so large and heavy it took two to lift it (as Alan Howarth and I regularly did, so he could polish the top of the harmonium). One wonders what happened to it. Cool in summer and delightfully warm when the boiler was in use on Saturday and Sunday, the church was a wonderful haven of peace and quiet, ideal for prayer and meditation. It was not unusual to find visitors who had come for just such a purpose.

The churchyard was a nightmare as the plan did not match reality and Harry Crompton, sexton for many years, often gave descriptions of the situation of a grave which meant nothing to others. Two examples are "West of Jim Turner's grave" and "Near Osbaldeston's grave". There is a wonderful story about a vault and a missing body, but alas, the man who could really tell the tale in all its hilarious details died many years ago.

People connected with the Church were as follows:

Churchwardens: Jack Coar and Milton Rossall

PCC Secretary: John Mares (he did the most wonderful doodles during meetings)

Treasurer: Jack Coar (he hated paying bills)

Organists: Dick Counsell and Eveline Mares

Headteacher: Miss Simcock, who actually lived in Blackpool and lodged in Darwen.

Sexton/Verger/School Caretaker: Alan Howarth. Later Terry Ackroyd

Mrs. Lang, the retired headteacher, lived in the School House

Following Mrs. Lang's death the new headteacher Mrs. Ward and her family moved into the School House.

Mrs. Rossall was the "grandmother" of the PCC and, besides Milton, had another son and two sons-in-law on the PCC. Milton and sons-in-law could be guaranteed to have different points of view from Mrs. Rossall! Mrs. Rossall and I claimed not to be gossips – we just liked to know. Nobody believed us. One of our pleasures in the gloaming of a winter's day was to pick a page in the Bible and one would read to the other a short passage and we would discuss it together. A tough farmer's wife she was a real character but one you soon came to love and admire – even when you did not agree with her and vice versa.

Tockholes is, as we know, full of history. Besides the various churches, which have stood roughly on the same site, there is one of the oldest Independent Chapels in the country, being formed in 1662. The present very pleasant building is not the original, dating from the 1700's. There used to be a small building not far away (below Victoria Terrace) that was built as the result of a bitter quarrel at the Chapel. The dissenting congregation continued for some time, but in the end their descendants returned to the fold. Relations between Church and Chapel were not always good in times past and in 1959 there was a definite 'us and them' on both sides. The new Vicar had other ideas. It was strange that despite the 'us and them' each attended (unofficially) the

300th Chapel Anniversary Celebration

Back Left to Right: Robert Leach; Mrs Walkden; Mrs. Jepson; Mrs Harrison; Mrs Clara Dawson; Harold Smith; Thomas Taylor; James Critchley; Fred Baron; James Blackledge; Alice Walmsley Front: George Gillibrand (Mayor of Blackburn); Unknown; Barbara Castle (Blackburn MP); Rev. P. G. Aspden; Rev. J. A. Figures (Moderator Lancs. Cong. Union) Rev. Hugh Gibson; Charles Fletcher-Cooke (Darwen MP); Unknown; David Davidson (Mayor of Darwen)

others harvest and anniversary services. A new Minister arrived in Darwen, who had responsibility for Tockholes and I soon became friends with Hugh Gibson. We loved sitting in the back room of the Chapel school building on a winter's night when the ladies had gone home from the United Class. There would still be a lovely fire and we would sit and chat for ages. Our great desire was that in 1962 when the Chapel celebrated its 300th Anniversary it should be done at a united service. It was hard work convincing people, but in the end, on a beautiful summer's afternoon the service was held and was a huge success. The two local MP's, Fletcher Cook and Barbara Castle, were present and I learned that the two MP's, despite their differences, were great friends and often collaborated when they agreed that something must be done both locally and nationally. I kept their secret – they relied on people getting the wrong idea about them. Not everybody was happy about the united service and some refused to attend, but in the end about 97% of the village thought it was marvellous and gave their support.

After I had been at Tockholes some two years I was told the truth about the Church – it had been condemned as unsafe ten years before. We had to move into the School, which was not convenient in many ways – we had to set to after a social on Saturday night and get ready for Sunday. Actually we thrived and enjoyed the feeling of closeness that we got in the School. The then PCC were marvellous. The Advisory Board was consulted and an architect obtained. We tried desperately to save the old Church but the roots of the dry rot were so firmly established in the walls that we had to let it go. The old National School was looked at but decided against and so the present building was planned. The PCC looked at the sketches for roughly half an hour and decided in thirty seconds to go ahead. Sadly, before the old Church was even demolished the Bishop, The Rt. Rev. Charles Claxton, decided he wanted me to set up a new parish in St. Annes on Sea. As we left workmen were digging up the main road – another battle had been won – Tockholes was getting mains water at last!

Thanks to Rev. Peter Aspden for the above account

55

HISTORIC CHURCH MAY HAVE TO CLOSE

A BLACKBURN country church that is steeped in history may have to be closed because of dry and wet rot. It is St. Stephen's, Tockholes, where evening prayer was held on Sunday, possibly for the last time.

Bare, ugly patches in the roof where the plaster has fallen show where the rot is at its worst. There are also damp and peeling patches on the walls.

Plans for the future of the church are uncertain. The present 100-odd members would never be able to raise sufficient money to pay for the extensive repairs, but if new inhabitants came to Tockholes the situation might be improved.

The Archdeacon of Blackburn (the Ven. A. S. Picton) told *The Blackburn Times* that the problem of St. Stephen's had been causing him, as well as the vicar, a great deal of worry.

"The future of the church hinges to a large extent on whether the Darwen water authority decide to bring tap water to the village. If they do, it could mean a revival of industry, more inhabitants, and the restoring and re-establishing of St. Stephen's. At present the church is far too large to be supported by the present population . . . but who knows, there *could* be need for a big church in the future.

"We can only wait and see," said the Archdeacon. "I don't think the church roof is in any real danger unless there is a heavy fall of snow in Tockholes. But we can't let the church remain in its present condition indefinitely."

SERVICES IN SCHOOL

The vicar, the Rev. P. G. Aspden, said that services would now be held in the schoolroom, where all the moveable church ornaments and fittings were being stored. Funeral services, however, might have to be held in the church, as the school was not licensed for that purpose.

It was only about **seven years ago**, he said, that St. Stephen's was completely redecorated, and though it was not realised the rot must have been well set in by that time. Church members had managed by really wonderful effort to raise £2,000 to pay for the redecoration, but could hardly raise the sum needed now for restoration.

The vicar estimates that there must have been rot in the church roof as long as 20 years ago, since when it must have been gradually extending, unnoticed.

He thinks that originally the roof was rather badly built, for he has records which mention that it was letting in water just above the organ only 12 months after the church was built in 1833.

The first patch of rot appeared about three years ago, above the organ. Later patches showed just above the balcony at the back of the church, and above the east window.

Church members are very worried in case any further falls of plaster in the near future should damage any of the church treasures. There is, for instance, a stained-glass window that cannot be valued. It dates from 1620 and includes, in brilliant colours, the coat-of-arms of Sir John de Radcliffe, whose ancient home was the manor house.

The east window is also a very beautiful one, worth about £4,000.

Also of historical interest in the church is an ancient oak chest, clamped with iron bands, which contains the church registers, and a strange old musical instrument looking rather like an outsized saxophone.

Just outside the church door is a stone monument, the upper portion of which is supposed to be a remnant of the old parish preaching cross, probably dating from 1684, while the lower portion is probably part of the ancient "toches" stone from which the parish takes it name.

The first parish church of Tockholes, St. Michael's, dates back to 640 A.D., was rebuilt in 1494 and restored in 1620. It was in 1825 that the old fabric was found to be unsafe and a fund was started for the new church to be erected a little to the north of the old one. The foundation stone was laid in February, 1832, by Mr. Lawrence Brock-Hollinshead, Lord of the Manor, and the church was completed and consecrated the following year.

Picture shows the damage over the east window.

THE GRAVEYARD contains a couple of things of interest in addition to the stone pulpit and sundial. These are the grave of John Osbaldeston and the Toches Stone.

John Osbaldeston: Not far from the Vestry door, stands the spindle shaped monument on Osbaldeston's grave. He was born at Snig Brook, Blackburn about 1777 and after some schooling he began work as a hand-loom weaver. He saw the power loom drive out the hand loom and the factory replace the cottage loom shop and it was this evolution which turned his active and inventive mind towards the problems of speeding up the various processes of cotton manufacture in the factories. He worked long hours and spent his spare cash working on his inventions, the most famous one being the Weft Fork. This was a device that brought the loom to a halt when the weft broke. Previously, the loom would have continued running without weft, leaving a gap and so spoiling the cloth.

He was known to have spent a great deal of time in the company of a man called James Bullough discussing his invention and explaining the operation at length, but it was James Bullough who eventually patented the invention in 1841 and who was subsequently accused of having stolen the idea. This offence rankled with Osbaldeston for the rest of his life. He also accused others of "being fattened and those still fattening" from the product of his exertions.

As well as losing a potential fortune from patent rights, he also lost a great deal of money investing in a public house at Four Lane Ends, Blackburn and eventually died in the Workhouse, penniless, at the age of 84. Some years before his death, a number of local cotton manufacturers agreed to contribute to a pension fund for his benefit, but as a result of his threats to commence legal action for the restitution of his patent rights, patrons withdrew their support. Towards the end of his life he even devised his own epitaph, but this was never used – "*Here lies John Osbaldeston, an humble inventor, who raised many to wealth and fortune, but himself lived in poverty and died in obscurity, the dupe of false friends, and the victim of misplaced confidence.*"

He was spared the indignity of a parish funeral thanks to three benefactors and the gift of a grave-space donated by the sympathetic vicar of Tockholes. A suitable monument was erected some years later and states simply "John Osbaldeston. Inventor of the Weft Fork"

The other monument is the **Toches Stone**, situated on the left at the top of the main pathway. The inscription reads "The upper portion of this monument is supposed to be a remnant of the old parish preaching cross probably dating from 684. The lower portion is probably a part of the ancient Toches stone from which the parish takes its name". With so many suppositions its authenticity is very much in doubt. However, *Baines History of Lancashire* of 1870 does refer to a 'perforated stone lying in the Churchyard which was supposed to be the remnant of an *ancient* cross'. No doubt the perforated stone now forming part of the monument is in fact that ancient stone, but there is no evidence to suggest the Village ever had a 'preaching' cross. According to the daughter of the Sexton the monument was built by her father and Rev. A. Corfield about 1909, the same time as the stone pulpit and the Rock Lane Well were erected. They used some old stones that had been lying around in the churchyard for many years. It is suspected *Baines'* reference to an 'ancient' cross was then used, to suggest it had been a 'preaching' cross.

Nightingale does not mention the monument in his book of 1886, but one of his many theories as to how the Village may have got its name could have been borne in mind when the wording of the inscription was under consideration. He referred to the Whalley Coucher Book in which occurred a reference to a 'bek under the Toghes Stone, 1457', but this particular reference related to a place in Great Harwood. Nevertheless, bearing in mind the area was once under control of the Danes, Toghes was thought to mean Tókis, a old Danish personal name, and an old Norse word, hóll, meant a hill or mound. String the two together and it is not too difficult to relate this same information to the name of Tockholes and its surroundings.

Monument to John Osbaldeston

The Toches Stone

CHAPEL

OLD INDEPENDENT CHAPEL, TOCKHOLES, ERECTED A.D. 1710.

Oliver Cromwell died in 1658 and his son, Richard, who succeeded him as Protector, was an ineffective leader and was forced to resign by the Army in 1659. This led to the restoration of the Monarchy the following year when Parliament invited the exiled Charles II to return to England as King. The religious situation at this time was very delicate. The Corporation Act of 1661 prohibited any non-conformist from holding office in any city or municipal corporation and was an attack mainly on the Presbyterians because they were seeking to modify the Episcopal Church Government. The Bishops and the King out-manoeuvred the Presbyterians by getting this Act through Parliament and many non-conformist influential laymen were adversely affected.

In 1662 the publication of a new prayer book and the Act of Uniformity meant that any dissenting ministers not previously episcopally ordained must be re-ordained and must also declare their "unfeigned assent and consent" to the new reformed book of common prayer. It also demanded canonical obedience to bishops on oath and renunciation of the "solemn league and covenant". This was an oath drawn up by Parliament in 1643 imposed on all Englishmen over 18, declaring they would enter into 'a mutual and solemn league and covenant' for the destruction of popery, prelacy, superstition, heresy etc. and also declare their intention 'to preserve the rights and privileges of the parliaments and the liberties of the kingdoms' though without any wish 'to diminish his majesty's just power and greatness'.

The immediate consequence of the Act of Uniformity was to deprive nearly 2,000 ministers of their churches and academic posts. These 'Non-conformists' would accept neither the book of common prayer nor re-ordination because they conscientiously believed that the prayer book was not warranted by scripture. It implied invalidity of their existing ordination and cast doubts on the nature of their ministry. It obliged them to kneel when receiving the sacrament; read lessons from the Apocrypha (books not recognised as canonical or authoritative scriptures); to use the sign of the cross in baptism and it prescribed god-parents to the exclusion of the child's own parents. The Act also affected schoolmasters, professors, university teachers and civil servants and caused terrible hardship and privation to such men and their families. This is the date which was considered as the break-away date from the established church and the one which is now noted on the Chapel Notice Board as being the date Non-Conformity was established in Tockholes.

Two further acts were passed putting even more pressure on the nonconformists; the Conventicle Act of 1664 which made it illegal for anyone over 16 to attend any assembly, conventicle, or meeting for religious purposes other than according to the Church of England, and the Five Mile Act of 1666 which forbade any nonconformist minister to live or visit within 5 miles of any place in which he had previously worked. All these acts did much to divide England permanently into conformists and nonconformists and from then onwards a clear line was drawn between those who accepted the teachings and disciplines of the established church and those who were determined to preserve their independence.

Undeterred by such hardships and persecution, and the threat of fines and imprisonment, the Independents still met for worship, led by ejected ministers, in woods and secluded retreats in the hills and moors. After the Conventicle Act of 1664 came into force it is understood that the people of Tockholes and Rivington frequently assembled to worship God according to the dictates of their consciences, in the open air, at a place called Winter Hill. Seats were cut out of the side of the hill, so as to form an amphitheatre, in the centre of which was a stone pulpit. Tockholes was a stronghold of independency, probably because of its isolation and therefore the lack of either too much pressure from one side, or too much influence from the bishops on the other side, and also to the devotion of its ministers. Its strength can be seen from the fact that it became the 'mecca' of non-conformity over a wide area - from Hoghton, Witton, Livesey, Withnell, Whittle-le-woods, Bolton and Blackburn.

However, in 1672 Charles II issued a 'Declaration of Indulgence' asserting his right to cancel all penal legislation against both Protestants and Catholics and as a result licences to preach were immediately taken out, amongst them, one to 'license John Harvie to be a Presbyterian teacher in a meeting-house in Tockley (Tockholes) erected for that purpose in the Parish of Blackburn, Lancaster' 1st May 1672. And so the story of non-conformity in Tockholes began officially. Nothing is known regarding the first meeting house and it was probably only a temporary structure. The terms of the licence, however, appear to suggest that a separate, purpose-built meeting-house was set up, even though most of the meeting-houses licensed at that time were private houses or barns and as the Act was passed on the 15th March 1672 and the Licence was taken out on the 8th of May the same year, it would imply that a building already in existence was used as a Chapel.

Prior to 1662, St. Michael's Chapel of Ease had at least two ministers with strong non-conformist views and as a result their ministries were cut short by the established Church, but their time spent in the village left a deep impression upon the people and shaped the future of non-conformity in Tockholes. St. Michael's also had several non-conformist trustees and as late as 1704 Bishop Gastrell wrote that money was in the hands of the Presbyterian Trustees, who gave no account of the Benefactors but paid the Curate punctually. He also referred to 'a School-house lately erected in Tockholes' administered by the same Trustees (along with others), but that sometime after the revolution of 1688, these trustees appear to have obtained the use of the Chapel for themselves and other dissenters on alternate Sundays, although tradition says one half day each Sunday and the Church of England the other half day. So what had happened to the 'meeting-house' of 1672 and where was the 'school house'? Whichever arrangement existed between Church and Chapel folk, it appears that relations between the two parties were very friendly. However, these arrangements were very shocking to the Bishop of Chester and he commanded that they be discontinued. The Non-conformists were therefore compelled to provide their own accommodation and as a result a chapel was erected in 1710 on the site of the present Chapel.

An Indenture made on the 10th July 1716 later transferred the Chapel building and the land upon which the edifice was erected from James Marsden Snr., Robert Etough and James Walmsley, all of Tockholes, Yeomen, of the first part to Henry Norris of Hoghton, Gentleman, Robert Bury of Hoghton, Yeoman, Edward Boardman of Witton, Robert Boardman of Livesey, Richard Dewhurst of Withnell, Richard Haydock of Tockholes and Thomas Marsden of Whittle, Yeomen of the other part, as Trustees of the Chapel, and confirmed that an arrangement had previously existed whereby the Dissenters had once been permitted to use the Church building. It recited that "whereas certain of his Majestie's Protestant subjects, dissenting from the Church of England, heretofore had the use of the Parochial Chappell in Tockholes aforesaid certain days monthly for the exercise of their Religious Worship, and being afterwards abridged thereof by the Bishopp of Chester, they have rather then contest their liberty thereto with his Lordshipp bought a parcel of land part of the close called the Upper Croft within Tockholes aforesaid, being about 20 yards square and thereupon have built an Edifice which is now certified, recorded and used for the worship of such Dissenters."

There is no picture of the building in its original form, but its description is as follows: "a low, thatched, oblong building with small square belfry tower at the west end. The windows had small, diamond-shaped panes". Two large square pews in the centre of the Chapel were owned by the Hoghton family, patrons of nonconformity in Tockholes. On the door panels were affixed the shield and monogram of Lady Mary Hoghton, widow of Sir Charles Hoghton, who died in 1710.

The first alteration to the building took place in 1777 because of increased congregations. Accordingly the west gallery was put in, but this necessitated removing the thatched roof and raising the walls about 3 to 4 feet. The original windows were replaced with small squares with mullions and the bell cot was fixed to the gable of the building, reached by a flight of steps. The gallery was also entered from the top of the same steps. The second or east gallery was added in 1780, and the front or new gallery in 1822.

No other serious alterations were made, but in 1870 the roof had become unsafe and was repaired, and the mullioned windows were replaced with larger, modern panes. Stained glass windows were inserted in the east and west ends and a new window created in the wall next to the pulpit. The greater part of the chapel was re-floored and the old pews dispensed with and long, single ones substituted. It measured 41 feet by 26 feet and seated about 300 people. One long aisle traversed it from east to west, a shorter one from each door intersecting. The one from the east door led into the vestry. The pulpit was fixed against the north wall and the singing pew was beneath the pulpit. Over the pulpit was a sounding board, hung by a chain or iron rod fixed in the ceiling. The pews were all made of oak, many of which were inscribed with dates and initials of pew holders.

In 1880, the roof was found to be so unsafe that a new one was imperative. The original scheme was to preserve externally, as nearly as possible, the antique appearance of the building, but to carry out internally a complete transformation. When the restoration was commenced, however, it became evident that the original intentions could not be carried out as the main-stays gave way and threatened to collapse and the

Old Independent Chapel

rest of the building was unsound. It was therefore resolved to raze it to the ground and erect a modern church on the same site.

Early chapel life will probably never be known, as documents relating to its history have vanished, including the old church book, which would have been priceless today. It is difficult to believe the story that almost 200 years ago the daughter of one of the ministers tore up its pages for curl papers!

A QUAINT TOCKHOLES RELIC

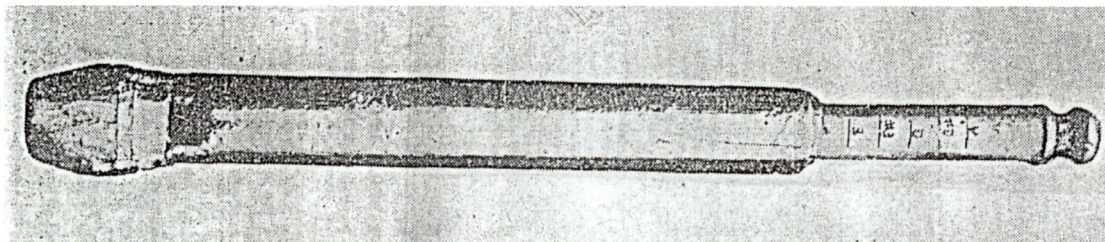

Some forty years ago, probably more out of curiosity than a sense of duty, the then caretaker of the Old Independent Meeting House at Tockholes made an inspection of the dark area under the floor of the building and lying almost buried among the dry earth and stones, he found the old and interesting musical instrument of wood illustrated here. Investigation proved it to be the original pitch-pipe used in the old 1710 chapel for giving the key for the hymns and psalms, and was, no doubt, thrown away by its then owner on the introduction of the more reliable metal tuning-forks. It consists of a small stopped diapa-on pipe with long movable graduated stopper, blown by the mouth and adjustable approximately to any note of the scale by pushing the stopper inwards or outwards. A pipe of this kind was so much influenced by temperature, moisture, force of blowing and irregularities of calibre, that it would only be depended on for the pitch of vocal music and not to be trusted for more accurate determinations. Apart from being a little worm-eaten, this interesting relic is in an excellent state of preservation.

The late Dr. Benjamin Nightingale, the well-known historian of North-west England Nonconformity, states in one of his books that in the early part of the last century the Old Independent Meeting House at Tockholes had several adherents who made a name for themselves as hymn and tune-writers, and the small orchestra of string and wind instruments appears to have formed an important part of the religious life of the district. Chiselled on an old monument in the graveyard of a former local musician is a hymn tune he composed. There are still treasured in distant households, whose ancestors were in the choir of this old and out-of-the-way worshipping place, musical instruments used for generations prior to the introduction of more modern means of accompaniment.

The old wooden pitch-pipe has now become a rare curio by reason of the small number in existence, and a short time ago a request was received by Mr. Critchley, of Livesey, to allow the one illustrated here to be placed in the museum of an old East Coast cathedral town, but it is intended to offer it, along with other old links with the past, to some local museum.

Blackburn Times 10th August 1935.

THE NEW CHAPEL

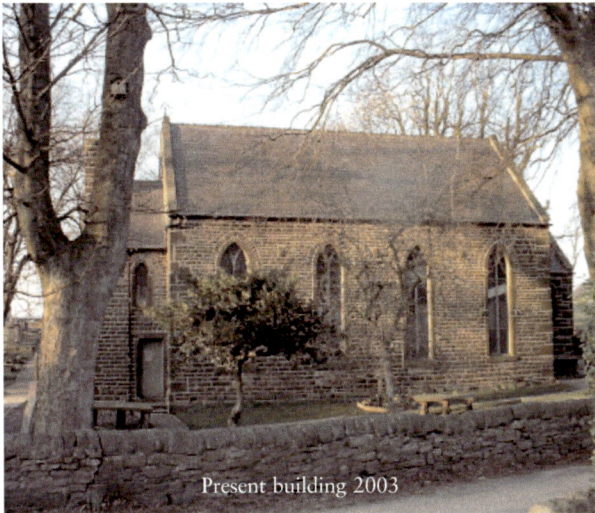

Present building 2003

Two corner stones were laid on 8th May 1880, just three months after demolition had started. One was laid by Miss Walsh, of Atlas House, Darwen and the other by Mr. J. Fish J. P. of Blackburn, both of whom were presented with a trowel and a mallet made from wood taken from the old building. Addresses were given by Messrs. W. Snape, A. E. Eccles and the Pastor A. Lee. Tea was served afterwards in the Silk Hall Room and in the evening an entertainment was given in the Bethesda Chapel. The collection at the ceremony amounted to £51.18.1½.

[6] "Its style is mixed gothic. In each of the two long sides are four long windows, worked in diamond-shaped pattern with pitch pine frames. It is entered at the east side by means of a porch, over which a stone has been placed containing the following inscription:- "Church formed A.D. 1662. Former Chapel built A.D. 1710. Rebuilt A.D. 1880.

An aisle runs from the porch down the centre of the Chapel to the pulpit, and on each side of this aisle lie all the pews. The pulpit, the gift of Mr. John Walsh of Darwen and erected in memory of his wife, rests on ornamental walnut columns, is finely upholstered and is made of best pitch pine and is the workmanship of Mr. T. Fawcett, formerly of Tockholes. In the communion is a handsome chair and table, made of polished pitch pine, the gifts of Mr. J. T. Gregson of Tockholes.

Behind the pulpit are doorways leading into two vestries, and above the vestries is the organ chamber. The organ is the gift again of Mr. John Walsh. There is only one gallery, and this is over the east entrance, a flight of steps to the right of the porch leads up to it. The pew doors from the old church, containing the initials and dates of the original seat holders, were removed and used in the new gallery.

The roof is supported by three sets of principals, well framed and bolted together and resting upon ornamented stone corbels. The ceiling is likewise boarded with pitch pine, and has between each set of principals spaces for ventilation, which has been planned upon the newest principle. Along the base of the roof there are plaster plinths, with quatrefoils set in colours. The walls are covered with plaster, while over the windows there are plaster mouldings, terminating in ornamental plaster corbels."

At the same time as the re-building, the burial ground was also greatly enlarged, and a new perimeter wall built. The whole undertaking cost £926.3.5d.

A major event in the life of the present building was the disastrous fire on 9th December 1945. This occurred in the Vestry and was thought to have been caused by faulty heating apparatus. A great deal of damage was done, including the destruction of the organ and organ loft immediately above the vestry and to the roof. The Chapel was eventually re-opened on 27th June 1948 and the organ was replaced in 1952.

Chapel Interior

Chapel Interior c.1900
Mr. Critchley (left). Mr. Edwards (right)

[6] *Extract from Rev. B. Nightingale's description of the finished building*

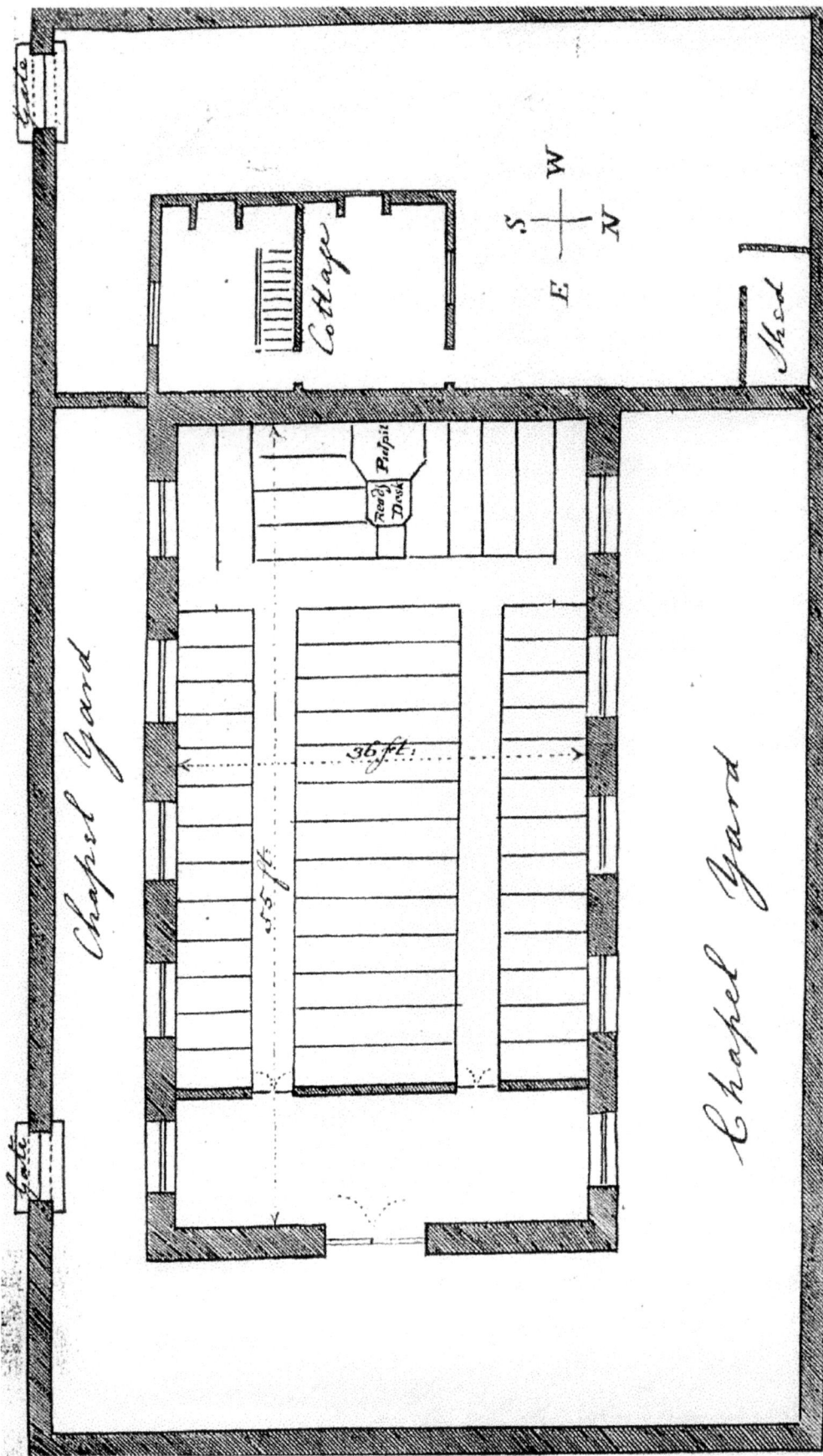

Plan of the Chapel, called "Bethesda" at "Tockholes" with the Chapel Yard, & cottage attached to it.

Nov. 16th 1831.

Scale 8 feet to an inch.

THE BETHESDA CHAPEL

BETHESDA CHAPEL, TOCKHOLES, ERECTED A.D. 1803.

This Chapel came into existence under unfortunate circumstances. Differences with the minister of the old Congregational Chapel led to the secession of a number of prominent families in 1803, amongst them the Cockers, Richardsons, Brindles, Smiths and Nightingales, who built themselves the Bethesda. This breakaway group joined the Countess of Huntingdon's Connexion, and had only three ministers during its short lifetime, the last one dying in March 1815. *Nightingale* records that very little was known of the first minister, the Rev. Thomas Pearson, whose name first appears in a Baptismal Register in 1805, except that on preaching his farewell sermon he used the most violent language, both about the chapel and the people. However, he does appear to have had the health of the children in the Village uppermost in his mind as his 'thank you' letter printed in a local newspaper shows:-

" *The advantages of Vaccine Inoculation in affording an absolute security against the contagion of Small Pox, having been ascertained with a degree of evidence which precludes all contradiction I have been long solicitous that the Children of the Poor, in the district of Tockholes, should partake of the benefits of this invaluable discovery.*

As the circumstances of a large proportion of the people in this neighbourhood rendered it impossible for them to offer a suitable remuneration to a Medical Gentleman, for the trouble and attendance necessarily connected with a general Inoculation for the Vaccine Pock, they were reduced to the necessity of seeking gratuitous assistance, or of exposing their Children as victims to a painful, loathsome and often fatal disease.

Being deeply impressed with the difficulties of their situation, I took the liberty of representing these circumstances to MR. BARLOW, Surgeon in Blackburn, and as the friend of the Poor, implored his assistance. With kindness and liberality, as honourable to himself, as to his profession, he readily undertook to communicate the Vaccine Infection to the Children of as many Poor as chose to apply; and on Friday last he Inoculated ONE HUNDRED AND TWENTY-SEVEN CHILDREN in Beshesda Chapel, of this place.

I feel it, therefore, my duty to offer him this Public Acknowledgement, in my own Name, and in the names of the Poor, for his benevolent exertions, and to assure him that he will have our prayers, that it may please God to enrich him with blessings infinitely surpassing those which have been conferred on us by his skill and humanity.

T. PEARSON – Minister of Bethesda Chapel, Tockholes" May 1804

From the copy of the engraving of that building it can be seen that the chapel was built very much after the style of the Chapel the dissenters had left. The entrance was on the east side, over which was inserted a stone with the inscription "BETHESDA CHAPEL 1803".

One long aisle led down each side of the building and on the wall sides were large square pews, the centre being filled with small, narrow ones. Originally it had three pulpits, but this was reduced to one, which stood on the west side immediately facing the entrance. Below the pulpit was the singing pew. The pews were all numbered and there were sittings for about 300 people. A large candelabrum hung in the centre. The Chapel had no gallery, but to the right, on entering, a flight of steps led to an upper room used as a vestry.

Externally there were two rows of windows with small square panes of glass running down each of the long sides; a bell cot, supported on pillars, stood on the east gable, but this was removed for safety reasons quite some time before the building was demolished, and adjoining the west wall was a little cottage used as a manse for the minister. There was a spacious burial ground surrounding the chapel and a goodly number of fine ash and plane trees, which gave it a 'picture postcard' look.

The date services were discontinued here is not certain, but it is known that shortly after Mr. Whiteley, (the old chapel minister with whom the original dispute had arisen), had removed from Tockholes in 1819, most people went back to the old Chapel.

In 1831 negotiations took place with a view to the Bethesda being licensed by the Bishop of Chester for use by the Church of England worshippers whilst their new Church was being built. Notes of an interview with Mr. John Cocker held on the 16th November 1831 at the Rev. Gilmour Robinson's Parsonage House and written by John Wm. Whittaker for the Church, explain the situation with regard to the building at that date, including an outstanding debt of £425 due to Mr. John Cocker. Mr. Cocker was unwilling to hand over the title deeds etc until indemnified of the above amount and Mr. Walmsley Richardson of Preston, was unwilling to dispose of the Ground Rent thereon of £1.8s 4d per annum. When asked *"for what sum the Trustees would convey the property to the Vicar of Blackburn for eventual consecration, entirely avoiding the place and retaining no rights and privileges in it"* Mr. Cocker replied that he was unable to answer the question, would consult his colleagues, and would deliver their reply to the Vicar. The reply was obviously unfavourable as worship continued in the dilapidated St. Michael's whilst St. Stephen's was being built.

In 1851 the Rev. Abram persuaded his people to purchase the building at a cost of about £40. Once the property was in the hands of the chapel authorities, the vestry was used for school purposes, and a short while after that, the house at the end of the chapel, formerly the manse, became the nonconformist day school. This part consisted of two rooms below and two above, one room on the ground floor being called "The Shop" where weaving was carried on, presumably by the schoolmaster in order to supplement his income. Services were held in the

Mortuary Chapel c. 1910

Bethesda again on Sunday evenings and at the old Chapel in the morning and afternoon. Occasionally, school sermons were preached in it and for many years it was also a Sunday School. Prior to the Lecture Room at Silk Hall being made, it was also used for tea meetings and other public gatherings. In the early 1860's the school ceased and the children were sent to St. Stephen's Church school.

In 1900 a small mortuary chapel was built on the site of the old Bethesda and the grounds were restored. The entire cost of this work amounted to £160 and was defrayed by John Pickop Esq., out of respect to his ancestors who were buried in the graveyard. A public service was held in November 1900 to commemorate the opening of the new Mortuary Chapel, also called the Bethesda, presided over by Mr. A. Eccles of White Coppice, a native of Tockholes, and tea and entertainment was provided afterwards in the new Sunday School (now the Village Hall). The Chapel was very small and had a fire-place where the altar would normally have been. Whether this place was actually used as a mortuary is uncertain – the word 'mortuary' was probably used as an alternative to 'memorial'.

For many years the building was disused, other than for the storage of old newspapers and waste paper collected to raised money for school funds. It was demolished in the early 1980's for safety reasons and because no money was available for repairs.

In addition to the trouble that led to the breakaway group of 1803 forming the Bethesda Chapel, a further upset occurred in 1853 which, for a short time, resulted in a second breakaway group being formed. The *Blackburn Standard* reported on 12th January 1853 as follows:-

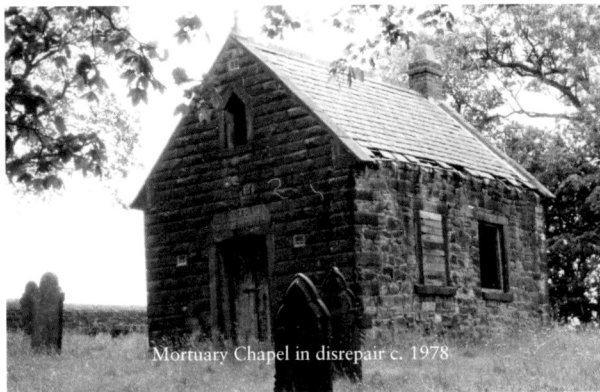

Mortuary Chapel in disrepair c. 1978

"SIEGE OF A CHAPEL.

Since the death of the late Mr. Abrams, minister of the Independent chapel, Tockholes, that village has been the scene of much disturbance between the members of his congregation. It appears that one part of the congregation, headed by one of the trustees, named Leigh, have invited a minister from Yorkshire to succeed Mr. Abrams, and have installed him into the chapel, and a house belonging to it, against the wishes of another portion of the congregation. The keys of the chapel were in the hands of Leigh's party, which is the more numerous one; and the "opposition" being unable to accomplish its ends by dint of numbers, resolved on more objectionable methods. One of the defeated party went to the sexton, and, under pretence of repairing the chapel, got possession of the keys, locked the doors and gates, and put the keys in his pocket. This enraged the "ministerial" party, and on Sunday morning, they gathered themselves together and proceeded to the chapel in a body, armed with hammers and chisels, and headed by a brother of Mr. Leigh. Meeting with no opposition, they speedily broke open the gate and doors. After having effected an entrance, they fetched the minister from an adjoining house, and a late service was gone through in a peaceable manner. During these proceedings, a large crowd of persons had gathered around the building, but some policemen were present, and no breach of the peace was committed.

THE NEW SUNDAY SCHOOL

The Independent Sunday School c. 1910

In 1899 it was found necessary to build a new Sunday School. Mr Eccles of White Coppice, Nr. Chorley offered the sum of £100 towards the project, as did John Pickop Esq. of Blackburn, but Mr. Pickop's offer was made on the condition that the new Sunday School be built on the site of the old Bethesda, that building then being in a state of decay, and the grounds being unsightly.

After much discussion it was decided that the site of the Bethesda was undesirable as it was most inconvenient to get to, and so Mr. Pickop's offer was unanimously declined. The site chosen was the one near Silk Hall, on the main highway. A building committee was formed consisting of the Pastor, Deacons and a few outside members, who were responsible for getting specifications and tenders etc. and who saw to the demolition of the old Bethesda. The Pastor persuaded the farmer members of his congregation to cart the stone and other materials from the Bethesda to the new site on the top road, and this they did free of charge.

The corner stones were laid by the Mayor of Blackburn, Mr. Eli Heyworth, J.P., Alderman T. Lightbown, J.P., Darwen, Mr. W. W. Richardson of Tockholes and Mr. Eli Smith of Withnell. Mr. Richardson was a member of the nonconformist family who had been prominent in the area for over 150 years at that time and whose ancestor had built Silk Hall. Mr. Smith was an old scholar. A car park was added in 1976 and several years later a new toilet block extension was built. The building is used today as a Village Hall.

Order of Service.

HYMN No. 1.   Reading of Scripture - Rev. H. IRVING.   Prayer - Rev. W. C. RUSSELL, M.A.

CHAIRMAN'S ADDRESS.   STATEMENT BY THE PASTOR.

Presentation of Trowel to the Mayor, by REV. R. NICHOLLS, Chairman of Lancashire Congregation Union.

ADDRESS BY THE MAYOR, who will lay the 1st Stone.

Presentation of Trowel by EPHRAIM HINDLE, Esq., to *Ald. Timothy Lighthown, J.P., G., who will Address the Meeting and lay Stone No. 2.*

HYMN No. II.   ADDRESS BY REV. B. NIGHTINGALE.

Presentation of Trowel by Mr. SAMUEL NIGHTINGALE, the School Superintendent, to *Mr. Wm. Richardson, who will lay Stone No. 3.*

Presentation of Trowel by Mr. JOSEPH GERARD, to *Mr. Eli Smith, of Withnell, who will lay Stone No. 4.*

ADDRESS BY REV. FRED HIBBERT.   COLLECTION.

VOTE OF THANKS, moved by Rev. WM. ANGUS.   Seconded by Rev. JAMES JOHNSTON.

HYMN III.   DOXOLOGY.

BENEDICTION -   Rev. F. L. SHILLITO.

Tea at 5-30, and Public Meeting.

SPLENDID ENTERTAINMENT BY THE DARWEN ORPHEUS BAND.

CONDUCTOR   R. WALMSLEY, ESQ.

SEVERAL MINISTERS AND FRIENDS WILL ADDRESS THE MEETING.

Chairman -   Rev. J. HORNBY, of Belmont.   ALL WELCOME.

Cockbolen Congregational Church

MAGAZINE.

CHURCH FORMED 1662.

TIMES OF SERVICE:—

MORNING at 10.30.   AFTERNOON at 2-30.   SUNDAY SCHOOL at 1.30.

WEEK NIGHT SERVICE on TUESDAY EVENINGS in SILK HALL at 7-15.

BAPTISMS any Sunday Afternoon.

Licensed for the Solemnization of Marriages.

For FUNERALS apply to the Pastor.

Church Officers:

Pastor—Rev. DAVID CRITCHLEY, Silk Hall.

Deacons:

MR. WM. W. RICHARDSON.	MR. GEORGE YATES.
MR. ELI SMITH.	MR. SETH MARTIN.
MR. WM. EDWARDS.	MR. S. NIGHTINGALE.

Secretary:

Mr. RALPH WHITE, Close Farm.

Treasurer:

Mr. WM. W. RICHARDSON, Crosslands.

Caretaker:

Mr. JOHN LONSDALE.

SUPERINTENDENT OF SUNDAY SCHOOL, MR. S. NIGHTINGALE.

PRICE ONE PENNY.

Inson & Son, Printers, Cort Street, Blackburn.

Dear Friends,

SATURDAY, August 5th, 1899, will find an important place in the very interesting history of our church, as it will provide for Mr. Nightingale, our historian, an important chapter for his next edition of his book, for on this day were laid the Memorial Stones of our New Sunday School. The weather was favourable, and a large number of friends came from far and near to make up one of the happiest gatherings ever held in Tockholes. The meeting was a grand one. In spirit, its order, the singing and addresses, and collection of £194 6s. 6d., made it a memorable meeting, and one long to be remembered. Councillor Ralph Yates, of Darwen, was an ideal Chairman. Right well did he conduct the proceedings, and all could see that his heart was with us.

The stones were well and duly laid by Eli Heyworth, Esq., J.P., of Blackburn; Timothy Lightbown, Esq., J.P., C.A., of Darwen; and by our trusted friends and deacons, Mr. Wm. W. Richardson and Mr. Eli Smith, of Withnell. Each of these gentlemen received a beautiful trowel, as good as beautiful, supplied by the celebrated silversmiths of London and Sheffield, Messrs. Mappin Brothers, on which were suitable inscriptions to remind these friends of the event in the days that are to come. Rev. Henry Irving read a portion of Scripture, and the Rev. W. C. Russell, M.A., offered up prayer. Then we had the capital address of the Chairman, who referred to the splendid work that had been done by the noble men and women who had laboured there during the past two centuries. The amount of influence for good that cause had exerted could not be measured, and he rejoiced to know that the present pastor and people were most worthily and successfully maintaining the best traditions which made that place sacred to free churchmen. He hoped all present would, in a practical way, express their appreciation of the good work being done.

The Pastor, Rev. David Critchley, next made a statement in which he said their cause occupied an unique position among the churches of that district. It was the parent of many children. Faithful men and women had laboured there for over two centuries, and had stood for Christ, and truth and freedom, on open bible and spiritual religion. Scores and hundreds of men and women had been blessed through the ministry there. The value or sacredness of a place did not centre so much in the fact of its external beauty, but by its spiritual associations and influence. They were indebted to the brave men and women who had witnessed there. The old Silk Hall had done splendid service and answered a most useful purpose, but was now out of date and unsuitable for successful Sunday School work, and it was mainly through a most distinguished son of Tockholes—a man who had devoted his life to the cause of human good, and who had ever been a genuine friend to that cause—A. E. Eccles, Esq., of White Coppice, that they were enabled to begin that good work. He had generously given £100 to commence with, and his kindness had been well supplemented by the kind help of others. He prayed that the new school would ever be a centre of life, power and blessing. Mr. Critchley also stated how the whole life had been moulded and blessed through the impression made upon him in his youth by Mr. Heyworth.

Mr. Heyworth, in his earnest address, said he was delighted to come, as was also Mrs Heyworth, to Tockholes, to encourage the pastor and the people who had had charge of the tea, and our lady friends who had kindly given the young men and women who kindly given was one, that Cromwell's influence had made its mark upon the people who had for long years been identified with that honoured cause, and he hoped it would go on and be abundantly prospered.

Mr. Lightbown next addressed the meeting, and said that Nonconformists in all the surrounding districts owed much to that grand old cause, for it had sent out good men and true to plant

had had many friends in the past. They would never forget the generosity of the late Mr. John Walsh of Darwen, and of Dr. Joseph Hacker and his mother of Blackburn, who had been true friends to their cause. The whole of the day's proceedings were a great success. The Lord be praised for His goodness to us.

We have now promised us over £500 towards our school funds. Let us strive earnestly to raise £200 more.

Our Prize Day was held on Sunday last, and was a most pleasing event. Over 80 prizes were given. *Particulars next month.*

those causes which had been such a blessing to us many. He rejoiced that on his father's and mother's side he could trace back his connection with puritanism for over 200 years. He prayed that school might over be a true memory-home for the church, and that out of it might come a splendid band of witnesses for the truth.

Rev. R. Nightingale, whose presence gave much pleasure to all of us, said he rejoiced to be present that day. His heart was made glad when he heard or saw that the cause he loved and that meant so much to him was doing well. He was pleased that two of his old schoolfellows—Mr. Wm. W. Richardson and Mr. Eli Smith, had laid two of the memorial stones that day. Their last two of them immortal stones had a splendid history, and Church at Tockholes had a splendid history, and they were proud of it. It had for over 300 years stood true to the great Free Church principles of their forefathers.

Rev. Fred Ibbison, in a humorous speech said, that when he was a boy an old teacher of his used to say that England was the greatest country in the world, that Lancashire was the best county in England, and that Tockholes was the grandest village in the county. He too rejoiced in the prosperity of that grand old church.

Rev. R. Nicholls, F. L. Shillito and Allen, Messrs. Ephraim Hindle, S. Nightingale, and J. Gerard also took part in the meeting. The Pastor thanked all present for their presence and help.

The Tea Meeting and Entertainment were a great success, stores could not get in the room; and it was a rich treat by their magnificent all the provisions, did splendidly. The Orphans all the provisions, did splendidly. The Orphans gave a rich treat by their magnificent Walmsley, gave a rich treat by their magnificent entertainment, as did Mr. J. Hornby, our ever welcome brother from Bolton, presided; and the Pastor, at the meeting, mentioned that they

On Thursday, August 17th, our two friends, Mr. Frederick James Nowson and Miss Alice Edwards, were joined in holy wedlock. The Pastor officiated. A goodly number of friends attended the interesting ceremony, and the presents were numerous and useful. The Bridegroom's brother acted as best man, and the Bride's sister Harriet acted as bridesmaid. We wish our young friends every blessing.

Helena Haythornthwaite, aged 4 months, daughter of William and Jane Haythornthwaite of Darwen. Died July 27th, interred July 29th.

Jane Ann Johnson, of 56 Princess Terrace Mill Hill. Died August 21st, interred August 24th. Aged 34 months.

Robert Johnson, of Henry Whalley Street, Mill Hill, killed at Mill Hill Station on Friday, Aug. 25th. Interred August 29th, deeply lamented by a sorrowing wife and family and many friends. Aged 52. "In the midst of life we are in death." "Be ye also ready."

Our sincere regards to all.

DAVID CRITCHLEY,
Pastor.

THE MEMORIAL LYCH GATE

Lych Gate c.1921

After the First World War several meetings were held to decide on an appropriate memorial to the young men of the village who had lost their lives. At first it was suggested that the memorial should be a united effort between Church and Chapel, but after several joint meetings, no definite plan could be agreed on, and as a result each place of worship carried out separate schemes. The Church installed the carved oak Communion Table, previously described, and still in use today, and The Chapel erected a fine oak Lych Gate over the entrance to the graveyard at the bottom of Long Lane. The official opening ceremony was performed on Saturday the 15th September 1920 by Mr. William Kay, J.P. of Livesey, Blackburn. A large number of people were present at the opening when Mr. Kay unveiled the brass plaque in memory of the soldiers who gave their lives:

Fred Nightingale	John Preston
Richard Hoskin	Roland Alston
John Beesley	Herbert Smalley

After the dedication and speeches a tea party and concert were given in the Sunday School to a densely packed congregation.

The following day, Sunday, Mr. Critchley, the pastor, preached a memorial sermon in memory of the old scholars who had been killed and again there was a large congregation. Mr. Frank Kershaw sang the solos "Nearer My God to Thee," and "Thou art passing hence my brother", and the choir gave an anthem. The final amount donated was over £150, more than enough to cover the cost of £140.

The Blackburn Times reported: *"The township of Tockholes, like other places, sent many of its sons to the country's service in the late war, and unfortunately has to mourn the loss of several fine young men. The question of providing some fitting token of the part these lads played in the great struggle, has occupied the attention of the villagers for some time. Originally it was suggested that the memorial should take the form of a united effort, but after several joint meetings, no definite scheme could be decided upon – a number desiring a monument, and the younger element a recreation ground. Ultimately the members of the Established Church (Rev. W. Hodgkin, B.A., vicar), and the members of the Congregational Church (Rev. D. Critchley, pastor), decided to carry out separate schemes, and both denominations have collected considerable sums of money to carry out the work. The Anglicans propose installing a carved oak Communion Table, and executing church improvements, and the Nonconformists have let the contract for the erection of a lych-gate at the entrance to their new graveyard"*.

In 1946 another plaque was added containing the names of two other villagers who had lost their lives in the Second World War, John Cooper and James Victor Catterall

The ravages of time and weather finally brought the life of the lych gate to an end and it was rebuilt at a cost of approximately £2,500 in 1989. The old tiles were re-used but the wood was replaced. It was re-dedicated on 1st October 1989 by the minister the Rev. Lois Sundeen.

Reverend David Critchley

Mr. Critchley was born in the mining village of Whiston, near Prescott, the son of James Critchley, a prominent nonconformist. From the age of 10 he was engaged in Sunday School work and received his education at Huyton Park Congregational School. As a youth he showed much promise and it was suggested he enter for the ministry, but Mr. Critchley decided to become a carpenter and joiner.

In 1871 he came to live in Blackburn and entered the ministry largely due to associations at the Paradise

United Methodist Church. He had previously worked as a colliery pumping engine attendant and journeyman joiner and in 1876 took up employment at the Joseph Dugdale Mills at Cherry Tree. In Cherry Tree he discovered there was no nonconformist cause in the village so with the assistance of several other men he started a Congregational movement and began preaching, at first in the open air and, later, in the Village Club Reading Room where he also started a Sunday School. His employer, Mr. Joseph Dugdale, was so impressed with Mr. Critchley's success, that he built the Congregational Church at Cherry Tree at a cost of £2000, all the woodwork in its construction being executed by Mr. Critchley.

In 1890 Tockholes Chapel had been without a minister for eight years and David Critchley was invited to take the services there for three months, and then for a further period of six months. During the second spell he was given a unanimous invitation to become the resident minister, a position which he accepted at the end of that year and which he held for the next 35 years.

The prospects were anything but encouraging. The Sunday School had practically ceased to exist and attendance at service had dwindled to a small number, but Mr. Critchley's enthusiasm to the cause and his dedication and determination soon brought people flocking back and congregations all through his ministry averaged 80 and 90 each service. During his ministry, problem after problem was successfully tackled; various organisations were placed on a sound basis both financially and otherwise; church and schools flourished; the Sunday School was built on the main highway; the mortuary chapel was erected; the organ was replaced and extensive improvements were made to both the chapel and the manse and more land was purchased to extend the graveyard. He was described as "a sincere and broad-minded man, who detested anything approaching ambiguity and narrowness. A plain man, with no pretensions to great academic learning, who demonstrated that success depended principally on honesty of purpose and integrity of character"

In 1912 Mr. Critchley was presented with a gold watch, and his wife a gold chain, on the completion of 21 years as minister of Tockholes, an event widely reported in the local newspapers. The occasion was celebrated with a tea party and concert.

In the minutes several resignations are recorded as having been made by Mr. Critchley but each time he was

Mr. Critchley
at Harvest Festival time

persuaded to stay on. However his resignation was finally accepted on 29th September 1925 and he preached his farewell sermon in chapel on Sunday 18th April 1926. A special tribute to his long service was made at a tea party and concert, in front of a large audience and many guests, when Mr. Critchley was presented with two oil paintings, by a local artist, of scenes in the Ribble Valley, and Mrs. Critchley received a mahogany hall stand, both gifts being suitably inscribed. A framed photograph should also have been presented at the same time, but due to the general strike the delivery of the picture had been delayed. Mr. Critchley did not long survive his retirement and died a few months later in 1926. In Chapel a commemorative plaque was erected to his memory.

1906? Tockholes Chapel May Queen
Back: L to R: Rev David Critchley; Lucy Mares, unknown; Mrs James Critchley; 2 unknown; Jane Mares, Ann Critchley; Elizabeth Mares; 2 unknown.
Middle Row: Janie Mares 2nd left. Rest unknown. Front Row: Fifth from left Ellen Mares; 9th from left Phoebe Mares – rest unknown

Standing left: Bessie Cooper. Right: Clara Baron
Seated L to R: Jennie Shorrock; Katie Whipp; Bertha Shorrock;
Nellie Norcross; Hetty Aspden

Mr Edwards Grave Digger
Circa 1900

Snow White 1940
Back L to R: Mary Smith; Marion Edwards; Unknown; Peggy Critchley;
Ada Parkinson; Joan ?; Betty Edmondson
Middle: Florence Norcross; Bessie Edwards; Unknown; Kitty Harrison;
Stanley Nightingale; Florence Nightingale

Ladies Weekend Concert 1960
L to R: Mr. Jepson; Marlene Smith; Jennifer Davenport;
Harold Smith; Norma Orton-Tracy;
Lorraine Berry

Snow White & the Seven Dwarfs 1921: Back L to R: Katie Whipp; David Critchley; Unknown; Mrs James Critchley; 2 Unknown;
2nd Row: Hetty Aspden; Edith Cooper; Unknown; Mabel Norcross; Laura Shorrock 3 Unknown; Alfred Edwards;
3rd Row: Jenny Shorrock; Wm. Edmondson; Clara Baron; Unknown; Alfred Mares; Harold Entwistle; John Harrison; Lily Cooper;
Ethel Ellison; Nellie Norcross; Walter Harrison; Front: Kitty Edmondson; Betty Edmondson; Lily Mares; Florence Norcross; Edna Baron;
3 Unknown; Bessie Edwards; Ann Whipp

70

The Darwen News, Friday, March 31, 1950.

"T' EVENTS O' T' VILLAGE"

THE FULL CAST.   ["NEWS" PHOTO.]

Every possible foot of floor-space in Tockholes Congregational School was occupied on Saturday night when the ladies of the Church presented "T' Events o' t' Village."

This entertainment was part of the ladies' week-end activities which have raised £30 for funds. The demand for tickets was so great that the ladies have decided to give a second performance to-morrow evening.

As the title indicates, the script is in dialect and the four principals—the gossips—are to be congratulated on the way they let themselves go. There was no sense of straining for effect in their interpretations. Through them the audience was given a commentary on what happens from a young couple's wedding day to the day of their first-born's christening.

Mr. S. C. Davis, who was joint producer with Mr. R. S. Leach and also stage manager, wrote the script for the first scene—outside the church—when some most perceptive and amusing observations were made by the gossips.

Costumes, not only of the four principals—Mrs. T. Counsell, Mrs. S. C. Davis, Mrs. R. S. Leach and Mrs. N. Walmsley—were well worth seeing, and the jet-trimmed capes and buttoned shoes must have been treasured for many a year. The prettiest scene was the bridal scene, when the beautifully gowned bride, Mrs. F. Harrison, and her attendants, Miss K. Leach, Miss V. Davis, Miss V. Harrison and Susan Haworth, walked down the centre of the hall, to the great delight of the audience.

A show within a show was given in the last act, when the audience joined with gusto in the choruses of songs sung by guests at the christening.

Make-up artists were Miss W. Waddicor and Mr. W. B. Grime.

Proceedings in the afternoon were opened by Mrs. S. C. Davis, who was introduced by Mrs. W. Haworth. A vote of thanks was proposed by Mrs. T. Leach and was seconded by Mrs. Norcross. Carol Harrison and Jessie Tillotson presented flowers.

After tea the Rev. G. M. Shaw introduced the entertainment. Those taking part and not previously mentioned were: Mrs. W. Harrison, Mrs. G. Pilling, Mrs. Miller, Mrs. S. Cooper, Mrs. Davies, Mrs. C. Harwood, Miss K. Leach, Miss Hargreaves, Miss I. Brewin, Mrs. W. Haworth, Mrs. A. Shuttleworth, Mrs. J. Tattersall, Mrs. L. Bowen, Mrs. J. Harrison, Miss E. Smith, Mrs. Dawson, Mrs. J. Critchley, Miss J. Croft.

Guest preacher on Sunday was Miss E. Jackson, of Morecambe. Solos were given by Mrs. J. Pickett, who also joined with Miss Pickett to give duets. Miss Brewin was at the organ.

Tockholes' Night of Comedy
(Darwen News 8th December 1950)

There was a happy and homely atmosphere in Tockholes Congregational School on Saturday when the ladies presented "The Charity Committee" as well as many other items of entertainment.

Though "The Charity Committee" was nominally the principal attraction it was another sketch "The Fashion Parade" which drew the loudest laughs. In this, shoppers Mrs. Leach, Mrs. Walmsley and Mrs. Davis hindered rather than helped by saleswomen Mrs. Tattersall and Mrs. Harwood, set about the complex business of buying clothes.

In this sketch, where they could use dialect to the best advantage, the ladies, particularly the three shoppers, were at their best. The dialogue had the attraction of becoming entirely spontaneous – as, indeed some of it was, for the ladies have an irrepressible talent for "ad-libbing."

A very warm reception was given to the songs of Miss Joyce Croft, who is pleasingly devoid of stage nerves.

She was not the only member of the cast whose singing voice pleased, and Mrs. N. Walmsley's smooth rich contralto, used with comedy effect in "I've got a Lovely Bunch of Coconuts" – a special request from the last show, would have sounded equally good in a more serious song. A hard-working member of the cast was Mrs. C. Harwood who as well as being the harassed hostess in "The Charity Committee" and a saleswoman in "The Fashion Parade", gave a very creditable impersonation of Gracie Fields.

The oldest member of the cast, Mrs. S. Cooper, put her heart and soul in leading chorus singing, as did the youngest member, Vera Harrison, in the solo, 'Little Old Lady'.

The most striking feature of the production came at the end of the evening in the form of a tableau. All lights in the hall were put out while preparations were made. When they were turned on, the audience saw, spotlighted at the back of the stage, Britannia, complete with glittering helmet and draperies and John Bull, a sturdy figure in high boots and top hat. These two characters were played by Kathleen Leach and Vera Davis, two younger cast members.

At their feet were Mrs. Leach (Queen Victoria) and Mrs. J. Miller (Queen Mary). The accompanist throughout was Miss H. Hargreaves.

Joint producers of the show were Messrs. R. S. Leach and S .C. Davis and the latter was also stage manager. The colourful wardrobe belonged to the ladies themselves.

The Rev. Edgar Jones, the minister, introduced the show and at the conclusion appreciation was expressed by Mr. J. Critchley and Mr. J. Miller.

A repeat performance was given on Tuesday evening in St. George's School, when the sum of £12 was raised for Church funds.

ST. STEPHEN'S SCHOOL,
TOCKHOLES.

THE ANNUAL NEW YEAR'S

TEA PARTY
AND
ENTERTAINMENT

WILL TAKE PLACE IN THE ABOVE SCHOOL,

ON ✦ NEW ✦ YEAR'S ✦ DAY, ✦ 1889.

REV. W. THOMASON, VICAR, IN THE CHAIR.

Conductor, Mr. J. Smith.   Accompanist, Mr. H. Catterall.

PROGRAMME.

CHAIRMAN'S ADDRESS.

GLEE	"Hail Britannia,"—(Dr. Spark)	Choir
RECITATION	"Let us be Happy,"	Master B. Isherwood
SONG	"A whet Sheet and a flowing Sea,"—(Ross)	Mr. John Turner
READING	"Donny at Hick's Wife's Buryin,"	Mr. Pomfret
PIANO DUET	"Palermo,"—(D'Albert)	Messrs. Catterall and Turner
SONG	"Needles and Pins,"—(Lohr)	Miss Pomfret
RECITATION	"Amos and Rath,"	Mr. Ed. Aspin
VIOLIN SOLO	"Bohemian Girl,"—(Balfe)	Mr. H. Whalley
DIALOGUE	"Handy Andy,"	Mr. T. Gregory & others
SONG	"White Wings,"—(Winter)	Mr. T. Hartley
GLEE	"The Moon Shines Bright,"—(Chard)	Choir

→✦ INTERVAL. ✦←

PIANO DUET		Messrs. Smith & Marsden
RECITATION	"Only a Tramp,"	Master Fred Catterall
SONG	"Uncle John,"—(Weatherly)	Miss Pomfret
READING	"Choice Pieces of Yorkshire,"	Mr. Pomfret
VIOLIN SOLO	"The Harp that once through Tara's Halls,"—(Farmer)	Mr. H. Whalley
DIALOGUE	"Mischievous Moses,"	Mr. Ed. Aspin & others
SONG	"They all love Jack,"—(Adams)	Mr. John Turner
RECITATION	"Heaw Johnny kept his Promise,	Mr. Jas. Turner
SONG	"Let me like a Soldier Fall,"—(Wallace)	Mr. Haworth
GLEE	"Five Bells,"—(Crampton)	Choir
FINALE		NATIONAL ANTHEM

TEA ON THE TABLES AT 4-30, ENTERTAINMENT TO COMMENCE AT 7 O'CLOCK.

TICKETS TO TEA & ENTERTAINMENT 9d. EACH.

ENTERTAINMENT ONLY, 6d.

PROFITS WILL BE GIVEN TO THE SCHOOL FUND

CHAS. KNOWLES, PRINTER, BOOKBINDER, &c., 72, DARWEN STREET, BLACKBURN.

CHAPTER 4

SCHOOLS & EDUCATION

General Education

In Britain the establishment of a system of schooling for the poor depended on voluntary effort, mainly by the churches. The idea behind these voluntary efforts was not so much the belief in the right of every child to an education, but an attempt to improve standards of morals and health. In 1802 a factory act was passed requiring factories to give their apprentices some part-time instruction in reading, writing and arithmetic for the first four years of apprenticeship. The education act of 1833 made part-time education for children in factories compulsory, but did nothing for the education of other children i.e. those in the coal mines

In 1870 the first real Education Act was passed, giving local school boards power to compel children between the ages of 5 and 10 years to attend school. School-attendance officers were appointed to visit the homes of children who did not attend to inquire into the reason for their absence and many such instances are recorded in the school record book for Tockholes.

School Boards were created to establish 'Board Schools', which at first made a nominal charge but in 1891 were made free by law. The setting up of Board Schools financed by the state, side by side with the voluntary schools financed by private societies, brought about a system known as the 'dual system'. In state schools non-denominational religious teaching only was allowed, and the school boards appointed the staff and saw to the upkeep of the buildings. In voluntary schools that were state-aided, the form of religious teaching, the appointment of staff and the upkeep of buildings were the responsibility of the school managers, though the State had the right to inspect the teaching of non-religious subjects in order to ensure that the school was efficient.

The idea that an education suited to his/her ability is the right of every child irrespective of his/her social class or financial position only became accepted in the 20th century, and it became an established fact as the Education Act of 1944 was implemented.

Education in Tockholes

The Independent Day School in Tockholes

The exact date of the commencement of the Independent Day School in Tockholes is not known, but it has been recorded that one existed in 1840. It began at Higher Hill, in a small cottage belonging to Moses

Old School built 1834

Aspden, who was the first teacher. From there it became a ragged school in a room in Silk Hall, where Moses Kershaw was the teacher, but the stipend being small, after a while Mr. Kershaw discontinued the work. A few of the children were then taught by Thomas Nightingale in his shop at Top o' th' Low, and later the school was transferred to Silk Hall for a second time, with Mr. Nightingale as teacher. When the disused Bethesda Chapel became the property of the Independent Chapel Authorities in 1851, the vestry was used for school purposes and shortly after that, the house at the end of the Chapel, formerly the Minister's Manse, became the school. This house consisted of two rooms below and two above, which by 1880, having become quite ruinous, was taken down and the materials used in the erection of the present chapel building.

The school was kept up for a considerable time in the Bethesda house in order that the nonconformists of the village might be spared the necessity of sending their children to the Church school. It closed a few years before the teacher's death and the children were then sent to St. Stephen's school.

The Old School, St. Stephen's Churchyard

Plaque on wall reads:

ST. STEPHEN'S SCHOOL
TOCKHOLES, WAS ERECTED
A.D.1834, UPON THE
GLEBE LAND BY VOLUNTARY
SUBSCRIPTION, AIDED WITH
A GRANT OF £150 FROM THE
NATIONAL SOCIETY, LONDON
GILMOUR ROBINSON, IN[t.]

The formation of this school was initiated by the Rev. Gilmour Robinson and whilst in the process of being built the Schoolmaster taught for some time in his own house. The School was opened in November 1834 and was erected at a cost of about £400. It was later extended several times and the building now remaining in the churchyard is only a portion of the original building. In 1854 *Mannex, 'History, Topography & Directory of Mid-Lancashire'* claims that 'connected to the Church is a neat school, 71 feet by 33 feet, erected in 1834 and now taught by Mr. Lawrence Ward'. The remaining building is approximately 40 feet x 17 feet.

For many years there was only the one Schoolmaster who was assisted by a monitor or pupil teacher, and also the Vicar, who taught religious education. Later, an assistant mistress was employed who also taught the girls sewing. The Master's salary was supplemented by the 'school pence' paid each week by the parents.

Inside the school the lighting was poor and skylights were added. The building also suffered from extremes of temperature - freezing in the winter and overpoweringly hot in the summer. During the summer the skylights were whitewashed to keep the heat down and in the winter months school often commenced with a singing lesson as it was too dark to see to read and write. One entry in the School Minute Book states that the school was closed on one occasion because the temperature was only 28º F and the children were crying with pain because of the cold!

The weather in those days was harsher than today and greatly affected school attendances judging from the numerous entries in the school minute book. On one occasion it was so wet the girls' toilets were washed down the embankment! On many other occasions, snow drifts prevented children coming to school. One year, snow started as early as October and another year the Village was snowed up in late March. School

rolls were also badly affected by illnesses such as cholera, typhoid fever, diphtheria, scarlet fever and the usual chicken pox, measles and mumps. Teachers, too, fell victim to sickness and school records often note the employment of relief teachers during such absences.

Problems also arose due to dampness and dry rot and eventually the building was condemned as being unfit for further use and the present day school was built.

A book entitled *"Darwen's Old School Tie"* by *Miss Annie Proctor*, a book outlining the history of education and all the schools in the Borough of Darwen, gives a brief history of the 1834 Tockholes School. In it she quotes *Abram* writing in 1877 – *"Early in the last century a Schoolhouse was built in Tockholes, the existence of which was reported to Bishop Gastrell about the year 1718, who records 'there is a school house lately erected in Tockholes, the only endowment is twenty shillings, the interest of which is applied to the repairs of the building by the Trustees, William Walmsley, James Marsden, James Walmsley and Robert Aytock. These last three are Presbyterians, and, as might be expected William Sanderson, a Nonconformist, is likely to come to teach at the said school."* Miss Proctor continues:- "Nothing was said of where the school was or even how it was maintained. When the Independent Chapel was established some years later there were day schools held in a variety of places from time to time e.g. Higher Hill, Silk Hall, Mister Nightingale's shop and for a period, in the old Bethesda Chapel. These schools were for Nonconformists but no child was excluded on religious grounds. ... Rev. Gilmour Robinson applied to the National Society for a grant to erect a school house on the Glebe Land. The estimated cost was £320 and the size of the school was to be 80 feet by 30 feet to accommodate 400 Sunday School scholars. In 1835 Returns for that year showed Tockholes credited with two day schools charging school pence. Between them they had 85 day scholars. The two Sunday Schools had 480 children between them out of a population of 1124. ... The master in 1869, Mr. Southworth, had 50 scholars and taught all ages in one room, his only assistance came from the Vicar who took Religious Instruction"

The Old School during renovation 1976

Then followed a list of some of the daily entries made by the teachers in the School Record Books :-

10th Sept 1880	Cholera in the Village – many away sick
28th Sept 1880	108 children present for Inspection. All the Managers were present too.
25th Nov 1880	Mr. Pickup (Manager) provided a new board and easel
7th Jan 1881	Alternate Day System altered for the Mill children. The half timers get through twice as much work as formerly. An improvement.
18th Jan 1882	Weather rough. Snow. No children at school.
27th Jan 1882	Heavy rain last night. School yard flooded causing the girls' toilets to disappear over the embankment into the stream.
28th Oct 1882	New Curate, and the workmen have finished paving the girls' yard.
31st Oct 1882	Gave a holiday this afternoon. Master moving into the new school house.
1883	A boy has been 5 years old since last April and his mother has been telling the Attendance Officer he was not 5 years old every visit he has made. (NB children under 5 were admitted free)
24th May 1883	Flooring under the Infant Gallery at the north end having been removed, the workmen are busy replacing it. There is not much teaching going on in all this noise.
11th Oct 1883	Workmen are resetting the water tub and putting in a tap for the convenience of the scholars.
June 1886	Skylights whitewashed on account of the heat
19th Nov 1886	New kettle has been provided so that those children who bring their dinners to school and who don't get hot water elsewhere can have it in school. Kettle used first time today.
6th Jan 1890	Mrs. W's children came without pence arrears. Vicar promised to pay it for them and set them on a fresh start for the New Year.
27th May 1890	Received a small load of coal. The school does not need warming but coal is needed to boil water for the children's dinner.
1st Sept 1890	Good school. The new fees begin today. Infants and Standard 1 free. Standards 2-7 two pence per week.
25th Oct 1892	Got an oil stove and three lamps – had them burning all day to warm the room a little. Walls damp. (The boiler had burst the day before)
6th Jan 1893	No fees taken today the school having been made free through the kindness of Mr. John Pickup Esq. of Blackburn. (A mill owner and school manager). Scarlet Fever in the Village. Drains examined.

The Annual Report of the Inspector in September 1893 ended with these words: "I hope there will be no long delay in the erection of the proposed new school. The present buildings are antiquated and I believe unhealthy and it is doubtful whether their continued recognition can be recommended".

1895	Extra week's holiday in the summer so that children could assemble in the new school on 19th August 1895
1904	Dinner had to be stored in the classroom owing to pilfering in the cloakroom. About 20 poor children were selected to go down to the Vicarage for a hot dinner on a very cold day.
25&30 Sept 1918	Twenty three children went to gather blackberries during school hours accompanied by the mistress.
2nd Oct 1918	Fifteen children absent this morning on a blackberrying expedition. No punishment meted out. (Gathering wild fruits and selling them was the way the country children did their bit towards alleviating the food shortages during the war years, whilst town children were sewing, knitting etc. and boys worked allotments).

St. Stephen's School, Tockholes, built 1894

The School was reorganised in 1931 into a Junior and Infant school under a head and one assistant'.

In 1893 Gilmour Robinson's Voluntary School was condemned by the Local Education Department. A plan for restoring the school had been formulated, but H.M. Inspector believed that the alterations would only satisfy the Department for a short time, so it was decided to erect a new school on a site in Rock Lane.

The corner stone of the new school was laid by W. H. Hornby Esq. M.P. on Saturday, September 15th 1894 and after the ceremony there was a public tea. The cost of the building amounted to £1500 and the building was eventually completed and in use by the summer of 1895. In October 1895 in an effort to raise the remaining £650 needed to clear the debt on the new school, a three day bazaar was held in the Exchange Hall, Blackburn.

GIFT OF LAND AT TOCKHOLES –

Mr. R. R. Rothwell of Bridge Hall Priory, Derbyshire, one of the Tockholes landowners, has given two acres of land on which is to be erected a Church School at Tockholes, in the place of the old one recently condemned by the Government Inspector. The School is to cost £1,000

Blackburn Standard 10th June 1893

GENEROUS GIFT BY GENERAL FEILDEN –

General Feilden has given £225 to the fund for building a new school at Tockholes, the present one having been condemned by the Education Department. Alderman Rutherford had previously given £50, Mr. Rothwell an acre of land for a site and Mr. Pickup an acre of recreation ground and £100, but £600 or £700 is still needed.

Blackburn Standard 14th July 1894

TOCKHOLES VICARAGE,

Darwen,

October 7th, 1895.

I am taking the liberty of bringing to your notice the position of our Church Schools. The Education Department last year forced upon this small and poor Parish the building of New Schools on a new site. The Schools have been erected at a cost of £1,500, of this sum £850 has been raised by a few outside subscriptions, and by the exertions of the Parishioners.

An effort is being made to pay off the remaining debt of £650 by holding a Bazaar in the Exchange Hall, Blackburn, on November 28th, 29th, and 30th. Donations, Contributions of Work, or Articles for this Bazaar will be most gratefully received by the following Ladies: Mrs. Corfield, The Vicarage; Mrs. John Coar, Yew Tree, Livesey; Mrs. Gregory, School House; Mrs. Knowles, The Farm, Livesey; Miss Janet Pomfret, Top of Low, Tockholes.

Hoping for your kind sympathy and assistance,

I remain,

Yours faithfully,

ASHLEY T. CORFIELD.

THE

FOUNDATION STONE

OF THE

TOCKHOLES ✦ CHURCH ✦ SCHOOLS,

WILL BE LAID ON

Saturday, September 15th, 1894,

—BY—

W. H. HORNBY, ESQ., M.P.

A Procession of Clergy, Choir, and Children, will be formed at the Old Schools at 3 p.m.

After the Ceremony there will be a PUBLIC TEA at 4-30.

Much earnest effort is being made to raise the £1,096 required for the building of these New Schools, and the Vicar and Building Committee would be greatly encouraged by your presence on this occasion.

TOCKHOLES VICARAGE.
SEPT. 3RD. 1894.   R.S.V.P.

CORNER-STONE LAYING AT TOCKHOLES.

THE FUTURE OF VOLUNTARY SCHOOLS.

SPEECH BY MR. W. H. HORNBY, M.P.

On Saturday afternoon Mr. W. H. Hornby, M.P., visited Tockholes for the purpose of laying the corner-stone of new Church schools, which are estimated to cost over £1,100, the present school by no means fulfilling the requirements of the Education Department. A plan for restoring the school at a cost of £500 had been formulated, but as Mr. Brewer, H.M. Inspector, believed that the alterations, as suggested, would only satisfy the Department for a short time, it was decided to erect a new school on a site in Rock-lane, kindly given by Mr. R. R. Rothwell. The new building, which is being erected by Mr. S. Harwood, of Darwen, from plans prepared by Mr. J. Bertwistle, architect, of Blackburn, and will be of stone, with brick lining, will consist of a mixed department capable of accommodating about 100 boys and girls, and an infants' room to accommodate 50. The school is to have an improved system of lighting and ventilation, and be fitted with every modern convenience. The whole of

THE VILLAGE TURNED OUT

to take part in the ceremony, and the number present was augmented by visitors from Darwen and Blackburn. The scholars, after walking in procession from the old school, opened the proceedings by singing the hymn "The Church's One Foundation," and after prayer by the Rev. G. R. G. Pughe, the Vicar of the Parish (the Rev. A. T. Corfield), in the capacity of chairman, recounted the circumstances which had led to the building of the now school. He stated that already the funds reached £500, or nearly half of the amount they required to raise. It was gratifying to note also that the money, to a great extent, had been contributed in small amounts—sometimes in pence and small silver—which was a striking commentary on the eagerness of the people of Tockholes to retain religious education.—Mr. Hornby then performed the ceremony of stonelaying, and in doing so referred to the difficulties of voluntary schools in these days when pressure was being put upon them by the Education Department, the friends of religious education not only being confronted by the cost of erecting schools, but having to meet the cost of maintenance as well. If they took the report of 1893, they would find that the cost per head in the Church Schools was £1 17s. 8d., and the

COST PER HEAD IN BOARD SCHOOLS was £2 8s. 4½d., or a difference per head of 10s. 8½d. If they took the question of maintenance last year, they would find that the board schools in England received from the rates in gross £1,705,624, or £1 1s. 2d. per head, while the Church of England schools received only £617,878, or 6s. 10d. per child from the consolidated fund. Therefore, he was strongly of opinion that unless some form of rate aid was adopted Church of England and voluntary schools in general would be crushed out altogether. It was perfectly impossible to have voluntary schools competing with board schools if board schools were to be in the position of those he had just alluded to—be able to spend £1 1s. 3d. per head as against 6s. 10d. in Church of England schools without any trouble or anxiety as to whence the money was to come. The result, unless rate aid was obtained, must be that sooner or later voluntary schools, that had been the pioneers of education and were still the greatest educational power in the country, would have to go down. He hoped that the managers of the voluntary schools would unite upon some scheme in order that they could force upon the Government the necessity of rate aid. The loss sustained by the Church of England schools throughout the country in 1893 was £41,590, and

THIS LOSS MUST CONTINUE to increase if board schools kept on spending money at the present rate. The supporters of voluntary schools had another claim on the rates, when it was considered that in keeping their own schools they also contributed to the rates from which the board schools received their money. Since the Education Act of 1870 came into force, some 861 Church of England schools had been transferred to the School Boards because they had not been able to find money to carry them on, and during the same time 5,838 new schools had been built by Church people. Mr. Hornby concluded an interesting speech by stating that he would give £25 towards the building fund, an announcement which was hailed with much pleasure.—The Vicar of Mellor moved a vote of thanks to Mr. Hornby.—Alderman T. E. Thompson seconded, and announced, amid cheers, that he had pleasure in contributing ten guineas to the building fund.—The Vicar of Tockholes, replying to a vote of thanks, stated that he had received several letters of apology for non-attendance from well-known local gentlemen, Mr. J. H. Hartley, a Tockholes landlord, enclosing a £5 note. (Applause.)—The proceedings closed with the singing of the National Anthem, and an adjournment was made to the old school, where tea was served, and a miscellaneous entertainment afterwards took place.

TOCKHOLES SCHOOL.

January, 10th, 1899.

MY DEAR SIR,

In submitting to you the Balance Sheet of our New School Building Fund, we beg to ask for your kind help and sympathy on behalf of this small and poor School. The accounts on the other side show that the Tockholes Church People have for the last three years raised more than £80 each year: Surely this is proof enough that we are striving to help ourselves, especially when you consider that each year about £100 is raised by Voluntary Subscriptions on behalf of the Current Account of the School.

We remain,

Sincerely yours,

ASHLEY T. CORFIELD,
JOHN HARTLEY,   } Managers.
JOHN COAR,

TOCKHOLES SCHOOL.

EXTRACT FROM "BUILDING FUND" ACCOUNTS.

RECEIPTS.	£	s.	d.	PAYMENTS.	£	s.	d.
In the year							
1894.—	549	4	5	Baron Harwood, Contract for School	1100	0	0
1895.—Bazaar	642	12	2	„ „ Building Walls, etc.	257	3	7
1896.—	102	0	0	James Birtwistle, Architect	45	0	0
1897.—Entertainments, etc. 36 0 0				Expenses of Bazaar	104	6	1
„ —Sunday School & Church Box 18 8 0				C. Knowles, Printing	2	11	6
„ —Subscriptions and Bank Interest 17 16 0				E. Catterall, Removing Old School	1	10	6
„ —Tea Parties, etc. 15 0 0				E. Shepherd, Repairing road	2	7	6
	87	4	0	Denham & Co., School Furniture	27	0	0
1898.—Entertainments & Sale 52 15 0				Low & Sons, Floor-blocking	35	0	0
„ —Sunday School and Church Box 29 13 0				Pearce & Brothers, Folding Doors	49	10	0
	82	8	0	Mercer, Heating Apparatus and Gates	56	9	0
Balance due to Bank	256	18	8	Bank Commission and Interest	39	9	0
	£1720	7	3		£1720	7	3

SIGNED.

Tockholes School,
January 10th, 1899.

A. T. CORFIELD,
JOHN HARTLEY,   } School Managers.
JOHN COAR,

A Grand Bazaar

IN AID OF

TOCKHOLES SCHOOL

Will be held in the

Exchange Hall, Blackburn,

Nov. 28th, 29th & 30th, 1895.

THE OPENING CEREMONY

Will be performed on Thursday the 28th, at 2 o'clock,

BY

THE VEN. ARCHDEACON RAWSTORNE, M.A.

The Bazaar will be opened on Friday the 29th,
at 2 o'clock, by

Mrs. W. B. HUNTINGTON.

And on Saturday, November 30th, at 2 o'clock, by

JOHN PICKOP, Esq., J.P.

ADMISSION :—

Season Tickets, 2s. 6d. Thursday, until 6 o'clock, 1s. ; afterwards, 6d.
Friday and Saturday, 6d.

(Children under 12 Half-price.)

AMUSEMENTS.

INSTRUMENTAL MUSIC
EACH DAY.

CONCERTS.

Will be given by

Messrs. Russel and Chadderton's Glee Party

On THURSDAY at 7 o'clock, and FRIDAY at 8 o'clock,

Also by the TOCKHOLES CHOIR,

Assisted by Mr. YEO, Mr. I. BURY, Mr. T. HARTLEY, Etc., Etc.

THE GIPSY TENT

Will be under the charge of

MISS FOX and MISS CHARLOTTE MORLEY.

"MY LORD IN LIVERY"

Will be performed on THURSDAY and SATURDAY
Evenings, at 8 o'clock, by an

Amateur Theatrical Party,

UNDER THE KIND SUPERVISION OF MRS. H. ROBINSON.

ENTERTAINMENTS.

Mr. E. S. Bellingham will give selections from his popular
Lecture, " Jokes & Jokers," on Thursday and
Saturday Afternoons at 4 o'clock.

The PHONOGRAPH will be under the charge of Mr. J. Westwell & Mr. F. Hartley.

CHARACTER FROM HANDWRITING

By the expert Graphologist, Mr. J. H. HAISE, 1s.

Your GIFTS, ABILITIES and WEAK POINTS clearly indicated.—WRITE YOUR NAME ONLY.

EXECUTIVE COMMITTEE.

Mr. J. S. Pollitt, Mr. H. Whittaker, Mr. G. B. Moore, Mr. C. Rennelley, Mr. John Hartley, Mr. H. Horsfield,
The Rev. A. T. Corfield (Vicar).

STALLHOLDERS.

The following Ladies and Gentlemen have kindly consented to assist at the
Various Stalls.

Contibutions in Money or Goods will be thankfully received by them.

No I.
The Vicarage Stall.

MRS. CORFIELD (SECRETARY).

MRS. MAUDSLEY.	MRS. STOCK.	MISS K. THWAITES.	MISS RADCLIFFE.	MISS DAVIDSON.
MISS M. DAVIDSON.		MISS PUGHE.		MISS A. G. PUGHE.

No. II.
Officials' Stall.

MRS. J. W. GREGORY AND MRS. JOHN COAR (SECRETARIES).

MRS. JOHN HARTLEY.	MRS. BARKER.	MRS. WORTHINGTON.	MRS. BAMFORD.
MRS. J. ASPIN.	MRS. H. TURNER.	MRS. D. CATTERALL.	MR. JOHN COAR.
MR. G. BARKER.	MR. W. WORTHINGTON.	MR. T. GREGORY.	MR. H. BAMFORD.
MR. JAMES ASPIN.	MR. D. CATTERALL.	MR. H. TURNER.	MR. H. CATTERALL.

No. III.
Congregational Stall.

MRS. KNOWLES AND MRS. MAGUIRE (SECRETARIES).

MRS. MOORE.	MRS. HORSFIELD.	MRS. RIGBY.	MISS MARY ANDERSON.
MR. & MRS. H. ASPIN (senior).	MR. & MRS. H. ASPIN (junior).		MRS. THOMAS COAR,
MR. & MRS. W. T. CHARNLEY.	MR. & MRS. WILLIAM ASPIN.		MRS. MICKLE.
MRS. BLACKBURN.	MR. ALFRED PARKER.		MR. JOHN MYERSCOUGH.

No. IV.
The Young Women's Stall.

MISS LIZZIE TURNER AND MISS J. POMFRET (SECRETARIES).

MRS. LOMAX.	MRS. INGHAM.	MRS. TURTINGTON.	MISS ELLEN SHARPLES.
MISS JANE BRINDLE.	MISS ALICE BRINDLE.	MISS MARY WHALLEY.	MISS ALICE PICKUP.
MISS ELLEN GREGORY.	MISS MARY SHEPHERD.	MISS ELLEN ASPIN.	MISS J. ASPIN.
MISS MARY CHEETHAM.	MISS ELLEN HORNBY.	MISS M. LINAKER.	MISS ALICE WHALLEY.
	MISS F. CATTERALL.		

No. V.
Refreshment and Flower Stalls.

MRS. ASPDEN (SECRETARY).

MRS. JOSEPH DUGDALE.	MRS. DR. ROBINSON.	MISS ALICE DUGDALE.	MISS ANNIE DUGDALE.
MISS ASPDEN.	MISS MAGGIE ASPDEN.	MISS FEILDING.	MISS A. FEILDING.
MISS LOWTHIAN.	MRS. BRINDLE.	MRS. PICKUP.	MISS HESTER ROBINSON.
MRS. GREGORY.	MRS. SUTTON.	MISS SHARPLES.	MRS. KENNELLY.
MRS. CATTERALL.	MISS M. A. TURNER.	MR. JOHN BAMFORD.	MR. THOMAS INGHAM.

No. VI.
Young Men's (Live Stock) Stall.

MR. MOORE (SECRETARY).

MR. HORSFIELD.	MR. E. CATTERALL.	MR. KIRKHAM.	MR. R. WHITTLE.

THE BAZAAR

Is under the Distinguished Patronage of

THE RIGHT REV. THE LORD BISHOP OF MANCHESTER, D.D.
THE RIGHT REV. BISHOP CRAMER-ROBERTS, D.D.
THE RIGHT HON. THE EARL OF DERBY, K.G.   VISCOUNT CRANBORNE, M.P
THE VEN. ARCHDEACON RAWSTORNE, M.A.

W. H. HORNBY, ESQ., M.P.	WILLIAM CODDINGTON, ESQ., M.P.
JOHN RUTHERFORD, ESQ., M.P.	R. YERBURGH, ESQ, M.P.
GEORGE WHITELEY, ESQ., M.P.	HERBERT WHITELEY, ESQ., M.P.

WILLIAM TATTERSALL, ESQ., J.P., C.C.

THE MAYOR AND MAYORESS OF BLACKBURN.

T. A. ASPDEN, ESQ., J.P.	THE REV. CHARLES GREENWAY, J.P.
J. ASTLEY, ESQ., J.P.	R. R. ROTHWELL, ESQ., J.P.
R. CODDINGTON, ESQ.	JOHN PICKOP, ESQ., J.P.
GENERAL CHANNER, V.C., C.B.	J. S. POLLITT, ESQ.
COLONEL CHANNER CORFIELD, J.P.	THE REV. G. PROCTOR, M.A.
CAPTAIN FEILDEN.	A. DUGDALE, ESQ., J.P.
COLONEL MOSLEY, J.P.	HERBERT ECCLES, ESQ., J.P.
COLONEL H. ROBINSON.	ROBERT RADCLIFFE, ESQ.
S. H. SHORROCK, ESQ.	

LADY CRANBORNE.

MRS. T. A. ASPIN.	MRS. ASTLEY.
MRS. WILLIAM CODDINGTON.	MRS. CRAMER-ROBERTS.
MRS. COSTEKER.	MRS. A. DUGDALE.
MRS. H. ECCLES.	MRS FOX.
MRS. GRAHAM.	MRS. GREENWAY.
MRS. W. B. HUNTINGTON.	MRS. HORNBY.
MRS. POLLITT.	MISS PICKOP.
MRS. RAWSTORNE.	MRS. H. ROBINSON.
MRS. S. SHORROCK.	MRS. W. TATTERSALL.
MRS. D. THWAITES.	MISS THWAITES.
MRS. J. THWAITES.	MRS. H. WHITELEY.
MRS. G. WHITELEY.	MRS. YERBURGH.

The following have kindly consented to act as Stewards.

THE REV. J. W. CLARKE, B.A.		THE REV. J E SAMUEL, M.A.
THE REV. T. W. WALKER, B.A.		THE REV. J. M. KINGSTONE, B.A.
MR. H. ASPDEN.	DR. WELLS, M.D.	MR. E. ASPDEN.
MR. J. W. CARTER.	MR. F. APPLEBY.	MR. R. CROOK.
MR. A. BERTWISTLE.	MR. G. RADCLIFFE.	MR. C. BARNES.
MR. F. THOMPSON.	MR. E. S. BELLINGHAM.	MR. WALTER FARNWORTH.
MR. G. POLLITT.	MR. HENRY WHITTAKER.	MR. H. SHEPHERD.
MR. A. YEO.	MR. P. C. WINTERTON.	MR. G. B. MOOR.
MR. J. BOTTOMLEY.	MR. T. ASPDEN.	MR. H. APPLEBY.
	MR. E. SAMES.	

ARCHDEACON RAWSTORNE ON EDUCATION.

For the purpose of raising £650 in aid of the new Church schools erected at Tockholes in compliance with the requirements of the Education Department, a three days' bazaar was opened in the Blackburn Exchange Hall, on Thursday, and in addition to a number of attractive stalls a novelty was introduced in the shape of some pens containing fowls and pigeons, the chief delight of the former being to lend a farmyard accompaniment to the speeches. Indeed, the birds were quite democratic, dividing their attentions between Archdeacon and Vicar with a most commendable impartiality. During the lulls our representative gathered from the Vicar (the Rev. A. T. Corfield), who was supported on the platform by the Venerable Archdeacon Rawstorne and a large number of clergy, that the parish of Tockholes had been dealt with

RATHER SEVERELY

by the Education Department. When they came to see the school the Authorities not only condemned the building, but the ground upon which it stood. Consequently they had to procure fresh ground, and erect a new school – a great undertaking for a parish containing, Nonconformists and Church people included, only 600 souls. The cost was £1,000 with £500 extra for enclosing the ground and other details. He announced that he had received £50 from Mr. William Tattersall – (applause) - £20 from Mr. Rothwell, and £10 from Archdeacon Rawstorne, whom he eulogised. The ARCHDEACON, who was well received, referred to the great esteem and affection he had for their Vicar, who was once a fellow-worker with him, and he hoped he would receive every encouragement in his good work at Tockholes. (Applause). Mr. Corfield seemed to think the new school was not so necessary. He (the speaker) had visited a good many schools in Blackburn and the neighbourhood to see whether the Education Department were right

IN THEIR DEMANDS

or not and he did not think in any one case the Department had been wrong. In this case he thought the new school was needed. They must not relax their efforts in the matter of education. In that large Archdeaconry they had done a great deal during the last two or three years, but there was to be done a great deal more which they must not shirk. If they had a Government in power which was favourable to Voluntary schools, they must not rest on their oars. The present administration, willing as they were to help Voluntary schools, only intended helping those who helped themselves. It was not right to expect them to do all that they wanted. They did propose to remit the 17s. 6d. limit, and to relieve schools from the rates. Still something more than that was wanted. Their Voluntary schools could not be carried on without more assistance than that. What they wanted was a proposal for the Government to supply funds to meet

THE ADDITIONAL EXPENDITURE

entailed on their schools through the requirements of the Department. If they could supply that, they would be able to carry on the schools as they formerly did, and they hoped the idea would be embodied in a bill to Parliament. They must not give up their Church schools to the Board. (Applause). The Board schools failed in one respect, which they valued more than any other, and that was in regard to religious instruction. They wanted teachers, earnest, able and willing, to teach the principles and doctrines of our Church, and they wanted them to teach them in a truly Christian manner. (Hear, hear). For that purpose they must retain the appointment of their masters and mistresses, and whatever happened he hoped the Government would always bear in mind the importance of religious training on the basis of Holy Scriptures. He had great pleasure in declaring the bazaar open, and acknowledged the vote of thanks passed to him on the motion of MR. G. B. MOORE, seconded by MR. GEORGE BARKER. It is interesting to note that the children of Tockholes collected no less than £17 in pennies in support of this commendable movement, which will be appealing to the generosity of the public up till to-night. The receipts amounted to a little over £200 on the opening day.

SECOND DAY'S PROCEEDINGS.

Mrs. W. B. Huntington opened this bazaar yesterday and was accompanied by Mrs. Herbert Whiteley. The Vicar (the Rev. A.T. Corfield) presided, and, in declaring the sale of work open, Mrs. Huntington expressed her sympathy with the movement, which she hoped would meet with every success. A vote of thanks was moved by the Rev. G. R. G. Pughe (vicar of Mellor), who made an allusion to the readiness with which Mrs. Huntington always came forward to lend her aid to good work. The motion was carried amid applause, and was charmingly acknowledge by the recipient.

Blackburn Standard 22nd September 1894

From the Blackburn Standard 7th December 1895:-

THE CHURCH BAZAAR AT THE EXCHANGE

On Saturday, the Bazaar which was held at the Exchange Hall, Blackburn, in aid of the new Church School to be erected at Tockholes, was opened by Mr. John Pickop, J.P. The Vicar (the Rev. Mr. Corfield) presided, and amongst the very small attendance was Mrs. Wm. Coddington, the Rev. Mr. Thomason. Etc. The Vicar, unfortunately for the object for which sale was intended, had to express his disappointment with the smallness of the receipts, as only some £325 had up to that time been received. On Friday, he remarked, £70 was the sum taken, and, owing to the small attendance, it would make an average of £1 spent by each person. One fact which he desired to emphasise was that the children at the Tockholes School were receiving free education in the full sense of the word; owing to the kindness of Mr. Pickop, the children did not pay one farthing for their instruction, (Applause). Mr. Pickop had handed him a cheque for £50. (Applause) – Mr. Pickop said no money was spent better than in education. They all knew that education could never be taken from a child, and he hoped that by its aid the poverty and distress which had existed so long would be very greatly diminished. (Applause). – A vote of thanks was accorded Mr. Pickop. The receipts up to Saturday night were £495. The total receipts amounted to £551.

The August 1895 Parish Magazine carried the following description of the plans for the Opening Ceremony of the new school:-

"Our exceedingly pretty little School is at last to be opened. The day fixed for this interesting ceremony is Saturday, August 17th. John Rutherford Esq., M.P. has been asked to 'unlock the doors', and we hope that his Parliamentary duties will enable him to do so. After the opening of the School at 3.30 o'clock, there will be a Tea Party in the Old School at 4.30, followed by an Entertainment in the New School at Seven o'clock. A Committee of young men has been formed to assist the Tray-holders, and another Committee have charge of the Tea Party. Tickets are being sold at 1/- each, which admits to the Opening Ceremony, Tea, and Entertainment. The date of our Great Bazaar in Blackburn Exchange is Thursday, Friday and Saturday, November 27th, 28th & 29th"

And the September 1895 Magazine reports on the activities which took place at the opening ceremony as follows:- *"The opening of our New School is rather a thing of the past, as we all read the somewhat lengthy reports from the daily newspapers. We will only remark that we were very pleased to have Mr. John Pickop and Mr. Rutherford with us, and to hear their addresses. Mr. Pickop expressed himself as very pleased with the building and said, 'All the arrangements had been well carried out for the advantage of the child.' All the Committee deserve the highest praise for their careful arrangements and hard work. Talking of the School, we should like to mention that there is one matter which has apparently escaped the notice of our friends the newspaper reporters, and that is the very comfortable room and arrangements made for the children from a distance having their mid-day meal in the School.*

The Committee having finished the building of the New School, are busy pulling down the old one. Our readers will be glad to learn that all this hard and rather dangerous work is being done gratuitously and after a hard day's work at the mill or on the farm. We give a list of the Committee who spend their evenings in this good way, and the number of attendances – Mr. Kennelly 10, E. Catterall 10, the Vicar 9, Henry Aspin (junior) 7, Thomas Gregory 7, Moses Catterall 7, Richard Corfield 7, John Hartley 6, William Aspin 6, Thomas Riley 6, H. Horsfield 5, Henry Aspin (senior) 5, Hugh Bamford 5, James Aspin 4, John Bamford 3, Edward Coar 3, Thomas Lowe 3, Edward Turtington 1, John Coar 1 and Thomas Ingham 1."

The first Headmaster at the New School was a Mr. Gregory. The School Minutes record several of his absences due to illness and he died aged 36 in 1896. His headstone in St. Stephen's churchyard reads *"In Loving Memory of WILLIAM JAMES GREGORY who departed this life March 28th 1896 aged 36 years. Erected by the members of the Malakoff Lodge No. 756 of the C.U.O. of Oddfellows to the memory of the above who for 12 years was their esteemed secretary. Deeply loved".*

The next appointed headmaster was Mr. William Tillotson who joined the school in May 1896 and left shortly after the death of his wife in October 1907. The copper jug near the altar in St. Stephen's Church is dedicated to "Mrs. Mary Ellen Tillotson aged 38 years, October 1907." Mr. Tillotson died on the 22nd August 1930 aged 62 and his second wife, also Mary, died on the 5th July 1930 aged 72 years. Alfred Tillotson, Driver in the 277th Brigade RSA was killed in action in France on the 13th October 1918 aged 21 years. All are commemorated on a headstone in the graveyard at St. Stephen's Church.

1895 – Headmaster Mr. J. W. Gregory
2nd Row first right – Lottie Duckworth.

Mr. &Mrs. Tillotson outside the School House with their son, Alfred, and teacher Miss Cooper. (*Left*) c.1902

The Church Magazine of December 1907 noted the death of Mrs. Tillotson followed by a report on the Day School:-

"We much regret to record the death of Mrs. Tillotson, the respected wife of Mr. William Tillotson. During her residence among us she took a deep interest in every good work, and by her gentleness and kindness endeared herself to all who had the good fortune to know her. Her patience and cheerfulness during her trying illness was really remarkable. She 'being dead yet speaketh,' telling us that kindness and gentleness is sure to win the love and respect of our neighbours, and that thoughts for others in their sickness and troubles is a sure comfort to us all in times of our tribulation. Our deepest sympathy is with her sorrowing husband and the little motherless lad.."

THE DAY SCHOOL: On the last day of November, Mr. Tillotson ceased to be the Head-Master of our day School. He resigned thinking that a change of School and parish might help him to bear his great trouble. Mr. Tillotson succeeded the late Mr. William Jas. Gregory – who is still affectionately remembered – in April 1896, and has done his best to impress on the many Scholars who have passed through his hands, the advantages of a good education, joined to a manly, straightforward Christian character. Our best wishes go with Mr. Tillotson in his new sphere of work. The Education Authority (The Lancashire County Council) has made a rule that no school with an average less than 74 is entitled to a Head-Master. Our Managers have therefore appointed as Head-Mistress Miss Genner who comes to us with the highest testimonials and qualifications. She was trained at Chichester Training College, and at her last School, Ovingdean, near Brighton in Sussex, she was a most successful teacher. We beg to give her a hearty Lancashire welcome to Tockholes, and congratulate the School Managers on their good fortune in obtaining the services of such a capable Teacher to train our boys and girls to become useful citizens, and good soldiers and servants of Christ. How thankful we should all be that in our Voluntary Schools our children can still be taught the faith of Jesus Christ. May all Tockholes parents continue to insist on their undoubted right to have their little ones brought in the "Faith of their fathers".

The School Log Books continued in much the same vein at the new school as at they had at the old school. Many references are made to the School being closed because of bad weather. Thick snows which began in December and sometimes continued into May often prevented access to the school and in February 1895, 8 degrees of frost was recorded **inside** the building. The most severe winters appear to have been 1922, 1936, 1940, 1942 and 1946/7 – the worst one being 1946/7. Mrs Lang, the headmistress, wrote in February 1947 "Very bad blizzard during the night. All the roads are blocked with drifts 6 and 7 feet in height. No children got to school; I got as far as the gate, but could not get in, the entrance was blocked by a six foot drift". March was pretty much the same and the village was isolated for 6 days from the 12th to the 19th.

School House c. 1902

The weather conditions not only affected the School. Over the years heavy snowfalls have caused many people to be cut off from their homes or marooned within them. Fatalities occurred in this area in the early years of World War I when three boy scouts got lost on Winter Hill and died of exposure. Flooding has also caused problems on several occasions. In the mid 1940's after a thunderstorm a torrent of water from the top road poured down the field above the School and hit the school boundary wall. In September 1963 another severe storm caused flooding in the school as water ran off the fields and a further flood was averted thanks to the Headmaster Mr. Jack Morris, the Vicar, the Caretaker and some volunteers who dug a channel to divert the water away from the building. Alas, in December 1964 the hall floor was badly damaged by a further flood.

Headmaster Mr. Wm. Tillotson and Teacher Miss Cooper c. 1905

School was also closed, or attendances sadly depleted, on many occasions because of serious epidemics of influenza, measles, chicken pox, scarlet fever, whooping cough, diphtheria etc. Happily, the improved conditions regarding sanitation and a water supply, coupled with the much improved standards of health care, including immunisation and visits to the school by doctors, nurses and dentists, greatly improved the general health of the children.

c. 1986

Children will be children, of course, and there are many instances of 'mischief' recorded and the punishments given. Before the introduction of school dinners in August 1945, brought from the Town by van each day, there were several instances of theft of food, but no mention of the culprits – the evidence having vanished! Also mentioned on several occasions were instances of stone throwing, and of school caps being thrown over the school wall. Bad language was another problem and being kept in during playtime seems to have been the punishment for this offence. There was a well in the school yard and several instances of children falling into it are recorded. Also in the yard was a water tub which some boys used as a fish pond after catching trout and minnows in the stream. The boys were duly cautioned and the tub had to be cleaned out. In the 1940's evacuees from Manchester caused disruption and were hard to deal with, they being unfamiliar with country ways. Mrs. Lang described them as being obstinate, insubordinate and impertinent. Various accidents are also noted, in particular cuts which needed stitching, trapped or crushed fingers, trips on the school steps, bruises, grazes and a broken leg, and an instance when a child pushed a bead up a nostril, resulting in a trip to the hospital and an operation to remove the obstruction!

One pupil, Ruth Crompton, daughter of the Sexton, attended the School along with her sisters, Alice and Dorothy. On one occasion when she was about 10 years old she got into trouble with the headmistress, Mrs. Lang, and whilst she was waiting to be 'dealt with' she hid the cane behind a cupboard. Mrs. Lang, well used to Ruth's mischievous ways, suspected what had happened and, with no more ado, sent Ruth to collect a replacement cane from the central store in the Cathedral grounds, Blackburn. Thinking this was her punishment, Ruth walked there and back and later admitted she had quite enjoyed the time out of school as it was a nice day. Nevertheless, on her return she still got the cane!

In 1969 an extension was added to the School giving a further classroom, headmaster's study, staff toilet, caretaker's room and kitchens, which meant school dinners could now be made on the premises. In 2002 a further extension was added giving another classroom, a new headmistress's study and a further office. The extension was officially opened by the Bishop of Burnley on Thursday the 13th June.

Flood c. 1946

Circa 1901. Mr. Tillotson (headmaster- back right)
2nd Row seated 2nd left Phoebe Mares 3rd left Ellen Mares

82

Tockholes Church of England
Primary School

✝

Dedication of the New Extension

by

THE RIGHT REVEREND
C. R. CLAXTON, D.D.

Lord Bishop of Blackburn

and

Official Opening

by

MISS M. V. SIMCOCK

(Former Headmistress)

on

THURSDAY, 16th JANUARY, 1969

at 3 p.m.

TOCKHOLES
CHURCH OF ENGLAND
PRIMARY SCHOOL

MANAGERS

THE REVEREND ALLAN LIVESEY
(Chairman and Correspondent)

MR. J. COAR   MR. M. ROSSALL
MRS. E. MARES
MR. J. BLACKLEDGE   MR. H. SMITH
Clerk to the Managers: MISS B. EDDLESTON

SCHOOL STAFF

MR. J. S. MORRIS (Headmaster)
MRS. L. POMFRET (Assistant Teacher)
MR. F. RILEY (Caretaker)
MRS. A. JEPSON (Cook)

DIOCESE OF BLACKBURN

THE LORD BISHOP OF BLACKBURN
THE RIGHT REVEREND CHARLES ROBERT CLAXTON, D.D.

CHAIRMAN, COUNCIL OF RELIGIOUS EDUCATION
THE RIGHT REVEREND G. E. HOLDERNESS, M.A.
Lord Bishop of Burnley

DIRECTOR OF RELIGIOUS EDUCATION
THE REVEREND CANON C. W. D. CARROLL, M.A.

LANCASHIRE COUNTY COUNCIL

Chairman, Education Committee:
COUNTY ALDERMAN J. R. HULL, C.B.E.

Chief Education Officer:
J. S. B. BOYCE, ESQ., T.D., M.A.

Chairman, No. 9 Divisional Executive:
COUNCILLOR MISS C. MARSDEN

Divisional Education Officer:
JAMES CLARKE, ESQ., M.A.

School 1969

C. 1918: Mrs. Lang (Right) : Back Row: John Harrison (middle boy): Row 3 first left: Mary Whittle (nee Rossall)
4th left Betty Miller (nee Rossall);.Walter Harrison 1st right : Front Row: Billy Critchley (centre)

1920's: Headmistress Mrs. Lang (Left); ? Booth; ?, ?, Benjamin Fish; John Harrison; Peter Knowles
2nd Row: James Hutchinson; John Cooper; Emily Harrison; Edith Horsfield; Clara Moscrop; Lilian Cooper;
Ann Parkinson; ? Kitchen; Harry Green; Miss Moon
3rd Row: Thomas Edmondson; ? Taylor; ?; Nellie Cooper; Dorothy Crompton; Ada Moscrop; Jenny Horsfield;
Mary Edmondson; Alice Harrison; William Critchley
Front Row: ?; ?Berry; Joseph Horsfield; Elsie Cooper; Dora Parkinson; ?; ?

84

June 1950
Back Row: Unknown boy; Betty Miller; Dorothy Coar; Unknown; Anne Smith; Christina Berry; Teacher ?:   2nd Row: Headmistress Miss V. Simcock;
Vera Harrison; Richard Smith; Billy Berry?' Rosamund Bowen; Jean Bowen; Tom Miller; Jessie Tillotson:
Third Row: Harry Whittle; Unknown girl; Unknown; Margaret Miller; next four unknown; Mary Whittle; Unknown boy; Lorraine Berry?:
Front: Unknown: Jacqueline Tattersall; Glynn Berry?; Carole Tattersall

1950's Pupils working on the flower-beds. Note the school yard was grassed at this time.
Left to Right: Jean Bowen, Jackie Berry?; Tom Miller; Billy Berry; Rosamund Bowen; Dorothy Coar; Richard Smith;
Anne Smith (seated); Jessie Tillotson (standing) ; Vera Harrison (standing) ; unknown girl

Lessons Are Enjoyed

Outside: The school of happy children

YOUNGSTERS who attend the little grey-stone school perched 900 feet above sea level in blustery Tockholes could be excused for failing to turn up sometimes.

For some of them getting to school means a two-mile journey from outlying farms and cottages; in winter the place is often completely snowed up; and if they intend to get there at all, the difficulty of catching a bus means that they have to be at the school at 8.30 in the morning!

For these florid-faced boys and girls, lessons start at 8.45 a.m. (And before they get down to work there are often stray cows to be chased out of the playground and geese to be shooed from the doorstep.)

Yet the 60-year-old Tockholes Church of England school has one of the highest attendance records in the area. For last month head mistress, Miss M. V. Simcock, proudly entered a 100 per cent. attendance figure in her register!

The reason ? " The kiddies here really enjoy school," says Miss Simcock, " and it would take more than snowstorms and icy winds to keep them away. The air here is bracing, too, and the children are extremely healthy."

As they cannot get home at mid-day, the 44 under-twelve's have their lunches at the school—and good ones they are, too.

Being only a small school, the pupils are able to receive personal attention from the teachers—which makes it practically a " home from home."

1946: Children left-right: Margery and Mollie Myerscough; Billy Harrison; Robert Harrison, Peter Robinson. Head Teacher Mrs. Lang standing left

1954: Back Row: John Whittle; ?; Alex McCarthy; Jimmy Mingay; Roger Rhodes; Glynn Berry; Trevor Berry; Middle Row: Stuart Houghton; Stephen Mares; Frank Worthington; Fred Rhodes; Gordon Kemp. Front Row: ?; Heather Strack; Edna Turner; ?; Lorraine Berry; Patricia ?

1958 Back Row L to R: Miss Freda Edmondson; Gordon Kemp; Frank Worthington; Dorothy Berry; Dorothy Jump;
Rita Fowler; Margaret Gibson; Marjorie Bailey; Heather Strack; Dorothy Jepson; Stephen Mares; Miss Simcock (Head);
2nd Row: Lesley Barker; Peter Berry; David Corran; Wilfred Bagley; ?; David Miller, Rodney Hanson;
Roger Davenport; Michael Corran; ?; John Lever; Peter Worthington;
3rd Row: Sandra Rhodes; Christina Bailey; Patricia Bagley; Joan Worthington, Margaret Smith;
Vivien Lever; Ann Wheatley; Ann Reilly, Helen Reilly, Susan Gibson;
Front Row: Bill Gibson; Geoffrey Smith; John Howson; David Mayoh; John Smith; Peter Berry; Ronald Kemp; Ian Haworth; Trevor Berry; Steven Corran.

1962:- Back L to R:Teacher Miss Vera Harrison (left); Kenneth Wilkinson; Peter Rhodes; Jennifer Ward, Christine Bowen;
Neil Smith; Nicholas Bowen; Headmistress Mrs. Ward.
Middle Row: Derek Wilkinson; John Lever; Peter Worthington; Roger Davenport; John Howson; David Miller;
Rodney Hanson; Graham Berry; Tony Wheatley; Kevin Davenport;
Front Row: Marion Jepson; Christine Worthington; Diane Berry; Sandra Rhodes; Ann Wheatley; Joan Worthington; Ann Reilly;
Helen Reilly, Susan Gibson; Claudine Jones; Andrea Butterworth; Alicia Lever

1968:- Back Row: Lewis Hebden; David Morris; Paul Butterworth; Tom Turner; Keith Morris; Kim Pomfret; Carol Taylor;
Billy Rhodes; John Turner; Mark Woods
2nd Row: Andrew Fielding; Lynn Beet; The Beet Twins; Dawn Mercer; Unknown; Alison Butterworth; Barbara Gibson;
Guy Pomfret; Glen Mercer; Sam Woods; Freya Jones; Susan Brodie (nee Jackson); Ann Reilly.
3rd Row: Raynor Jones; Tony Taylor; Andrew Bland; David Woods; Unknown.
Front Row: Janet Ward; Carol Coar; Chris Beet; Carol Worthington; Becky Griffiths; Jeanette Coar; Beverley Fleming; Jane Aspinall;
Kerion Jones; next 3 unknown; Anna Griffiths; Margaret Turner

1978: Back: Mrs. Braithwaite; Mrs. Pomfret; Paul Aspinall; Jonathan Ward; Susan King; Hazel Gilbert; John Bland; Gillian Jump; Liam Robinson;
Erica Gilbert; Sonia Butler; Ruth Cank; Laura Aspinall; Peter Farnworth; Michael Meadows; Nigel Morris; Victoria Knighton; Emma Robinson;
Mr. Jack Morris; Peter Aspinall;
2nd Row: Samantha Tuley; Melanie McConnell; Karen Meadows;?; Jonathan Knighton; Paul Gillett; Gillian Salthouse; Katie Jacklin;
Helen Gordon; Diane Clarkson; Ewan Gilbert; Anne Farnworth; Karen Cleary; ?' Catherine Smith;
3rd Row: ?; Emma Jump; ?; ?; Richard Clarkson; Derek Crane; Saul Ward; Caroline Salthouse; Jason Riding; Adrian Shannon; Mark Navesey;
Denise Butler; Janet Gordon; ?; Christopher Smith; Clare McConnell; Karen Riding; Kathryn Bentley;
Front Row: Louise Aspinall; Madeleine Aspinall; Joanne Jump

1984: Back Row: Nichola Pateman; Elizabeth Smith; Christopher Smith; Naomi Walkden; Karen Riding; Sarah Gibson; Claire Pateman;
2nd Row: Mr. Harrison (Head); James Horrocks; Graham Prescott?; Marie Prescott; ? Underhill; Caroline Salthouse;
Emma Jump; Richard Clarkson; Pamela Cleary; ?; Mrs. .L. Pomfret;
3rd Row: Ruth Stott; Anna Willis; Louise Aspinall; Lisa Crewdson; Peter Isherwood; Guy Woolford; Nichola Miller; Lisa Foster; Lindsay Gillett; Richard Rosthorne;
Front Row: Nancy Smith; Duane Healey; Ruth Talbot; Michael Weale; Leigh Fuller; Simon Dean; Shaun Hedley; Jonathon Ashton; Zoe Fuller

TOCKHOLES C.E. PRIMARY SCHOOL

1894 1994

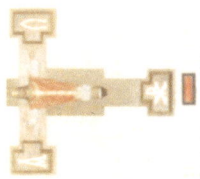

1994: Back Row: Rachel Talbot; Lindsey Jackson; Gemma Pearson; Amy Houghton; Philip Gaul; Matthew Reilly; Haley Brown; Philip Callaghan; 2nd Row: Kelly Aspin; David Hebden; Lauren Farnworth; Lisa Hebden; William Smith; Michael Riding;; Lucy Brown; Jackie Aspin; William Gaul; Ben Turner; 3rd Row: Heather Critchley; Vicki Houghton (Catering); Marilyn Turner (Secretary); Brenda Fleming (Catering); Mrs. Sue Gleave (Headmistress); Mr. Alan Reilly (Teacher); Anne Smith (Catering); 4th Row: Amy Callaghan; Elisa Ikin; Emma Jarrett; ? Leighton; Michael Brown; Sophie Farnworth; Jonathan Lindley; Ben Abell; Katie Turner; Katie Lindley; Jessica Coy; Front Row: Aaron Dawber; Luke Marriner; Holly Riding; Deborah Coy; Adam Waite; Laura Bond; Jill Hebden; Claire Critchley; Tom Woodward; Dean ?

90

2002:- Back Row L to R: Lydia Monk, Marilyn Turner, Zac Margerison, Ulysees Woods, Rosie Hanson, Jonathon Marriner, Liron Aharoni, Daniel Ayto, Liam Monaghan, Angus Treadwell.

2nd Row: Ben Holmes, Rory Pickering, Daniel McDonough, Kieron Monaghan, Sam Marriner, Rachel Waite, Jack Thompson, Jon-Michael Christopher, Gary Walsh,
Matthew Ayto, Anne Smith, Vicki Houghton, Barbara Cocken (Head Teacher)

3rd Row (standing): Matthew Jarrett, Tom Connell, Katie-Beth Christopher, Becky Abell, Jade Tolen, Becky Taylor, Lydia Harwood, Jacob Marriner

4th Row: Linda Kennish, Charlotte Roberts, Daniel Holmes, Rachel Walsh, Joseph Adams, Harriet Hanson, Emily Lathom-Taylor, Jenny Allman,
Luke Thomas, Kirby Todd, Marley Goldthorpe, Tony Thompson, Isobel Kirby, Lorraine Catchpole

Front Row: Matthew Rhodes, Elizabeth Schofield, Lottie Lathom-Taylor, Celine Woodburn, Matthieu Woodburn, Joshua Proctor, Joshua Barlow, Bethan Goldthorpe, Kimberly Cowan, Beth Holmes, Dylan Mayor.

Photograph courtesy of The Nick Clarke Studio, Sough Road, Darwen.

CHAPTER 5

ROADS & TRANSPORT

Over the years the bad state of the roads in Tockholes has been a frequent topic of conversation, most of them being just cart tracks until the beginning of the 20th Century.

As long ago as 1770 an Arthur Young described the roads in the County and in particular the one between Preston and Wigan as follows: *"I know not in the whole range of language terms sufficiently expressive to describe this infernal road. To look over a map and perceive that it is a principal one not only to some towns, but even to whole counties, one would naturally conclude it to be at least decent, but let me most seriously caution all travellers who may accidentally purpose to travel this terrible country to avoid it as they would the devil, for a thousand to one but they break their necks or their limbs by over-throws or breakings down. They will here meet with ruts which I actually measured four feet deep and floating with mud only from a wet summer. What, therefore, must it be after a winter? The only mending it in places receives is the tumbling in some loose stones which serve no other purpose but jolting a carriage in the most intolerable manner. These are not merely opinions, but facts, for I actually passed three carts broken down in these eighteen miles of execrable memory."* No doubt the Tockholes roads were of the same ilk even in 1833 when, as previously mentioned, the Bishop of Chester was asked to attend the opening ceremony of the new Church and was advised not come by coach.

Packhorse Road from Higher Hill to Victoria Terrace May 2003

One ancient road, still traceable in parts, came from the Rossendale area through to Preston and is the packhorse road dating back to Saxon times known as Limersgate. The road cut through Darwen from east to west and ran through Whitehall, Printshop, Bury Fold, Kebbs (Bold Venture), Turn Lane, across what is now the Earnsdale Dam and up Dean Lane at the side of Fine Peters. From Fine Peters it crossed to Higher Hill and then down the hill on the present un-made road to the cross roads at the junction of Old School Lane and Chapels Lane. A walk-way on the West side of the path from Higher Hill is a good 3

feet higher than the rest of the road and some of the old stone slabs of the original surface can still be seen under the undergrowth. Both this road and Dean Lane are now impassable except on foot or by horse. At the cross roads the road turned left, past Lower Hill and then across the field to Lower Crow Trees Farmhouse and on to Preston. In *Darwen & Its People*, the author, J. G. Shaw writing in 1889 described the road as *"wide and clearly marked by the remains of ancient scraggy-looking hedges on each side, but almost impassable despite its width, and on one side deeply sunk below the level of the adjacent land. This was once the only road for horse or cow from Darwen to Tockholes, except by going round the Golden Cup and it is today the only direct public road to Tockholes."*

Another road from Darwen to Tockholes came over the moors and began in Darwen Town Centre. It continued up Tockholes Road, past the Sunnyhurst Pub, the Waterman's House, Wenshead, Stepback and to the Royal Area where Hollinshead Mill was situated. In 1899 *Shaw* stated it was *"a private thoroughfare known as Tockholes Road, made by Mr. Eccles Shorrock nearly forty years previously at a cost of £2,000. Shorrock's tenants, and those of Mr. Duckworth, lord of the manor, were allowed the free use of it, but the general public were subjected to a toll charge which they gladly paid in preference to going round by the Golden Cup, or along the neglected bridle road of their forefathers."* Presumably, Shorrock built the road to create easier access to his estate, Hollinshead Hall, and between his Mill at Tockholes and his Mills, the Railway Station and the A666 in Darwen. Until recently, the post van still used this track and token tolls were collected twice a year in order to maintain its designation as a privately owned road.

The main road from Blackburn to Bolton through Darwen, now the A666, was constructed in 1797. Prior to that date it is said that the main road from these two towns ran through Tockholes, past Lower Pasture Barn Farm, Catherine Edge, Longworth Moor, Stones Bank and probably to Dimple and Egerton. Bolton at that time was a busy town with a weekly market held on Monday and no doubt this road would have been filled with travellers and the small manufacturers from surrounding districts with their packhorses taking goods for sale and purchasing their yarns for making new cloth. A map made for Tockholes by Thomas Whitaker in August 1724 shows the then main roads to Blackburn from Tockholes. The top road joins 'four lane ends' at what is now the Black Bull cross roads and a left turn is the route to Blackburn via Preston Old Road, a right turn down 'Bog Bank' leads past Earcroft and through Lower Darwen and then to Blackburn, and the route straight ahead led through Ewood, joined the road from Lower Darwen and ran past St. Mary's Church (now the Cathedral).

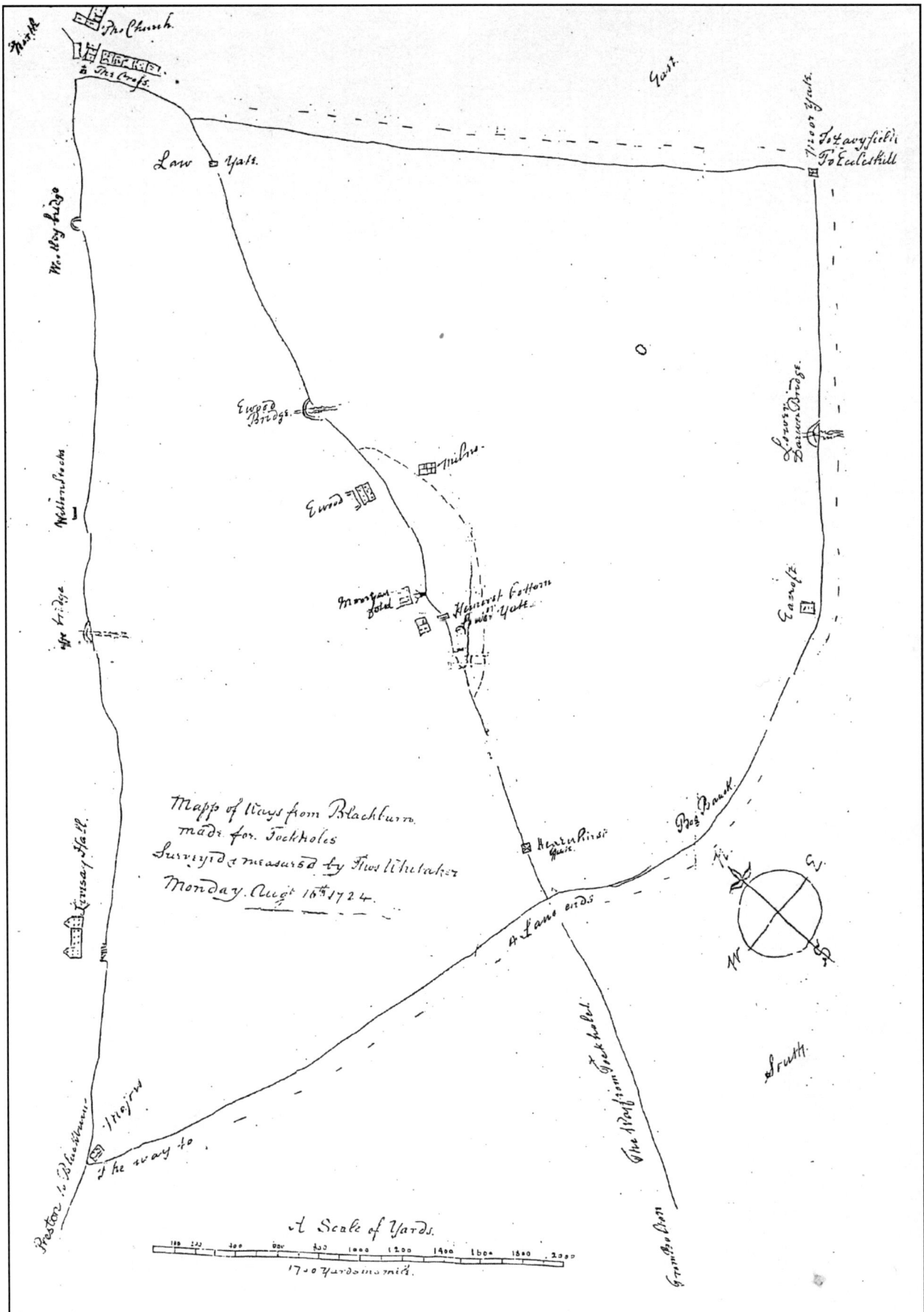

TOCKHOLES SCHOOL

A GRAND

CINDERELLA

SOCIAL

Will be held in the above School on

SATURDAY, FEB. 22, 1908.

DOORS OPEN AT 6 O'CLOCK,

TICKETS, 1/- EACH.

A very small charge will be made for

REFRESHMENTS.

Proceeds on behalf of the "Rock Lane Repair Fund."

However, with the construction of the A666 in 1797, followed four years later by the construction of another major turnpike road from Bolton to Preston, now called the Belmont Road, Tockholes became 'stranded' between the two and whilst Darwen thrived and expanded and Abbey Village and Belmont Village developed, Tockholes began to steadily decline, the state of its roads being one major reason. Hopes were raised in the mid 1860's when it was stated that a branch line of the Lancashire and Yorkshire Railway was about to be made, giving a station to Tockholes, but there was bitter disappointment when the station was eventually given to Withnell. This line was begun on the 6th December 1866 and opened on the 1st December 1869. Had the line gone through Tockholes no doubt the Mills, and possibly the coal mines, would have survived and it may have led to further development, both industrial and residential. Whilst our predecessors suffered greatly from the lack of progression the railway would have brought, Tockholes would not have remained in the 'time warp' enjoyed by the inhabitants of today.

By 1894 Tockholes had its first Parish Council and over the years the Council successfully dealt with numerous complaints regarding bad roads. In the early 1900's it appears to have been a thorn in the side of the Rural District Council in its attempts to get Pickop Brow, Morris Brow, Rock Lane and Long Lane taken over and made repairable at the expense of the R.D.C. The Rev. Ashley T. Corfield was appointed first Chairman of the Council and it was he who led the 'attack'. In October 1907 he was spokesman on behalf of a deputation from Tockholes at the monthly meeting of the Blackburn R.D.C., which meeting was fully reported in the newspaper. The initial discussions were unsuccessful.

However, the Parish Council and Church Officials continued to fight to reach a solution and by Spring 1909 the newspaper was reporting *"It will be good news to visitors to Tockholes and also to the inhabitants to know that the improvements in Church Lane which had been in progress since last December, will be completed by the end of June. The road and fencing are to be entirely reconstructed, the former having a foundation of rubble on top of which will be a thick layer of blue-stone. On the north side the wall will be set back some four feet, thereby making the roadway a uniform width of twenty feet. The cost of the improvements, which will approximately reach about £400, is being borne partially by the wardens of St. Stephen's Parish Church, Mr. R. Rothwell, estate proprietor, and by public subscription. Within twelve months of completion the roadway and its appurtenances will be formally taken over by the Rural District Council. The contractor for the wall is Mr. Lenz, of Tockholes, while Mr. Richard Mayers, also of Tockholes, is laying the road. The improvements have found employment for a considerable number of men during the quiet portion of the year and when completed will make one of the finest roadways in the district, removing what has hitherto been an eyesore and a death-trap to pedestrians and vehicular traffic. It reflects great credit on the wardens of the Parish Church.*

The ceremony at Rock Lane, Tockholes, on Saturday afternoon last, when the thoroughfare to be known as Church Lane, widened and repaired, was formally opened by Mrs. Corfield, wife of the Vicar, is practically the end of a controversy which at times has greatly excited the Blackburn Rural District Council. The road in question is the only thoroughfare to Tockholes Church and it was formerly in a dangerous state of disrepair. Attempts innumerable were made to saddle the Council with the responsibility of putting the road in order, but the Clerk pointed out that the evidence and the law were against this contention and the Council refused to make itself liable....Landowners and the adjoining farmers were approached in vain, and it began to look as if nothing ever would be done, when the whole difficulty was settled by the offer of the County Council to take over the road if somebody would first put it into a thorough state of repair and keep it so for a year. Nobody seemed to be under any legal compulsion to do this, therefore a subscription list was opened and the replies being satisfactory, the work was begun and the job was finished on Saturday, to the profound relief of all concerned.

Blackburn Times 7th August 1909

Top Road near The Rock c. 1946

The road was opened with due ceremony by the Vicar's wife and reported in the Blackburn Times on 7th August 1909. Rock Lane was finally taken over by the Blackburn Rural District Council and the Church contributed £25 per year for a period of four years towards the expense involved in the undertaking.

Morris Brow also caused great concern on many occasions in the 19th and 20th Centuries and it was thought that levelling it would make access to the Village easier and would eventually bring new housing and possibly create more work for the villagers. In 1859 the Blackburn Standard reported that Eccles Shorrock of Darwen was building a Mill at Tockholes and had subscribed to the Morris Brow Committee for the improvement of that road. In the early 1860's the American Civil

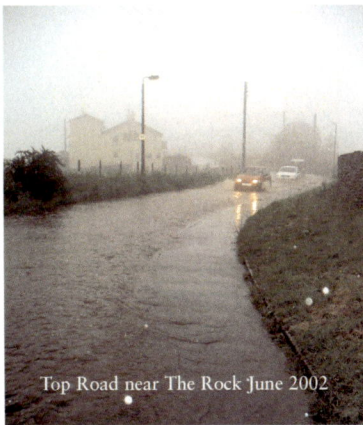

Top Road near The Rock June 2002

War had caused many mills to close due to the lack of transport of raw materials from the Southern States and as a result there was high unemployment. The employment figures for Blackburn and district in January 1863 made dismal reading – 12,376 full-time workers; 2,819 short-time workers; wholly unemployed 12,585 and 27,780 usually employed. The unemployed were found work on the construction of a new Workhouse and the Infirmary, the laying of over 21 miles of sewers and the flagging and paving of several miles of road, Morris Brow being one such road.

In March 1900 the Council Minutes reported on *"the shocking condition of the road after the cutting of the last heavy snow falls and remarking on the fact that many mill operatives had had to wade through pools of slush to get to work and stand the whole day in soaked conditions, endangering health."* In March 1921 suggestions were made that the Rural District Council be approached requesting them to culvert the brook at the bottom of the Brow with a view to the eventual improvements of the gradients of both Morris Brow and Pickop Brow. It was thought to be an opportune time for the carrying out of such work as, yet again, so many able bodied men were out of work. By October of that year the Parish Council was urging the R.D.C. to bring forward a scheme for the improvements in view of the recent Government decision to make large grants towards such work.

November 1924 shows the Parish Council was still nagging the R.D.C. with a view to improving the *"double twist in the roadway at the bottom of the Brows"* as they were most anxious something should be done at an early date to avoid the chance of a serious accident which they felt must happen sooner or later. By March 1926 the R.D.C. had actually commenced work, but the work was progressing far too slowly in the opinion of the Parish Council because of the number of road accidents at that time and the ever increasing traffic then using the roadways. It was suggested that the request to expedite the matter be linked with the problem of the narrow corner near Barker Fold and the very bad state of the highway's surface throughout the whole length of our Township, but in particular from the Livesey end to the Victoria Hotel, the potholes on this length being very numerous and dangerous to traffic. It was proposed that a small portion of land belonging to Barker Fold Farm be acquired so as to make the road wider on the *"very dangerous twist in the Highway at the point where our Parish joins the Livesey Parish ... which is a great danger to the traffic using the roadway, particularly in dark and foggy weather."*

Unfortunately, the R.D.C. refused any further improvements at that time. The problem was eventually solved in the late 1990's by the building of the M65 motorway that runs across the bottom of the Brows, and the creation of a new Morris Brow, which is now a fly-over across the motorway. The chance of being stuck on one of the steep gradients due to snow and ice has now been greatly reduced.

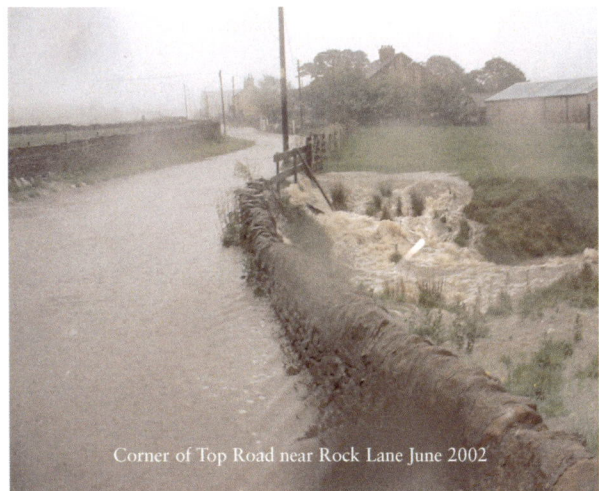

Corner of Top Road near Rock Lane June 2002

Back o'th' Low 1940

Other stretches of road that caused concern due their bad state of repair were the road from the Royal Arms to the boundary near the Finger Post on Belmont Road and the road between Lodge Farm and Chapels Farm owned by the Rothwell Estate. During rainy weather two places on the top road were prone to flooding and were brought to the notice of the R.D.C. One was near the Victoria Hotel and the other was near the Rock Inn and in September 1909 a thunderstorm caused chaos when the roads flooded. Nothing changes! On Friday 14th June 2002 the Village was subjected to another deluge which caused widespread flooding and much damage in the Village and neighbouring towns and woodlands. Again, the road near The Rock was flooded and Rock Lane, Long Lane, Weasel Lane and many other lanes looked like rivers at the height of the storm. A lake formed in the Lych Gate outside St. Stephens, but the weight of water amassed in the road outside the URC Chapel caused the perimeter wall to collapse, flooding the southern end of the graveyard and subsequently washing away part of the back boundary wall. Several homes were also flooded.

To bring the story up to date in 2002 the Borough Council circulated the Villagers with its proposals to build an elaborate traffic calming scheme extending from Morris Brow to The Royal Arms. The scheme included the creation of numerous chicanes, mounds and rumble strips and speed limits of 20 and 30 m.p.h. in an attempt to prevent the use of the top road as a 'rat run'. Work on this project commenced in January 2003.

The condition of various footpaths and bridges such as the bridge crossing the brook in Healds Wood on the Tockholes/Feniscowles footpath, known as Sheep-bridge, (jointly repairable by the Feilden & Rothwell estates), the Red Lee Footbridge and Engine Bottoms Bridge were all considered to be dangerous in the mid 1920's and brought to the attention of the Parish Council who took to task those responsible and saw that repairs were effected.

However, by 1951 the County Council had agreed to accept responsibility for the future maintenance of three more roads:- Old School Lane, from its junction with Tockholes Road at Victoria Inn to its junction with Chapels Lane at Victoria Terrace, a distance of 310 yards; Long Lane, from its junction with Tockholes Road to its junction at Chapels Lane, length 390 yards; and Chapels Lane from its junction with Old School Lane at Victoria Terrace to its junction with Rock Lane, length 717 yards. The information was received 'with great satisfaction and approval' by the Parish Council.

Outside the Post Office 1940

The question of street lighting was raised several times in 1935 and 1936 but by April 1936 it was proposed and accepted that the matter be dropped. It was not raised again until May 1946 when it was proposed that enquiries be made regarding the cost of having lights erected at various points in Tockholes. Ten sites were suggested by the Parish Council but after much correspondence between North West Electricity Board, the Police and the Parish Council only eight sites were agreed, the Police objecting to the ones at Higher Hill and Hollinshead Terrace. By May 1957 the 8 lights were in place:- Barker Fold, top of Rock Lane, bottom of Long Lane, junction of Rock Lane and Pickering Fold, Shirley Gardens, Victoria Terrace, Victoria Hotel, junction of Weasel Lane and the top road. It was 1960 before Higher Hill eventually got a light and August 1963 before one was erected at Hollinshead Terrace. Since then others have been erected at Back O'th Low, Weasel Lane, Lower Hill, the Church and Brookfield Farm.

Motorway fly-over Morris Brow and Pickop Brow
May 2003. Note the old Pickop Brow now a cul-de-sac

Top Road 1979. Snow was piled high and there was only one lane of traffic with 'passing places' for several weeks

Tockholes has a reputation for some spectacular snow falls and over the years the Village has been stranded for several days at a time on many occasions. The wind blows the snow off the fields and fills the roads between the dry stone walls and also causes many huge drifts. On one occasion in the 1940's food had to be passed to the occupants of a house at Back o' th' Low through the upstairs back window until a 'channel' was dug to their front door.

A near fatality occurred in the Winter of 1947 when Mr. & Mrs. Robert Leach, who had a business in Mill Hill, decided to come home early because of a blizzard. By the time they reached The Rock visibility was almost nil, but as they were so near to their village home they decided to continue the last few hundred yards and headed towards a light. They lost their bearings and ended up at the top of Weasel Lane where they collapsed, exhausted, into a deep snowdrift. About the same time Mr. William Baron, a neighbour who lived in Weasel Lane, decided to fetch some coal and take a peak at the weather, but being extremely deaf did not hear the cries for help. Fortunately his wife did and the couple were rescued.

SNOW SCENES 1940 - 1995

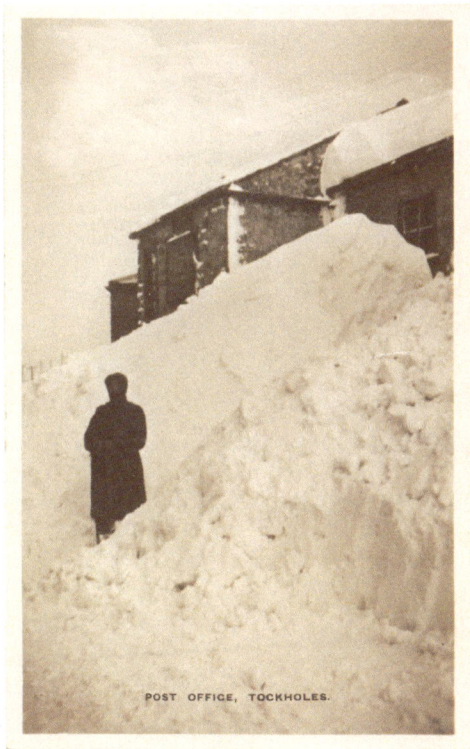

1940

Top o' th' Low 1940
Note gable on the right of old cottages which once
stood on the Victoria Inn Car Park.
Nook Cottage (left) Golden Stoney in background

Road at Barker Fold c. 1982

Barker Fold c. 1982 - Vine House in background

Higher Hill c. 1940

Cotton Hall 1984

Cotton Hall 1979

Chapel's Barn c. 1995

Chapel Lych Gate 1979

THREE HOUSES, TOCKHOLES.

TRANSPORT

Until the 1920's the only transport was 'shank's pony' or a horse and cart if you were one of the lucky ones! The dozens of footpaths that still criss-cross the parish are testament to the fact that most people walked every-where. As previously mentioned, carts were constantly getting stuck in the potholes and ruts of the Tockholes roads, but in the 1920's the roads must have been con-sidered adequate enough to commence a bus service from Blackburn. The first Parish Council minute men-tioning the Blackburn Bus Company is in October 1926 and records a complaint on behalf of the people of Tockholes regarding the inconvenience experienced as a result of *"the lack of proper accommodation and the overcrowding, at times, on the bus service between Tockholes and Blackburn"*. Many, many such similar complaints followed over the years, especially regarding overcrowding on the return journeys after work; also grumbles over the lack of buses; the late arrival causing passengers to miss connections at the boundary of Darwen and Blackburn; the changing of time-tables; the timing of the last bus home on a Saturday at 10.30 p.m. and the Sunday schedule! Today's bus operators would probably leap with joy to be in such demand.

In April 1930 the Parish Council wrote to the Blackburn Bus Company and the Darwen Tramways Company asking for a reduction in fares on behalf of the Tockholes people. Why they thought Tockholes was eligible for a reduction is not clear but in April 1933, after many requests, Darwen Tramways eventually granted a reduc-tion. The Blackburn Bus Company appears to have ignored all letters.

The first bus terminus was at the Victoria Hotel and it was several years before the route was extended as far as Hollinshead Terrace. Today, of course, with almost everyone independently mobile with their own motor cars, the bus service through the Village is very much reduced, but a bus does now go right through the Village and on to Belmont.

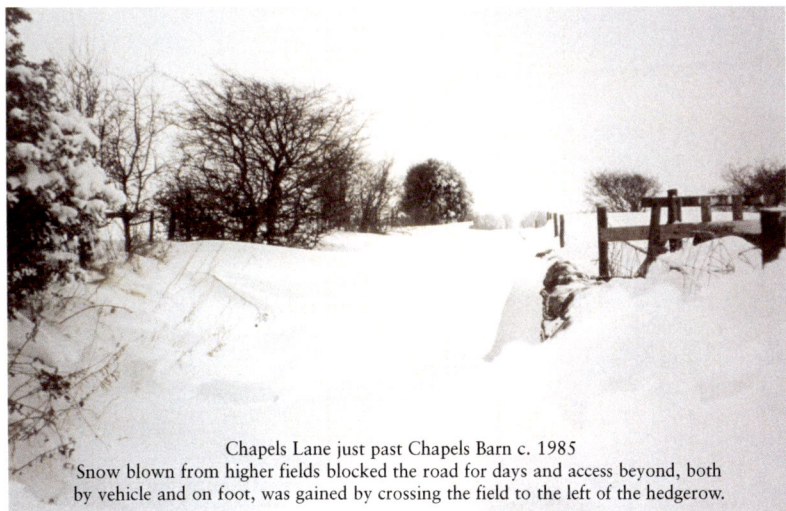

Chapels Lane just past Chapels Barn c. 1985
Snow blown from higher fields blocked the road for days and access beyond, both by vehicle and on foot, was gained by crossing the field to the left of the hedgerow.

FOR AN
AFTERNOON OUTING

Visit

TOCKHOLES

BY BUS.

Special Parties
catered for.

TRAVEL BY THE

B. B. C.
Lion Coaches.

SPECIAL PARTIES
CATERED FOR.

Particulars and Prices will be
given on application at the Office
—or phone 6684.

TOCKHOLES TIME TABLE.

Mon., Tues., Wed., Thurs., Frid.		SATURDAY.		SUNDAY.	
Blackburn	Tockholes	Blackburn	Tockholes	Blackburn	Tockholes
dep.	dep.	dep.	dep.	dep.	dep.
a.m	a.m.	a.m.	a.m.	a.m.	p.m.
6 30	7 5	6 30	*7 5	1 35	2 5
6 35	7 15	6 35	7 15	2 35	3 5
10 30	11 0	10 30	1l 0	3 35	4 5
p.m.	p.m.	11 50	p.m.	4 35	5 5
1 15	2 0	p.m.	12 15	5 35	6 5
2 30	3 0	1 5	1 35	7 5	7 35
4 15	5 0	2 5	2 35	8 5	8 35
5 35	6 15	3 5	3 35	9 5	9 35
7 5	7 35	4 5	4 35	10 5	10 35
9 15	9 45	5 5	6 5		
*10 30	11 0*	7 5	7 35		
		8 5	8 25		
		9 10	10 0		
		10 30	11 0		

* Wednesday and Saturday only.

BLACKBURN BUS COMPANY TIMETABLE 1928

100

A SELECTION OF NEWS REPORTS RELATING
TO THE STATE OF THE ROADS

IMPROVEMENTS IN TOCKHOLES AND LIVESEY.

The scheme for levelling a steep brow in the township of Livesey, near Tockholes, called Morris Brow, which has been talked of for more than a dozen years, is now, we understand, likely to be accomplished. Subscriptions have been entered into by the principal landowners and most of the tenants in Tockholes. Mr. J. Fielden, of Witton, and Mr. Eccles Shorrock, of Over Darwen, have contributed most liberally. The state of the roads in many parts of these townships is so bad that at times they are scarcely passable. It is anticipated, at an early date, if Mr. Hardy's highway bill (which has been read a second time) does not meet the difficulty, that the surveyors will be empowered under an existing act of parliament to borrow a sum of money to be paid by regular instalments and spread over a certain term of years. In our columns of to-day an advertisement will be found from which it appears that the committee to whom the alterations are entrusted are about to proceed without delay. We also understand that the weaving shed in Tockholes, for 350 looms, now in course of erection by Messrs. Eccles Shorrock and Co., of Over Darwen, will be completed by the Autumn. Mr. Rothwell, of Sharples Hall, near Bolton we are informed, is about to fix upon a suitable site for a shed for 250 looms on his estate. These new sheds, together with the improvements about to be made by Mr. Ward in his works have raised the hopes of the inhabitants of this sequestered place.

Blackburn Standard 23 February 1859

1907
"TOCKUS" ROADS
An Urgent Matter for the Village

'...*The Rev. A.T. Corfield thanked the Council on behalf of the Tockholes people for receiving the deputation. ... There were three things, he said, that they wanted remedying. The first was that "old, old annual" Pickop Brow. The other roads, Rock and Long Lanes, were also in a very bad state of repair. It was suggested that the Council pay £300 to the cost of repair and that Tockholes residents would find the other £100. Rock Lane, continued Mr. Corfield, one of the chief thoroughfares of the parish, as was Long Lane. He was asking them to do so because several of the deputation were prepared to swear before a magistrate that a mile of road was repaired by the rates up to a few years ago. It was not taken over by the Council and they simply wanted the Council to take over half a mile, which was the distance of those two roads. There were over five miles of public roads in Tockholes, and of these the Council only repaired two, only half a mile of which latter were used by the Tockholes people. If that was not an injustice, what was?*

Rev. D. Critchley, another of the deputation, said he came to voice the opinions and feelings of the largest public meeting representing all classes that had been held in Tockholes during the seventeen years he had known it. Tockholes was one of the healthiest places in this part of the country, and he certainly believed that if the roads were put in better repair there would be some building done. Farmers had to keep two horses, where in an or dinary place one would be sufficient. Their village was worth helping and if they made the approach to the district better they would confer a very great boon on the residents. Sixteen years ago his rate was a little over 10s. and now it was over 30s. for the same house, with very

TO CONTRACTORS AND OTHERS

TO BE LET, BY TENDER, the ALTERING and LEVELLING of part of MORRIS BROW, in the Township of Livesey, with the Erection of Fence Walls, Forming of Culvert, etc. etc.

Plans and specifications may be seen at the "Rock Inn," Tockholes, after Friday the 25th inst.

Sealed Tenders, addressed "Morris Brow Committee," must be sent on or before the 8th OF MARCH NEXT, addressed "Morris Brow Committee," care of Mr. T. SHARPLES, Rock Inn, Tockholes

Blackburn Standard 23 Feb 1859

little more improvements, and it was not unreasonable to ask the Council to expend some £300. The village would find the other £100 and would be perfectly willing to do its best, if the Council would help them.

Mr. Turner said he was a Tockholes farmer and as a resident who had lived there all his life made a strong appeal for some action to be taken by the Council. It was no uncommon thing to see horses and carriages in difficulties; in fact there was hardly a day last winter that passed without some accident or other. He himself had been called out at all times of the night to assist strangers who were in difficulties. The condition of the roads also kept many of the children from school. He had even seen at various times, when a funeral cortege was going towards the chapel, the coffin taken out of the hearse and carried across the fields, in order to evade a possible accident in Rock Lane. This kind of thing, he thought, was a disgrace and he hoped the Council would give it their full consideration.

Mr. Birch (the Clerk): Did you ever hear in your life of the parish highway surveyor spending a penny on these roads? – No.

Mr. Birch: It has never been claimed in the district that it was a parish highway repairable by the inhabitants at large? – Not to my recollection.

A long discussion followed between the deputation and members of the Council, after which Mr. Smalley pointed out that they were committed by a resolution which stated that nothing could be done in the way of carrying out these improvements in Tockholes until the property-owners of the district offered to cover almost the whole of the expense.

The Chairman: I think it would be better to pass a resolution ordering the Clerk to go into everything and report as to the legal aspects of the case.

The Rev. A. T. Corfield: If you postpone the matter it will mean knocking it on the head. I move that the resolution that the Council supply the £300 be passed.

Mr. Smalley: That is out of order.

Mr. Corfield: I am very sorry that you should have to stop it merely on a point of etiquette. I move that the former resolution be rescinded and also that a special Council meeting be held a fortnight hence to take the matter up. He was sorry Mr. Smalley had blocked it.

Mr. Smalley: I strongly protest against that statement. Personally I do not care a scrap about the matter. I was merely pointing out the true facts of the case. If Mr. Corfield thinks he will make political capital out of it he is mistaken, because politics do not enter into the Council's work in the slightest degree and I protest against his selecting one individual in this way.

Mr. Corfield: I have never taken the slightest part in the work of this Council from a political motive. Mr. Smalley's attack is most unjustified and I ask you not to take any notice of it. The people that want this improvement are not only Conservatives, but Liberals and Socialists also. If Mr. Smalley is a Progressive, why does he not allow Tockholes to progress.

After Mr. Corfield's resolution that a special meeting be held, the matter was allowed to drop."

....

Blackburn Times 20th January 1923
'THE DEVELOPMENT OF TOCKHOLES
*Road Gradients which have hindered Progress
Villagers Discuss £4,500 Scheme'*

To ease the steep gradients of Morris and Pickop Brows, Tockholes, and thus make less difficult the approach to this healthy, moorland township, was the subject of discussion at a specially convened public meeting at St. Stephen's School, Tockholes on Thursday evening. Over 60 property owners and residents, many of whom had tramped a considerable distance, carrying their own hurricane lamps, attended. The Rev. D. Critchley, Chairman of the Parish Council, presided.

Mr. J. Birch, (Clerk to the Blackburn R..D.C.) broadly outlined a scheme which had been prepared by Mr. L . D. Brothers (Surveyor to the Council). He said all were agreed that a practicable scheme should be embarked upon. The R.D.C. had considered the question for many years; in fact it exercised the minds of the old parish authorities long before the Highways Act was passed giving control of roads to the District Councils. It had been 'suggested' that the present time was most opportune, because the Government were prepared, in respect of approved schemes, which had in view the employment of unskilled labour, to contribute 60 per cent of the wages bill of such unskilled labour engaged through the Employment Exchange. The Government would not contribute to the cost of skilled labour or materials. The Government advisors would require to

be satisfied the scheme was one of utility and likely to be of permanent benefit to the inhabitants. The proposal roughly was to lower the top of Morris Brow by eight feet and raise the bottom between Morris and Pickop Brows by nine feet, thus taking away 17 feet of gradient. The only difficulty was the cost. The estimate appeared high, but was arrived at having regard to the enhanced cost and difficulties in regard to the absorption of unskilled labour on work which the men were unaccustomed to. In round figures the total cost would be about £4,500, the proportions for unskilled labour being about £1,900, which would probably rank for a grant of some £1,100 from the Government. How to find the £3,400 was the question before them. In November 1921 the R.D.C. stated they could not entertain the idea of expending a large sum of money unless the immediate neighbourhood concerned was prepared to make a voluntary contribution of a considerable amount. At present he was directed to approach the landowners, whose land might be expected to be improved by the carrying out of the scheme. If Tockholes was made more accessible for traffic the value of the land for building purposes would be considerably enhanced. Tockholes was undoubtedly a healthy neighbourhood, and if claims in that respect could be brought to the notice of builders a garden city might spring up. He attended a meeting of landowners that afternoon and a small committee was formed to interview owners not present. In a lesser degree the individual property owners would benefit if Tockholes could be developed into the fair district it was hoped for. It was not possible for him to say what proportion of the cost would satisfy the R.D.C., but the better the offer was the more likelihood there would be of the Council sympathetically considering the wishes of the inhabitants.

Mr. Brothers, surveyor, gave details of the scheme, stating that the gradient of Morris Brow would be reduced from one in 9.75 to one in 11.75 and Pickop Brow from one in 13.5 to one in 15.

The Chairman said he had been in the district 32 years, during which time repeated efforts had been made to impress the authorities to deal with that great hindrance to the progress and welfare of the neighbourhood. It was generally agreed that the demolition of the two cotton mills in existence years ago at Tockholes could be traced to this drawback. He was pleased his recent appeal to the local authority appeared to have had serious consideration. In regard to the Government relief of unemployed he would rather pay his money towards maintaining those men on productive work than allow them to stand at street corners smoking their pipes and doing nothing. If the work was done it would put a new aspect on the life and future of this district. It was one of the healthiest districts in the county, and if the scheme was carried through new houses would be built. One friend had already agreed to commence building from four to seven houses. One sum suggested as their contribution was £500. United effort and sacrifice were needed. It was estimated that – a 3/4d rate throughout the whole rural district over 20 years would cover the cost, and he would be agreeable to increase the demand to a twopenny rate and shorten the period. Two landowners, Mr. Stanley King and Mr. John Turner, had agreed to make a free gift of land required for the work.

Mr. T. Whipp, representative of the R.D.C., said the problem was one which his grandfather, as surveyor under the old Highways' Act was concerned with, and which was also dealt with by the Council at the time his father was their representative.

In answer to questions, Mr. Birch said the Liverpool Corporation, who owned considerable stretches of land, had declined to do anything. Apart from what the Government granted and the amount Tockholes contributed the cost would have to be raised by loan, be chargeable to the whole of the Blackburn Rural District and repaid by rates. If the balance to be met from rates could be reduced to £2,400, the rate would be two-thirds of a penny for 20 years. It was, of course, no easy matter to persuade people in the Ribble Valley if they were not going to derive any benefit from the expenditure of money in Tockholes. During the time he had been connected with the Council, since 1894, small road improvements had been carried out in various parts, but this was the largest undertaking of its kind. There was no chance of a grant from the Roads Board as well as the Unemployment Grants Committee of the Government.

Mr. Brothers was also questioned and said inconvenience on the road would be experienced for 12 months. He knew nothing of the original scheme said to cost £800, but the present was somewhat similar to one prepared by Mr. William Sames.

A vote of thanks to the Chairman, Mr. Birch and Mr. Brothers was moved by Mr. T. Whipp, seconded by Mr. T. Edmondson, and unanimously carried.

A large and representative committee was formed."

• •

Blackburn Times Report
of R.D.C. Meeting February 1923

TOCKHOLES SCHEME NOT SUPPORTED
Rural District Council Fight Shy of Cost

The monthly meeting of the Blackburn Rural District council was held on Saturday, Mr. A. E. Troop J.P. presiding.

The suggested scheme of improving gradients at Morris and Pickop Brows, Livesey, was discussed. At the Highways Committee the previous Wednesday, the Clerk (Mr. J. Birch) reported on the meetings at Tockholes, and gave estimates of the cost and possible grant from the "Unemployment Committee". Mr. T. Whipp, representative for Tockholes, attended the committee, and stated that he was authorised to make an offer to contribute the sum of £600. This left the sum of £2,800 to be defrayed by the Council. If the repayment of this sum was spread over a period of twenty years it would involve an expenditure of £224 per annum for that period. "Having very carefully considered this question in all its bearings, the Committee do not feel themselves in a position to make any recommendation to the Council, and therefore leave the matter as an open question for the decision of the members, generally" was the resolution passed.

When the minutes were considered, Mr. Whipp said he was sorry they had come to that decision, for he had expected some material result. The prosperity of Tockholes depended on the improvement of the roads in the neighbourhood. If nothing was done the ratepayers in that district would be quite justified in passive resistance over the payment of rates. The scheme would have proved the greatest boon and blessing ever conferred upon Tockholes. Apparently if Tockholes residents had been prepared to find £4,000 and left a deficit of £500 only, there would have been croakers objecting to the undertaking. He moved that the matter be referred back to the committee for full consideration. He also required a return of what certain townships paid in rates, and the amounts spent in those townships, for the past five years.

Mr. M. Ainsworth seconded.

Mr. H. Smalley, J.P., said it would not do to look too closely of what each township paid and received in respect of the upkeep of the roads. Looking at a scheme of such magnitude he did not think the ratepayers as a whole would be justified in paying £224 a year for two decades on the capital outlay. Then it was estimated that a further expenditure of £120 to £130 per year for ten years would be required towards the cost of maintenance of the roads in the Tockholes district. Already they were spending £60 a year on the Tockholes roads.

Mr. Whipp: Since the war began there has not been half the money spent on Tockholes that has been paid.

Mr. Smalley said the heavy expenditure on Balderstone and Clayton-le-Dale roads was owing to through traffic. If Morris and Pickop Brows were so improved as to greatly increase traffic through Tockholes they would have to face similar heavy expenditure. It was no use referring the matter back to the Highways Committee, for they had considered it fairly and fully.

The Chairman said there were several parishes where the receipts were greater than the expenditure, and Billington was one.

The motion to refer the scheme back was defeated by six votes to two, and in regard to the suggestion that the Surveyor should tabulate receipts and expenditure of certain parishes for the past five years there was equal division between the four members who voted. The Chairman then declared the motion as not having been carried.

NINETEEN NEW HOUSES

The Surveyor (Mr. L. D. Brothers) presented plans for 19 new dwelling-houses to be privately erected. Five were intended for Tockholes, eight for Livesey, four for Mellor, and two for Salesbury. It was mentioned that this was a record number for private enterprise since pre-war days.

Blackburn Times 20th June 1923

The healthy upland township of Tockholes has hopes of becoming prosperous again if a long deferred scheme of road improvement at Morris and Pickop Brows is undertaken. The villagers turned up in large numbers on Thursday evening to discuss a £4,500 scheme for easing the gradients of the two slopes of a basin-like road, which makes it difficult to get to Tockholes from Blackburn and Darwen. The Brows are situated in Livesey and the road is the main highway through Tockholes to Bolton. The Rev. D. Critchley, who during his 32 years' residence, has always advocated that the work should be done, said the demolition of two cotton mills could in some measure be traced to this hindrance to road transport. He hinted that the erection of a number of dwelling-houses was contemplated, and that there was a prospect that the value of the land and buildings would increase. How to raise the money is the present chief concern, for unless Tockholes residents make a fair contribution to the cost the Rural District

Blackburn Times 10th February 1923

The Rural District Council on Saturday last turned down the officer of the Tockholes people to raise £600 towards the cost of £4.500 required to improve the gradients at Morris and Pickop Brows, Livesey. It was hoped to get the work done by the unemployed, and therefore to obtain a grant of £1,100 from the Government, leaving £2,800 to be met out of the rates on the whole rural area. To this the representatives of the other townships objected and an argument followed as to each township's share of expenditure out of the total rate. It was admitted that some of the townships contributed more in rates than they got back in any form, and that others did not contribute as much as was spent on them, but in the later case, it was pointed out, the townships were called upon to bear the cost of roads upon which there is heavy through traffic. On Morris and Pickop Brows, on the other hand, the traffic (it was alleged) is entirely local. But this argument did not satisfy the representatives from Tockholes, who hinted at passive resistance to the further payment of rates if nothing is done to meet their wishes. The R.D.C. as a whole were against them, and the scheme was rejected. The official view of the case is that there is no possible chance of a Government grant for the work referred to as grants are only made to expedite work which has been under contemplation, and to recoup the local authority for the difference in cost involved by hurrying it on and using unemployed labour. The easing of the gradients at Morris and Pickop Brows, it is stated, has never been considered as work to be done by the R.D.C. at any time.

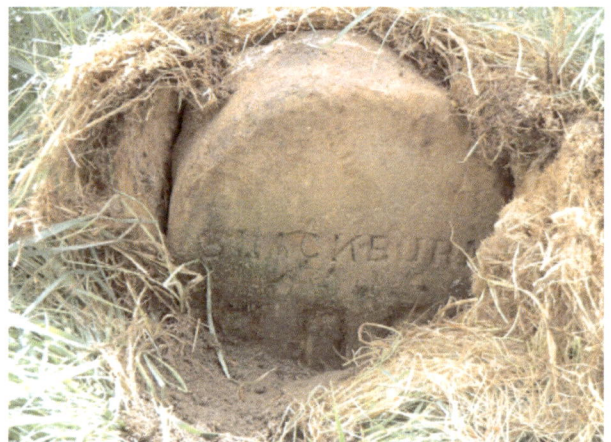

The only known remaining Mile Stone in the Village

council is not likely to be encouraged to embark on the scheme, even though a Government grant of about £1,100 may be obtained to relieve unemployment.

CHAPTER 6

EMPLOYMENT

A glance at St. Stephen's Burial Registers for the 19th Century shows almost everyone is described as "Weaver". Firstly, of course, people were handloom weavers but in the mid 19th Century power loom weaving was introduced to Tockholes when Redmayne's Mill, the first of the Tockholes Mills, opened on a site to the South of Fine Peters. In 1859, the Mill which became known as Hollinshead Mill, was built to the South of The Royal Arms. These two mills employed a good deal of the population of Tockholes and their eventual closures were the main reason many families finally deserted the Village to find work in Darwen and Blackburn. Other occupations listed on the early census returns show many people to be farmers, but most were connected to the cotton industry in some way or another. As well as weavers there were warpers, winders, overlookers, warehousemen and heald knitters etc., all put out of work with the closure of the mills.

In the early part of the 19th century handloom weaving was still extensively followed and a stroll around the Village on a dark night would have given a glimpse into most of the village houses where Villagers would be seen working in their "shops" by the dim light of candles suspended from cords. They toiled long hours in order to finish their pieces of cloth and so earn enough to provide for their families. In the 1820's wages had fallen very considerably and at one point a number of men visited the village, broke all the shuttles of the weavers and cut their warps to prevent them from working for low wages. As a result many families became totally dependent on charity and, weakened by starvation, their children died from common childhood diseases.

In 1825 serious loom-breaking and rioting was reported in many towns in the area including Blackburn and Darwen. In Blackburn on the 24th April 1826 several thousand workers marched on Mills in the town, smashing the looms and tossing the warps and twist into the canal. The Dragoons were called upon to quell the riots and during one encounter one soldier was seriously hurt, a rioter was shot dead and several others were fatally injured or seriously hurt. The Riot Act was read out at 3.30 p.m. and again at 8 p.m. In the evening of that day 10,000 weavers jubilantly paraded in the streets proudly boasting that not a single power-loom remained unbroken, and the Dragoons were ordered to clear the streets. This was done by a charge through the crowd, soldiers striking the rioters with the flat edge of their sabres. The next day a similar fate befell mills in Darwen.

[7] On the 27th of April 1826 the last of the loom-breaking riots in this area took place at Water Street, Chorley. The 'arrangements' for this act were made somewhere in Tockholes by a group of rioters who had been in Blackburn a couple of days previously and amongst the leaders was one, Thomas Sharples, aged 24, a Tockholes handloom weaver. He had been hiding from the law somewhere in this area, sheltered by family or friends, but still desperate

[7] Information taken from "Riot" by William Turner.

enough to continue the loom wrecking. Early on the 27th the armed group, led by Sharples, left Tockholes, along with their supporters, and made their way across the fields via Withnell, Brinscall and Heapey to Water Street, Chorley. Sharples had cleverly led the marchers over the local footpaths so as to avoid the Dragoon Guards positioned on the main road. More supporters had collected along the way and a sizeable mob had formed by the time it reached Water Street Mill. Here, as before, the Riot Act was read but nevertheless fierce fighting took place and 80 looms were destroyed. During the fighting the leaders ran off back to Tockholes, leaving the locals to continue the stone throwing and fighting.

Arrest was inevitable though, and two days later Sharples was amongst those taken before the magistrates and subsequently imprisoned in Lancaster Castle and later tried at the Assizes. The Assizes were held the following August as a result of which several rioters were deported to Australia and many more received prison sentences. Thomas Sharples received the death sentence, commuted to 18 months imprisonment.

In the 1851 Census there appears the name of a Thomas Sharples, then aged 49, living at Higher Hill with his wife and four children aged between 21 and 4, and described as 'handloom weaver', born in Tockholes. Could this the same Thomas Sharples who led the rioters to Chorley?

Some years later Rev. Gilmour Robinson wrote *"Nearly all the people (of Tockholes) are handloom cotton weavers, and have passed through most abject poverty."* The desperate plight of all hand-loom weavers was graphically described in a letter of 1826 when the Blackburn Weavers' Union Society sent a written address to Robert Peel, the then Secretary of State for the Home Department, outlining the immense hardships and suffering caused by the introduction of power looms and also by the operation of the Corn Laws which had raised the price of imported wheat, so making bread, the staple foodstuff, much more expensive.

Also in January 1826 the Blackburn Mail wrote of the Weavers' plight - *"in the severity of a cheerless winter, they have further to endure all the positive pain of the extreme rigour of the climate and insufficient clothing. They feel themselves thoroughly wretched, without all present comfort and totally hopeless for the future. Could we look beneath the roofs of many hundreds of the houses, we should see many thousands of individuals, men, women and children, suffering under the accumulated ills of poverty, hunger, cold, nakedness and sickness. Many of them do not expect that their sickly wives and children can last out the famine and misery of the passing day."*

In April of that year 2233 families in Blackburn had taken poor relief. One of the Workhouses reported that 76 new inmates had been admitted in one week, bringing the total workhouse population to 678. Workhouses were looked upon as an absolute last resort, the fear being that, once inside, there would be no getting out.

"FIRST WORKHOUSE was at Grimshaw Park from 1700's to 1860, then a new one was opened at Queens Park for 700 people. The poor, the homeless and orphans went to these establishments. The Workhouse was supposed to prevent the poorest people from starving by giving them food and a home in return for their work. In reality it was like a prison. Workhouse inmates were known as paupers and had to dress in workhouse uniforms.

Families were split up, the food provided was often substandard and the work given was often hard, repetitive and dirty. It included sorting through refuse for bones or cotton rags to be resold, breaking stones for road surfacing and being hired out to mines and mills.

When paupers died they were buried with little ceremony and no headstone was put on their grave. Poverty was never far away and it was normal for families to sell or pawn almost all their possessions to keep out of the workhouse."

Workhouses slowly began to cater more for the infirm and those who could not look after themselves, and so care for the destitute gradually turned into care for the sick and Blackburn Workhouse became Queens Park Hospital in the 1930's.

WEAVERS' ADDRESS:

TO THE RIGHT HONOURABLE ROBERT PEEL, HIS MAJESTY'S PRINCIPAL SECRETARY OF STATE FOR THE HOME DEPARTMEMT

Sir,
We, the Operative hand-loom Weavers of Blackburn, presuming upon the public spirit, and love of justice, which distinguish your political character, have ventured, in the unadorned language of British Mechanics, to lay before you a statement of a part of our numerous grievances, in the firm persuasion, that His Majesty's Government, need only to be informed of the sufferings of the people, for full and complete justice to be administered to them.

It is well known that the Cotton Weavers received, for many years, wages, sufficient to procure in moderation, all the necessities of life, and thus were placed on a footing of equality with the rest of the working community; but within the last eleven years, we have experienced repeated reductions in the price of our labours and often when there was not the least reason, until at this time, we cannot procure more than one or two meals a day. Our dwellings are totally destitute of every necessary comfort. Every article of value has disappeared, either to satisfy the cravings of hunger, or to appease the clamours of relentless creditors; our homes where plenty and contentment once resided, are now become the abodes of penury and wretchedness. This, however, is only a faint picture of the situation of those who are *fully employed*. No adequate idea can be formed of the sufferings of those who are *unemployed*, of whom there are upwards of SEVEN THOUSAND in this town and neighbourhood; - thousands who were once possessed of an honest independence, gained by laborious industry, are now sunk in the lowest depths of poverty; - thousands, who once looked forward with confidence to a decent competence to support themselves in old age, are now reduced to the melancholy alternative of subsisting on casual charity, or becoming the inmates of a workhouse. Were the humane man, Sir, to visit the dwellings of four fifths of the Weavers, and see the miserable pittance which 16 hours hard labour can procure, even of those who are fully employed, divided between the wretched parents and their starving little ones, he would sicken at the sight and blush for the patience of humanity!

The principal causes, Sir, which in our opinion, have conspired to produce that wretchedness and misery, which reign universally amongst the Weavers, are, the *Corn Laws* & *the introduction of Power Loom Weaving*. The former by enhancing the price of provisions, afforded a pretext to avaricious Manufacturers to reduce the wages of their workmen, in order that their quantum of profits might still be the same; and all the others were soon necessitated to follow their example, and, by preventing the admission of foreign grain, they contributed effectually to deprive us forever of thousands of our best foreign customers, by forcing them in retaliation to manufacture for themselves. But whatever may have been the evils inflicted by the operation of the Corn Laws, they vanish into nothing when compared with those which followed the adoption of Power Looms. This was the grand blow which struck at the root of our domestic happiness, – this completed what the Corn Laws had begun – and, like the tenth Egyptian plague, this exceeded all the commercial evils which had ever visited this once-happy country. This machine produced a new epoch in our Manufactures; one boy or girl was able to perform as much work as several hand-loom Weavers – immense numbers were in consequence thrown out of employment – the hand-loom Manufacturers were forced to reduce their wages, that they might be able to meet their rivals in the market – reduction followed reduction, until at this time our wages are 80 or 90 per cent less than they were 20 or 25 years ago. The power-loom has done incalculable injury to the country; - it has forced thousands to the workhouse – the land has been taxed to support them – rents have consequently risen – and, we venture to assert that three fourths of that opposition which has been manifested to any alteration in the Corn Laws, may be traced to the power loom, and the recent improvements in machinery, as its parents. Were land the common property of all, then any improvement in machinery, which would tend to abridge human labour, would be a national benefit; but while every new discovery in the art of diminishing manual labour, tends only to enrich those by whom the improvement was introduced, and to spread an equal proportion of poverty among the working classes, we cannot refrain from protesting against such innovations, as calculated to sap the foundations of society, and to transform a happy, well-fed, and independent peasantry, into a race of grovelling, mean-spirited paupers.

We are aware of the slippery ground on which we stand, when we address persons in office, in the language of simple truth, but when we reflect, that almost all the Officers of his Majesty's Government, have had their salaries advanced, and in many cases more than doubled, upon the plea of an advance in the price of provisions; whilst, for the same reason, amongst many others, we have had our wages repeatedly reduced, until they are no more than THREE or at most, FIVE SHILLINGS per week; when we contrast our present circumstances with what they once were, and when we look upon our starving wives and children, and have no bread to given them; - we should consider ourselves still more degraded than we are – as undeserving the name of Englishmen, were we to withhold our complaint from His Majesty's Government, or to abstain from speaking in proper terms of what we consider the causes of the present unparalleled distress, which exists amongst the weavers, and, we implore you, Sir, by all the ties which bind the patriot to his country – by that anxiety for the welfare of England, which you have frequently evinced – to use that influence, which you possess with his Majesty's Government, towards producing an amelioration of the condition of the most injured and oppressed class of His Majesty's subjects.

By order of the Committee
Of the Weavers' Union Society. JOHN LANCASTER

REDMAYNE'S MILL ALSO KNOWN AS VICTORIA MILL

The introduction of steam looms gradually replaced handloom weaving and the factory system was born. Here in Tockholes, the first mill, Redmayne's Mill, was erected about 1838 and this provided employment for a considerable number of villagers. The mill was sited on the field between Fine Peter's and Four Houses. Leonard and Hannah (*nee Peacock*) Redmayne had moved from Cumbria to Horwich about 1777 where Leonard took up the position of Minister of Lee Congregational Chapel, Horwich. One of their sons, John Peacock Redmayne, resided in Tockholes for some time and was a member of the Chapel, but he left in 1840 to live in Preston. He and his first wife, a Miss Brownlow of Horwich, had three sons, one of whom was lost at sea when young. The two remaining sons, Richard Brownlow Redmayne and John Redmayne, are the ones who built Tockholes Mill.

Richard was transferred from Belgrave Congregational Church, Darwen, to Tockholes Church (Chapel) on 6th July 1845. He married Mary Cocker, a member of a prominent Chapel family, and died 6th June 1853 aged 42 years.

Notices in the local newspapers show that the brothers parted company in 1849 and the business was then carried on by Richard Redmayne alone. After Richard's death at the relatively young age of 42, it appears his wife carried on the business for a couple of years but by 1856 the Mill and all its contents were advertised for sale. One month later, their home, Fine Peter's, was also on the market.

The properties must not have sold at the first Auction as similar advertisements were placed on the 29th April 1857, under the charge of a new firm of Auctioneers. The advertisement re-listed the Machinery and effects at Tockholes Mill together with similar machinery and effects at Duke Street Cotton Works, Blackburn. The Tockholes estate contained additional details relating to the "newly erected Power Loom Cloth Manufactory, Engine House, Boiler House, Warehouse, Sizing House, Store rooms, Smithy and Workshops." The Redmaynes also owned other buildings in Duke Street and Blakey Moor including a four storey Power Loom Cloth Manufactory with Warehouse, Mechanics shop, Counting House, Dwelling-houses, Grocer's Shop and other Buildings, Water lodges, Yards and land comprising a total of 5969 square yards.

NOTICE IF HEREBY GIVEN

That the partnership heretofore subsisting between us, the undersigned, RICHARD BROWNLOW REDMAYNE and JOHN PEACOCK REDMAYNE, carrying on business at *Tockholes Mill*, in the township of Tockholes, in the County of Lancaster, under the firm of "R & J. REDMAYNE," as Power-Loom Cloth Manufacturers, has been this day dissolved by mutual consent. And that all debts owing to or from the said Co-partnership, will be received and paid by the said RICHARD BROWNLOW REDMAYNE, who will in future carry on the said business at Tockholes Mill aforesaid. Dated this twenty- second day of august one thousand eight hundred and forty-nine.

RHARd. B. REDMAYNE
JOHN P. REDMAYNE

Signed in the presence of
THOS. AINSWORTH, Solicitor, Blackburn.

Blackburn Standard 29th Aug 1849

SALE THIS DAY
BY ORDER OF THE MORTGAGEE

TO BE SOLD BY AUCTION
By Mr. GRUNDY

At the "Old Bull Inn" in Blackburn in the County of Lancaster, on **WEDNESDAY (THIS DAY)** the **10TH DAY OF SEPTEMBER 1856, at Six** o'clock in the Evening, subject to such conditions of Sale as will be then and there produced:-

ALL that very desirable and handsome RESIDENCE, Garden and Orchard, situate in *Tockholes* in the County of Lancaster aforesaid, and commonly called "FINE PETER'S" and also all that COTTAGE and WAREHOUSE adjoining the same Messuage, together with the Barn, Shippon and other Outbuildings, and Fold Yard, situate thereto.

And also all those THREE CLOSES or PARCELS of MEADOW LAND and small NURSERY, situate near to the said Residence, comprising six acres, or thereabouts; and also all those TWO CLOSES or PARCELS of LAND, comprising six acres, or thereabouts, commonly called the "PICKERING FIELDS", adjoining thereto.

And also, all that desirable FARM commonly called "GREEN HILL", comprising 9 acres of Meadow and Pasture Land, and situate in *Tockholes* aforesaid, together with Dwelling-house, Barn, Shippon and other Outbuildings; and also, all that desirable FARM commonly called "HOWCROFT" comprising 4 acres or thereabouts of Meadow and Pasture Land, together with Dwelling-house, Barn and Shippon thereto; which said two last mentioned Closes or Parcels of Land Buildings, etc. are part of the Estate called "FINE PETER'S", comprising in the whole 24s. 3r. statute measure, Freehold Land and Buildings.

And also all that POWER-LOOM CLOTH MANUFACTORY, Boiler-house, Engine-house, Warehouse, and other Buildings erected upon one of the Closes of Meadow Land above-mentioned; and the Steam Boiler, Steam Engine and other fixed Machinery, Gasometer, and Water Lodges within and upon the said Power Loom Cloth Manufactory, or thereto belonging.

The whole of the said Premises are Freehold of Inheritance, and very advantageously situate on the Blackburn and Bolton Highway, as respects the supply of coal, water, and labour.

Further particulars may be obtained from the AUCTIONEER, 86 King Street; or Messrs WORTHINGTON and EARL, Solicitors, Bond Street, Manchester

Blackburn Standard 10th September 1856

Redmayne's Mill eventually passed into the hands of Henry Ward of Blackburn, who added a shed for an extra 260 looms at the rear of the existing building. In September 1863, Benjamin Sandford and John Willacy Haydock purchased the property from Henry Ward and during this time employed some 150 people. The Mill was then known as Victoria Mill.

A Minute in the School Diary for Friday 23rd April 1869 reads "One of the Mills in the vicinity stops work" and in June of that year an advertisement appeared in the Blackburn Standard for sale of the effects of the Mill.

In March 1872 the Mill was up for Auction again and was bought by Thomas Brooks of Blackburn for the sum of £545. Whether Brooks actually took possession is unclear as *Nightingale* stated the property passed from Sandford and Haydock to a man named Hindle and that Hindle was the last owner who eventually had the building demolished.

The O.S. map (left) shows the site and size of the Mill in 1848 and presumably the 4 cottages, now known as Four Houses, contained within the same complex. Today, the remains of the gateway into the grounds can still be seen on the northern gable of the terrace and some of the present rear garden walls appear, in part, to have been built with dressed stone, probably from the demolition of the Mill.

Pleasant View (Four Houses) 1978

Pleasant View 2003
The four cottages mentioned in the Auction Notice below

Pleasant View 2003 showing the remains of
the Old Mill Gateway

At the "Old Bull Hotel" in Blackburn —— in the County of Lancaster, the twenty seventh day of March ——— 1872.

Conditions for Selling by Auction, by Messrs. Salesbury Hodgson

All that power loom Cloth Weaving Mill called "Victoria Mill" situate on the Easterly side of the old highway leading from Blackburn to Bolton in Pockholes in the County of Lancaster with the Engine House Boiler House Gas House Stables outbuildings privileges and appurtenances thereto belonging Together with the Steam Engine of 25 Horse power Boiler of 35 Horse power Shafting Gearing Steam Water and Gaspiping Gasmaking Apparatus Roberts Gasometer and other fixtures therein an Inventory whereof is now produced. ———

And also four cottages adjoining the said Mill with the backyards and conveniences thereto belonging ———

The property is freehold of inheritance contains 9630 superficial square yards of land or thereabouts and is free from ground rent ———

HOLLINSHEAD MILL

There is no known photograph of Hollinshead Mill but a plan of the Mill and grounds was made for a survey of the property carried out in March 1903 which gives an excellent description of the whole site. The Survey described the buildings as being old and very much worn with the exception of the large Weaving Shed. The floors were generally in very bad condition and required some renewal. The Engines, Looms, Steam Pipes, Fans and other machinery in the Mill were also old and in some instances practically worn out, the life left in them being estimated at about 25 years.

The Lease expired in June of that year and the Annual Rental was £230, including the Mill, power and machinery, the Tenant having to repair the Machinery and the Landlord being responsible for the building and power. The estimated value of the premises and machinery for compulsory sale was £1948.

Key to Plan references:

A, B & C – Office, Store-room & Warehouses, with Waste Room at one end, all one story high

D. Skip Yard, Cindered Floor

E. Two Storey Building, comprising Weft Store or Yarn Warehouses on ground floor, with Tape-room and Sizing Room above, approached by Step Ladder and Power Hoist

F. Store-room for bobbins etc. and Winding and Warping Room with Flag Floor and Weaving Shed Roof; one Storey high

G. Small Weaving Shed 15 Looms

H. General Weaving Shed with 318 power looms, Driving Gear. One Storey high

I. Small Gas House

J. Boiler House, one storey high

K. Engine Room, one storey, with Beam Engine, 250 i.h.p.?

L. Octagon Factory Chimney

M. Gasometer

N. Mill Lodge with Stone built sides and all piping

O. One storey Stable and Office with weighing Machine by Hodson with 6ft x 5ft table

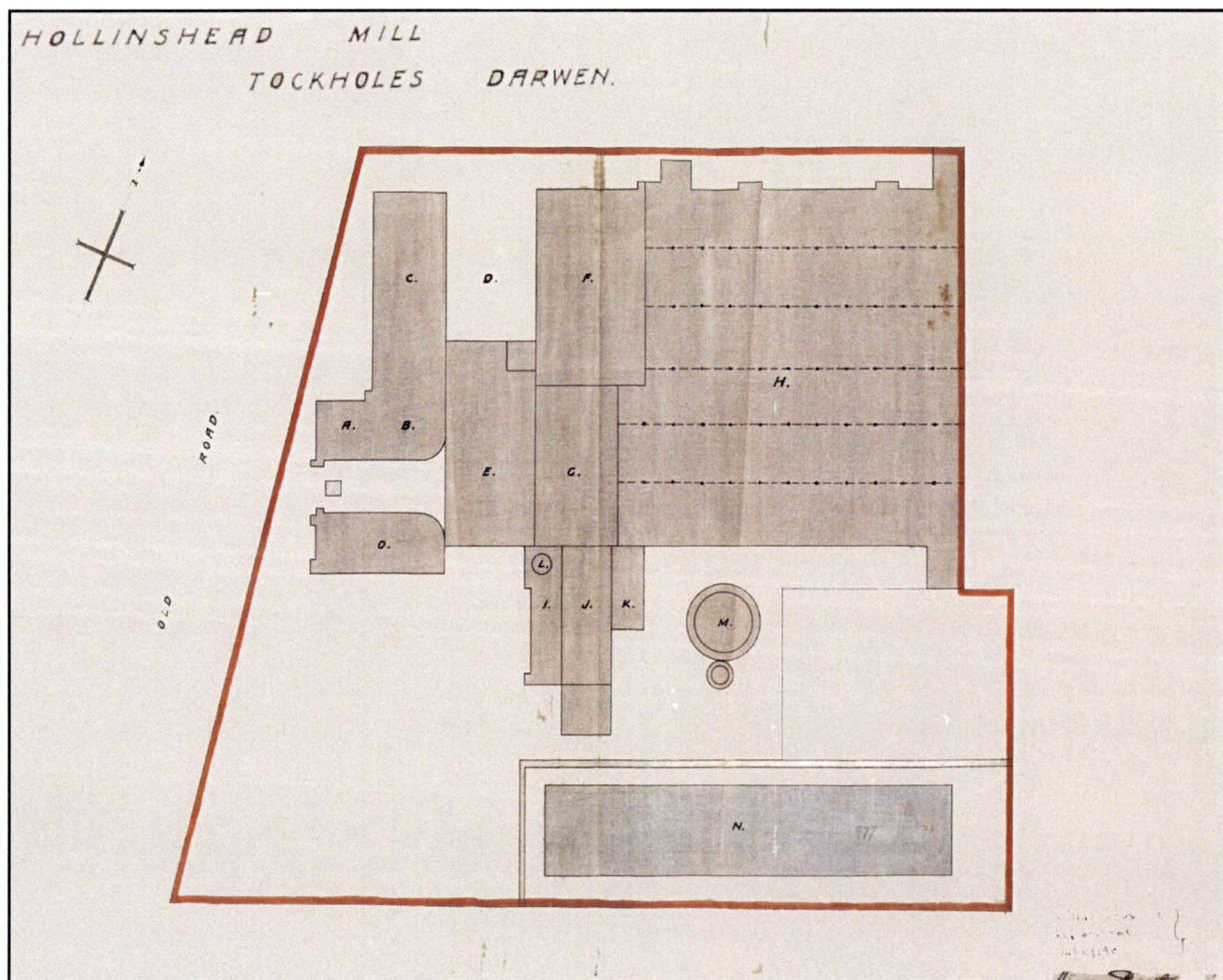

HOLLINSHEAD MILL TOCKHOLES DARWEN.

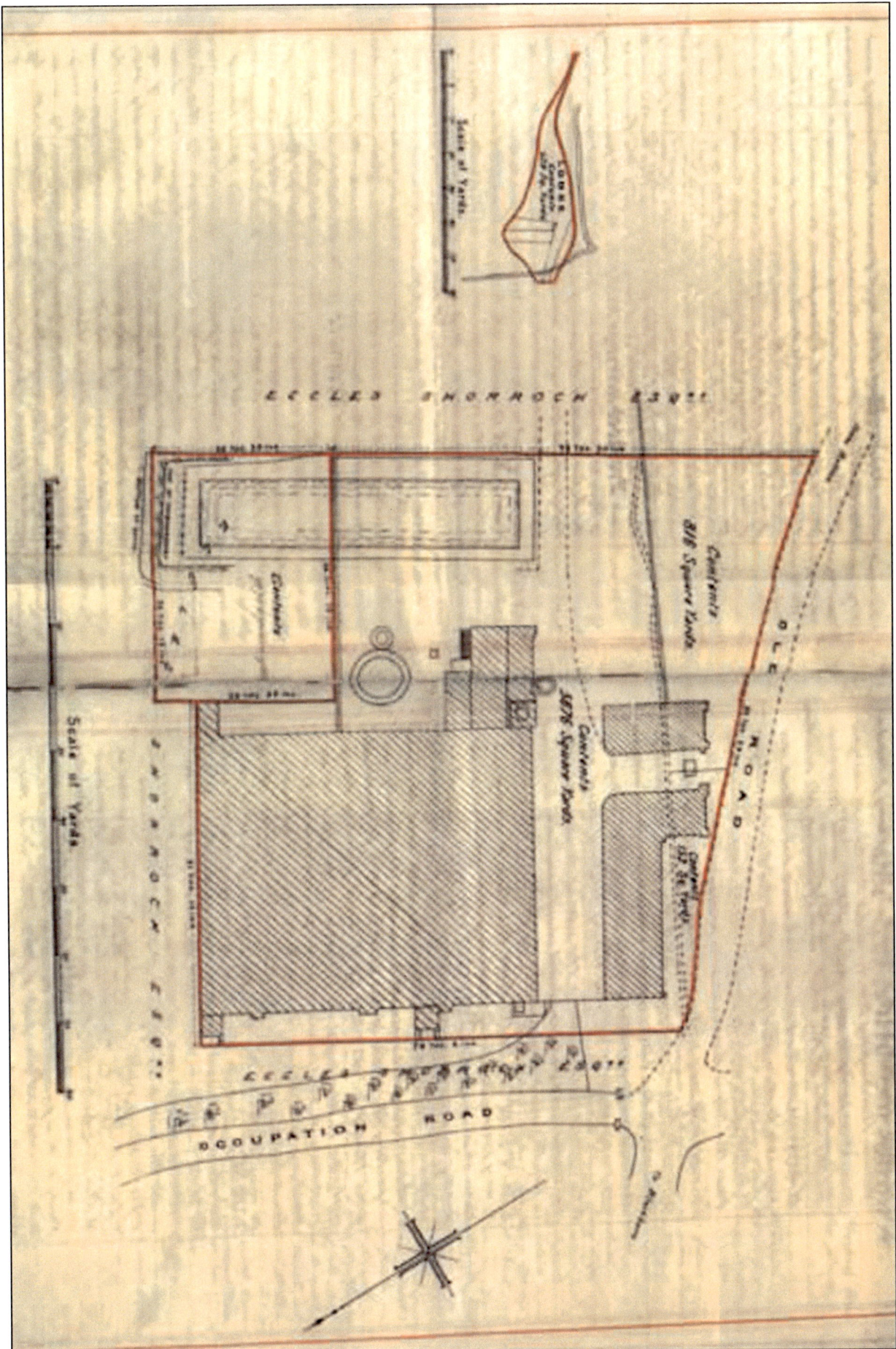

Deed Plan of the Site of Hollinshaed Mill

Originally built in 1859 by Eccles Shorrock Bros. of Darwen, this Mill contained 318 looms and employed about 150 people. Within two years of its construction the American Civil War had broken out, an event which hit the Lancashire Cotton Industry with tremendous force. The supply of raw material dried up and as a result whole towns and communities were thrown out of work. Tockholes was no exception and suffered the effects along with many other places. The spectre of famine brought together the Church people and the Dissenters in the Village and they worked together on common committees for the relief of the poor and opened soup kitchens to feed the starving. Many unemployed men were engaged to do work for the township by mending the roads, Top o' th' Low to Three Lane Ends being one, which was levelled. The levelling of this road then brought the suggestion that similar work should be carried out on Morris Brow, as this steep road had long been the main barrier for traffic between Blackburn and Tockholes, but the undertaking was considered to be too big a task for that time.

The Civil War ended in 1865 and for the next few years, work at Hollinshead Mill appears to have run relatively smoothly, or at least our research has not shown otherwise. A note of alarm occurred in 1873, possibly unknown to the workers at the Mill, when by an Indenture dated 10th April 1873 Eccles Shorrock mortgaged all his properties and land in Tockholes, along with other properties in Darwen, to raise a loan of £13,000, all secured by a life insurance policy for £13,500. This deed contained some very interesting maps of farms and buildings, long since demolished, which formed part of Shorrock's estate in Tockholes.

Nine years later the firm of E. Shorrock Bros. & Co. was in dire trouble and the Blackburn Standard for 14th October 1882 reported:- "**HEAVY FAILURE of COTTON MANUFACTURERS.** *A very heavy failure of cotton manufacturers was reported at the County court, Blackburn, on Wednesday afternoon. Mr. Charles Costeker, solicitor, filed a petition for liquidation on behalf of Eccles Shorrock, Ralph Shorrock Ashton and William Shorrock Ashton, of Over Darwen, cotton spinners and manufacturers, trading under the style or form of 'Eccles Shorrock, Bros., and Co.,' at New Mill and Brookside Mill, Over Darwen and Hollinshead Mill, Tockholes. The liabilities are estimated at £95,000. The assets, consisting of mills, stock-in-trade, cotton in course of preparation, cloth, yarns, mill furniture, and effects, are put down at £50,000 or thereabouts. Mr. John Adamson, of the firm of Messrs. Adamson, Son & Co., accountants, Norfolk-street, Manchester, was, on the application of Mr. Costeker, appointed receiver and manager of the business until the first meeting of creditors, the date of which has not yet been fixed. There are rumours that the mills will be stopped, which if it take place will be a sad calamity for Darwen."*

By November of that year the Blackburn Standard carried the Sale Notice for all the Shorrock properties, including Tockholes Mill:

At School on the 17th November 1882 the Headmaster recorded that the following children had left that week due to their parents having left the village on account of the mill being stopped: Nancy, Jane &

PRELIMINARY NOTICE of IMPORTANT SALE of VALUABLE MILL PROPERTIES and WEAVING SHEDS, at Over Darwen and the neighbourhood

NOTICE is Hereby Given, that during the month of December next, the following Valuable **MILL PROPERTIES and WEAVING SHEDS**, at Over Darwen, will be offered for Sale by Public Auction, as going concerns, namely:-
NEW MILLS containing 19,848 Mule Spindles, 17,860 Throstles, and 810 Looms, with the Reservoirs and water privileges thereto belonging. These Mills are in the centre of Over Darwen and are close to the Railway Station
DARWEN MILLS, containing 49,728 Mule Spindles, with the Reservoirs and water privileges thereto belonging. These Mills are very compact.
BROOKSIDE MILL containing 843 Power Looms, and valuable water privileges
TOCKHOLES MILL containing 318 Power Looms, and valuable water privileges
Further particulars will be published in due course, meantime any person requiring further information can obtain same from **MR. JOHN ADAMSON** of No. 5 Norfolk-street, in the city of Manchester; or from me, the undersigned

CHARLES COSTEKER,
Solicitor, Church-street, Over Darwen
Blackburn Standard 18th November 1882

William Holden and Sarah Marsden, but a few days later he records that Mary Brindle left school on the 1st December to become a full time hand at the Mill, aged 14 years. Also he recorded that many children were absent through sickness that same week and as if all that wasn't enough to cope with, on the 7th December there was such a severe snow-storm that not a single child attended school that morning and the school closed for a couple of days. The Diary continues – 12th December – "Owing to the removal of families consequent upon the closing of Messrs. Shorrock Bros. & Co's Mill and the severity of the weather, the average weekly attendance has fallen from 96 on 20th October 1882 to 63.1 on 8th December." In fact the school was closed for 3 more days that week due to the bad weather, and finally it was closed on the 21st December until the 3rd of January 1883 for the Christmas Holidays. The Census of 1881 also supports the facts relating to the decline in population. Seven of the eighteen houses then at Hollinshead Terrace were empty, as were eight other dwellings in Victoria Terrace and Shirley Gardens.

By February 1883 the papers were reporting that the Cotton Trade was re-starting in some of the Shorrock Mills, but sadly not at Tockholes Mill, which *"still remained idle and the village almost deserted,"* but happier news in the Blackburn Standard of 2nd June 1883 reported that *Hollinshead Mill, had been let to Messrs. E. and G. Hindle of the Commercial Mills, Bolton Road, Blackburn, who intended commencing work immediately after the repairs were finished, which were then being extensively made. It was understood, however, that a road was being formed from Tockholes to Withnell for the better convenience of the work-people and the public generally. This, together with the re-starting of the mill, would no doubt revive Tockholes once more, as ever since the stoppage of the mill in November last nearly all the houses in the locality had been empty and the place deserted.*

A further report of the same date described the events which led up to the closure of the Mill:-

A "Convivial Meeting" was held in December of 1883 to commemorate the re-opening of the Mill. *"Villagers and ex-villagers met at the Victoria Hotel on a Saturday in the middle of the month to have a party, towards which D. Thwaites Esq. and J. Haydock Esq. of Blackburn had each kindly contributed. About 100 people sat down to an excellent meat tea, served up in Mrs. Haydock's usual style. During the tea a miscellaneous programme consisting of songs, recitations etc. was drawn up and after ample justice had been done to the good things provided, the cloth was removed and Mr. J. Livesey was called to the chair, a position which he filled in a very creditable manner. A little before ten o'clock a vote of thanks to Mrs. Haydock and family was carried unanimously and then the meeting terminated after the singing of the National Anthem."(Blackburn Stan*dard 15th Dec 1883)

Things did not remain quite so cordial for very long though, as the settlement of a strike at Tockholes Mill was reported by the Blackburn Standard on 7th February 1885. Unfortunately, the earlier report on the reasons for the strike has failed to come to light.

IN a great industrial community like Blackburn and East Lancashire where vast commercial interests are at stake, it is always gratifying to be assured that the cotton trade is in a fairly prosperous condition. Up to very recently reports of the most gloomy and foreboding nature have reached us, and although the accounts are now of a more cheerful description the industry cannot be said to have recovered the protracted period of depression through which it has unhappily passed. The margin between the prices paid for cotton and those paid for yarn is nothing to boast of, but the general state of trade is such as to afford ample employment for the workpeople with the present liberal rate of wages. After some delay all the mills in the town, with one exception, are now in full operation, and on Monday next work at the Albert Mill will be resumed. Darwen and the neighbourhood have recently suffered severely on account of the failure of Messrs. Eccles Shorrock, Bros., and Co., and in that town likewise a more hopeful period has apparently set in, work being now plentiful owing to the successful exertions that have been made to re-start the closed mills on the part of large-minded employers of labour. Perhaps no locality around Blackburn has experienced the full force of these untoward circumstances so keenly as the village of Tockholes, where the stoppage of the mill has driven forth from their native homesteads numerous families, their only means of subsistence having been cut off. To such an extent has this migration been carried on that for some time past Tockholes has presented the appearance of a "deserted village". The hearts of hundreds, therefore, who formerly resided in this healthful district will be gladdened by the announcement which we are this week enabled to make that on Monday next the Mill will be re-started. Doubtless those who through stress of circumstances left the locality will return to their former abode and dwell among their own people in the village around which cluster many cherished recollections of the simplicity of home life on the country-side.

Blackburn Standard 2nd June 1883

Mrs. Haydock & Family outside the Victoria Hotel

SETTLEMENT OF THE WEAVERS' STRIKE AT TOCKHOLES

"A settlement of the weavers' employed at the Hollinshead Hall, Tockholes, by Messrs. E. and G. Hindle, who struck work on Tuesday week, under circumstances fully reported by us, was affected on Monday which resulted in work being fully resumed by all the workpeople on Tuesday morning. The Darwen weavers' secretary, Mr. Entwistle, and a deputation consisting of some of the weavers, again waited upon Mr. George Hindle, one of the firm, last Monday, when Mr. Hindle, as on all former interviews, declined to grant Mr. Entwistle permission to work up any of the sorts, (sic) and absolutely declined to give any information whatever. The weavers have therefore had to return back to their work without having gained any advantage or satisfaction whatever. Between forty and fifty of the weavers were last Saturday enrolled as members of the Darwen Weavers Association, and others have promised to do likewise, in order, as we are informed, that the matter can be again taken up by the Weavers Association, without much loss being incurred to the weavers. It is fully anticipated that by next Saturday upwards of 80 of the weavers will have joined the Society."

Two breaches of the Factory Act were reported in 1892 (*See Chapter 9*), but the next major event was the acquisition of the remaining land and buildings of the old Manor of Tockholes by the Liverpool Corporation in 1903, Hollinshead Mill and Garstangs being parts of the remaining estate. A record taken from the Chapel Minute Book documented the closure of the Mill: *In August of this year the Liverpool Corporation purchased the Mill at Tockholes and closed it. In September the whole of the machinery was sold by Auction and cleaned out, leaving the Mill, where most of our villagers worked for a livelihood, a desolation. As a consequence, many families have been compelled to leave the district, leaving our village poorer. It is a sad blow to us. For it has seriously affected both places of worship in our Village. But we need not despair if our remaining adherents will be true to our cause, and to their duty. The Lord has ever blessed us – He will bless us still if we prove ourselves worthy and prayerful and true."*

Eventually Liverpool Corporation demolished the Mill in 1903/4, together with the houses on one side of Hollinshead 'Street'. Once known as Factory Row, Hollinshead Terrace is in fact the remains of the only 'street' in Tockholes. These were houses built in 1859/61 to accommodate workers at Hollinshead Mill, and the first house in the remaining row was an ale house known

Hollinshead Terrace April 2002

as The Royal Oak. The front room had built-in wall seats which were still intact as late as the 1970's, but which were then removed to create more living space when the house was divided into two dwellings. The ale

house was first listed on the 1871 census, the son of the household being a bookkeeper at the Warehouse and his father the 'beer seller'. At this time 19 houses were recorded in the Street, two of them with occupants who were listed as Grocers, but ten years later only 12 houses were occupied and the row was then called Hollinshead Terrace. One house was a Grocers and Out Licence. In 1891 eighteen houses were once again recorded as occupied but the ale house was empty. The Grocery business prospered a little longer and by 1901 was still run by the Brownlows, the same occupants as on the previous Census. This time Mr. Brownlow is not listed as a Grocer, but as an Employer - Grocer/Colliery Master, his wife is the Grocer and their 19 year son, Ralph, is a newspaper seller, all working at home. Several of the houses are recorded as having been used for Sunday school purposes and religious meetings, especially during in spells of bad weather, for use by children considered too young to walk to the Church.

Garstang Terrace 2002

Garstang Terrace, or Garstang Row as it was first called, was also built as housing for workers at the mill and was probably named after the ancient farm/manor house known as Garstangs, or Gerstaine Hall, which stood opposite at the time the row was built. Another row, built at a similar time, is Ryal's Cottages.

The population of the Village declined even further when this second Mill closed and from an all time high of 1269 in 1821, there are now less than 400 people in the village today.

Ryal's Cottages 1975

Ryal Cottage and Shippon c.1970

Ryal Cottage c. 1975

Ryal's Cottages 2002

RYAL COTTAGE, RYAL FOLD

Whilst not a listed building this house is late 17th Century, probably built at a similar time as Ryal Farm, and contains many features associated with buildings of this period. A report on the properties in this area carried out in 1975 revealed that the original windows were once mullion windows, the shallow, front upper left having three lights and the upper right having four lights. The ground floor front windows also each contained four light mullions, this time with hood mouldings. (The mouldings are still intact.) The central porch contained very large quoins, and had a flagged roof with kneelers and the door, originally facing South, had been replaced with a modern window. The original large stone lintel over the former door remained, above which was, and still is, a square shallow recess suggesting the position of a date stone. The new doorway was re-sited on the east side of the porch.

To the east of the farmhouse was an attached shippon with a first floor opening to the hay-loft, and evidence had been found in the shippon indicating that there had once been windows in the east gable, at both ground floor and first floor level, traces of mullions and mouldings still being visible at that time. This indicated the shippon had been a later addition to the house, but no date was given as to its possible age. The windows have since been re-instated. The barn was in an advanced state of decay by 1975 and was demolished and replaced with an attached garage. The farmhouse was restored at the same time.

115

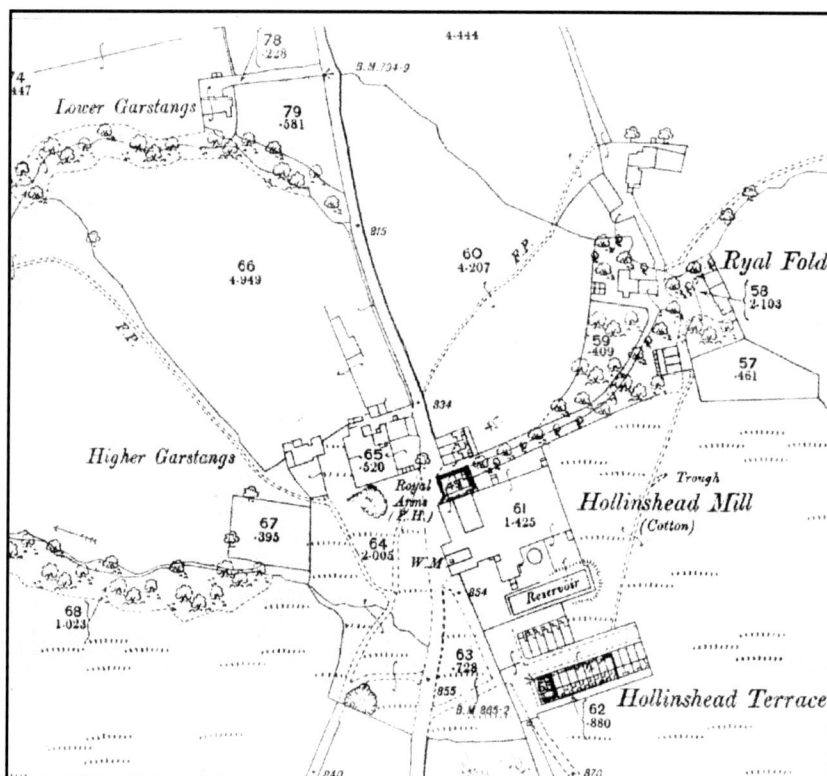

1894 Map showing the layout of Hollinshead Mill and both sides of Hollinshead Terrace.
Also note the layout of Higher & Lower Garstangs, both now demolished

PRINTING WORKS AT HALLIWELL FOLD

PRINT-WORKS AND FARM
TO BE LET BY PRIVATE CONTRACT
FOR A TERM OF YEARS

ALL those desirable Print-works, Messuage, Farm and Tenement situate in Tockholes in the County of Lancaster, called **HALLIWELL FOLD**, consisting of Print-Shops, Dye-houses, and other buildings; a Stream of Water and other Privileges convenient and necessary for carrying on the Printing Business; a Farm-House; several Cottages, Barn and other Outbuildings and *(a illegible quantity of)* Land, of the Measure there used or thereabouts, be the same more or less, and late in the Possession of Mr. Duxbury.

Halliwell Fold is situate about four Miles from Blackburn and eight from Bolton, and near to the Turnpike Road leading from Bolton to Preston, and Possession may be hand immediately.

For further Particulars apply to J. & A. HAWORTH, Attorneys-at-Law, Bolton, who are authorised to treat for the same.

Blackburn Mail 6th February 1818

Also connected with the cotton industry was a Calico Printing Works once belonging to Lawrence Brock-Hollinshead, situated in the Roddlesworth Valley near to Halliwell Fold Bridge. Today it is very easy to walk past the location without realising there has been a thriving business on the site. An old survey book written between 1805 and 1815 describes it as a wash-house or dye house for printers, a fat-house and latterly a printing house. A further survey book written about the same time states that "the Printworks at Halliwell Fold are empty and destroyed", yet in 1818 the printing business, farmhouse and other buildings at Halliwell Fold were offered for sale as a going concern. It is assumed, therefore, that the printing side ceased to operate sometime between 1815 and 1818. The farming side remained until the land was acquired by Liverpool Corporation at the beginning of the 20th century. The occupants recorded on the 1891 Census were Ralph and Sarah Ann Mares, thought to be relatives of Richard Mares, farmer at Higher Hill Farm at the beginning of the 20th Century.

116

PLAN OF
HALLIWELL FOLD
IN THE TOWNSHIP OF
TOCKHOLES

Copied in 1901 for a Deed between
Eccles Shorrock III and Howard Shorrock
& Others to The Liverpool Corporation
(Original plan was attached to a deed of
1874 made between Eccles Shorrock
and Sir Wm. Foster Bart & Others

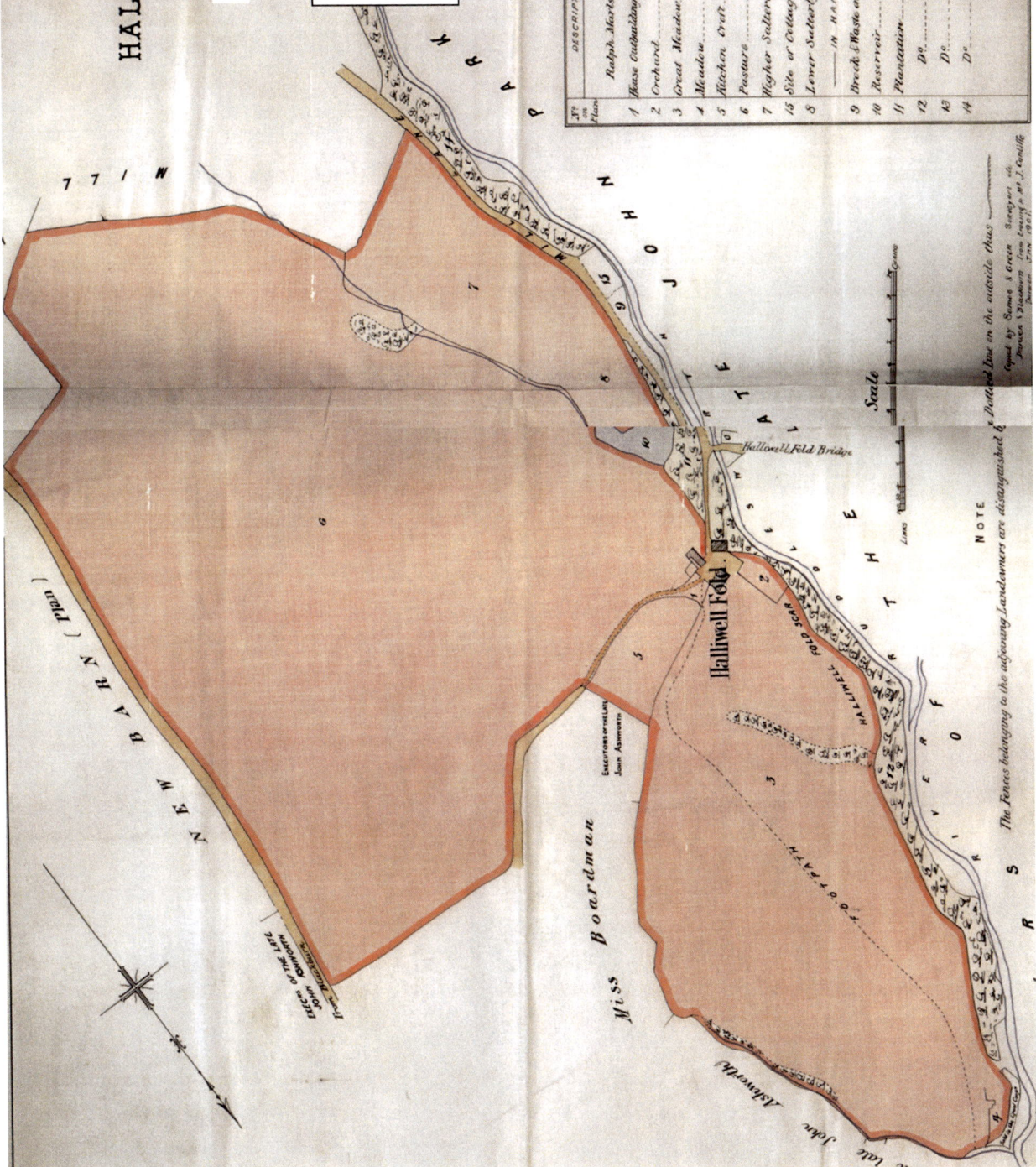

Reference

No on Plan	DESCRIPTION	STATUTE		
1	House Outbuildings Garden Fold & Road			
2	Orchard			
3	Great Meadow			
4	Meadow			
5	Kitchen Croft			
6	Pasture			
7	Higher Easterly			
15	Site or Cottages			
8	Lower Easterly			
	— IN HAND —			
9	Breck & Waste on side of Mill Lane			
10	Reservoir			
11	Plantation			
12	Do			
13	Do			
14	Do			
	Total			

Scale

NOTE

The Fences belonging to the adjoining Landowners are distinguished by a Dotted line on the outside thus

New Barn (Plan)

Miss Boardman

Executors of the late John Ashworth

Halliwell Fold

Halliwell Fold Bridge

RIVER ROD OR THE

CORN MILL

The Ordnance Survey Map of 1848 shows the site of a Corn Mill upstream of two cottages on the East side of Mill Lane, situated near the river, but nothing remains of the building today. However, there is a deep, water filled ditch near the site, which could possibly have been used in connection with the Mill. At first glance the ditch seems to be a natural formation with rough rock encircling about two thirds of the pool, but at the north end, stopping the outflow of water, is a wall with a trough cut into one of the capping stones, obviously used to channel the water for some reason long since past. It is now difficult to believe that corn could have been grown in the vicinity, but before the reservoirs were built and the woodland planted, the valley was farmland and remnants of gateposts and field boundary walls can still clearly been seen. Corn would probably have also been brought in from the lowlands.

COAL MINING

Coal Mining appears to have been quite extensive in the Tockholes area and in 1877 *Abram,* wrote that 'coal had been got in Over Darwen, Eccleshill, Tockholes and Lower Darwen for at least three centuries, probably longer, and that there were traces of old abandoned pits and workings in many places upon the hill-sides.' Several Villagers are described as Coal Miners on the 1851 Census Return, one being John Crook, aged only 15, of Bethesda Row, and another even younger boy, Joseph Warburton, aged 9, living at Top o' th' Low, listed as a Drawer in the Coal pit. A drawer's job was to pull tubs of coal from the coal face to the pit entrance, often by crawling on all fours pulling the tub behind them.

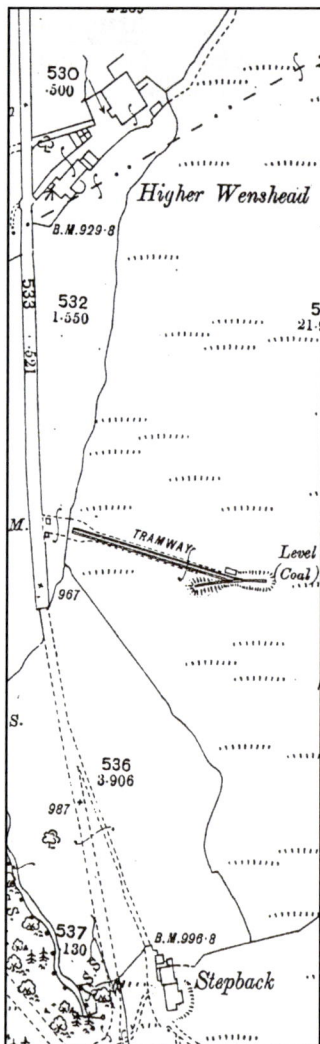

The 6 inch Ordnance Survey map of 1848 shows numerous pits around the east side of Winter Hill and also defines Coal Pit Lane leading to that area, a lane still known by that name although now a footpath and bridle way. Several more old shafts are marked to the south end of the Village on the east side of Cartridge Hill and also around Stepback. Old Lyons Colliery and its many pits are clearly shown, as is an engine and a weighing machine, and another Coal Pit Lane. The myth that Tockholes had 'Treacle Mines' in the area probably arose from the black sticky substances which were often found around the coal seams and which looked like molasses, but today, only mounds and traces of the old shafts, many of them fenced off, still exist and the area has reverted back to moorland. The industry probably ended when the seams ran out or because the remaining coal was of poor quality.

Remains of Lyons Farm 2002. Site of the weighing machine can still can still be seen on the edge of the road to the left of the ruins.

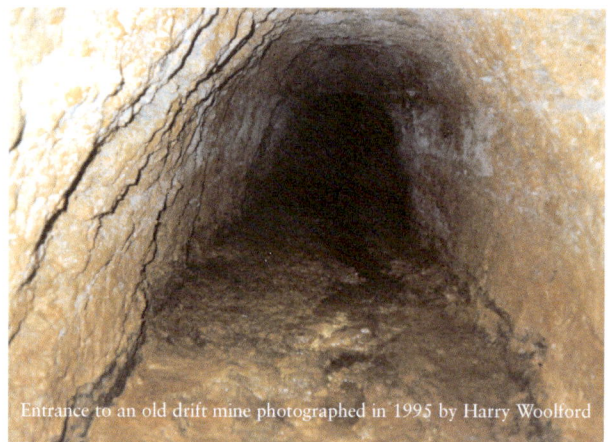

Entrance to an old drift mine photographed in 1995 by Harry Woolford

QUARRYING

Again, the 1848 Ordnance Survey Maps tell us more about this occupation than the recorded history of this area. Sandstone quarries are marked to the south and west of Old Lyons Farm on the southern boundary of the Village and in the fields beyond Weasel Lane and Coal Pit Lane at the northern boundary, with many more shown in between at places such as Stepback, Higher and Lower Wenshead, Halliwell Fold Scar and Higher Hill. All these pits must have provided a fair amount of employment in their day and no doubt also gave rise to the "Quarryman's Arms" ale house at Higher Hill, and to the further occupation of stone-masonry. Stone masons have been listed living at Higher Hill, Lower Hill, Midge Hulme and Back of the Moss – all near marked quarries. Most of the houses in the area are supposed to have been built from locally quarried stone, but no working quarries now remain.

THE GARAGE

Aerial View of the Garage c. 1979

c. 1971

The Garage was built in 1947 by Mr. Leslie Bowen and a colleague. The first owner was Mr. John (Jack) Cross who lived for a time on Pickop Brow, but later moved into Sea View, the house next to the Garage. He ran the business for over 20 years until its sale in 1970. The next owner was Mr. Alan Haworth and Alan continued the business until the late 1980's when it was eventually sold for development. A detached bungalow and a pair of semi-bungalows now stand on the site.

Development on Garage site 2002

POST OFFICE

In 1897 one of the first projects of the not long formed Parish Council was to petition the Darwen Post Master for a Post Office in Tockholes and to have an evening mail collection. In March 1900 the situation had not been resolved and the tenant of Bradley Farm complained that with only 3 deliveries per week to his farm he frequently missed business deadlines and was suffering pecuniary loss, so would the Council do all in its power to obtain a six days a week delivery service. By February 1901 it was being reported that the request for 6 deliveries per week had been granted. A further proposal for a local Post Office was made at a meeting in September 1901 and the request was eventually granted but no record of the date was made. The post office counter was opened in the grocery and general store run by the Gregsons, a post box having been sited in the wall of the shop for many years previously. In July 1923 another request was made that a Public Telephone Call Box be installed in the township and this was subsequently placed outside the Post Office, where one still stands to this day.

These premises were shop premises for well over 150 years. On the 1841 Census, Ellen Leaver, aged 60, was listed there as a Grocer. By 1851 the business was owned by William Gregson, aged 31, Grocer & Joiner and wife Ruth, 24, Grocer, living there with their son Edward, aged 1 year. This couple appear at the property on the next 3

Old Post Office 2003

Census Returns and by 1881 had six children, one daughter working in the shop and one son working as a joiner. By 1891 Ruth was widowed and living at another property at Top o' th' Low, but her second son, John T. Gregson, took over the business and styled himself as 'Shop General Trader'.

During her stay in the years of the First World War, Margaret Tapley described the Post Office and shop as "an Aladdin's cave of good things. I never objected to go and fetch a pound of butter or a bag of flour from there. The smell inside the shop was a delicious mixture of cheese, dried beans, peas, raisins, prunes, bacon, butter, potatoes (still earthy) and cabbages and kale fresh from the farms. Then there were floury tea-cakes, scones, bags of coffee and cocoa and brown sugar, tins of black treacle and condensed milk. Further into the darkness of the shop were the poultry and pig foods. Great zinc bins with lids tipped open, corn, maize, oats and bran. 'What's thee doing, child?' would be the call from over the bacon slicer. 'I've lost my penny in the corn bin.'

'Well, be sharp and find it 'afore I measure it away.' Then began the glorious dip of bared arms thrust into the shifting corn, scooping out the middle to pile it up round the edges and then letting it slither like a landslide back again until even the elbow was deep in corn. The trick was to have your coin in your pocket all the time ... it was a wonderful game and once I found a sixpence as well as my own penny."

The last Post Mistress was Mrs. Beryl Farnworth who ran the counter and the general store for 25 years and it was a great loss to the Village when Beryl retired and closed the shop. A long time resident of Tockholes, Mr. Robert Lee, a retired headmaster, penned the following poem and dedicated it to Beryl.

Sadly, Beryl did not have a very long retirement. She died in 1996.

After Beryl's retirement the Post Office Counter was moved to the home of Mr. Ken Kershaw in his dining room at Silk Hall Cottage, but this, too, was closed on Ken's retirement in 2000.

Ode to Mrs. Beryl Farnworth
by Mr. Robert Lee
(late of Four Houses, Tockholes)

CLOSING DOWN

Goodbye, farewell, you Village dear P.O.,
We're deeply saddened thus to see you go,
For countless years you've been the Village friend
Whose services are hard to comprehend.
You've been the centre of our small community,
The focal point of harmony and unity.
'Twas there we'd meet our friends and local folk
And pass the time of day and crack a joke.

Attending to the needs of every patron
With pleasant, calm efficiency was Matron.
The wise presiding genius we grew to love,
Controlling with an iron hand in velvet glove,
And so, dear Beryl, as you now retire
To take your ease before your winter fire,
We hope you'll plan to utilise your leisure
To do whatever brings you greatest pleasure.
Keep well, live long, enjoy your welcome rest
-For you, our friend, we all just want the best!

Robert Lee 23rd August 1994

Post Office and Grocery Store Circa 1930

THE CAFÉ

In the early part of the 20th century the first owners were Mr. & Mrs. J. Hartley who acquired the land and had a house built with a shop, tearoom and bakehouse combined. By 1911 the shop was chosen by the Gala Committee to supply 500 pies and 500 buns for the event held to celebrate the coronation of King George V, Mrs. Cooper at the Post Office Store providing coffee and sugar. The Café itself was in the room above the shop and could be hired for functions such as birthday parties. Mr. & Mrs. Hartley retired to 'Sea View', next to the Garage, and their business was then taken over by their daughter and son-in-law Mr. & Mrs. Entwistle, who ran the café for many years before selling it to sisters, Bessie & Marion Edwards

Peggy Haworth in the Victoria Stores c. 1984

Bread, cakes, pies and other homemade delights were made on the premises, for sale in both the shop and café, and huge potato pies could be ordered for special Village functions. On occasions the bread supply was augmented with deliveries of "Veget" bread from Worsley's Bakery at the bottom of Bog Height Road. Cooked meats could be purchased from both the Café and the Post Office, but during and just after the First World War fresh meat was provided by Mr. Lord the Butcher, who came to the village twice a week in his blue van filled with rows of swinging legs of lamb and rounds of beef. From the 1930's fresh meat was supplied by Clarkson's Butchers from Mill Hill who ran a similar delivery service.

After the death of Bessie Edwards in 1980 and the retirement of her sister, Marion Edwards two years later, the Grocery business was taken over by Mrs. Peggy Haworth who kept a well-stocked store for several more years, before it was finally closed and converted into a house, now known as Old Victoria Stores.

In the days when the Village was more self sufficient, as well as the two main shops there have also been several other establishments in some of the cottages. The two small shops at Shirley Gardens have already been mentioned, but there has also been a Clogger at Top o' th' Low, a Boot and Shoe Maker living on Bethesda Row, a Tailor in Duck Hall Cottages, and several Dress and Bonnet Makers, one at Chapels Farm in 1851, one at Hollinshead Terrace and another at Gorses both in 1871. Several Blacksmiths are also mentioned on the Census Returns.

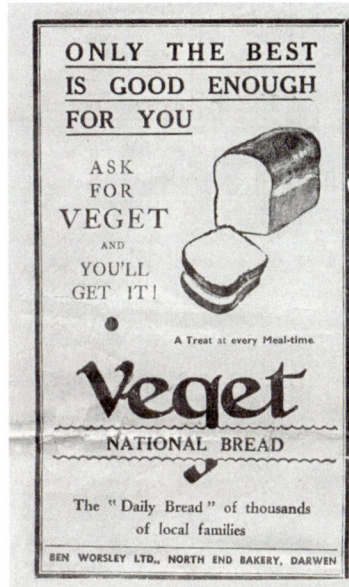

ONLY THE BEST IS GOOD ENOUGH FOR YOU

ASK FOR VEGET AND YOU'LL GET IT!

A Treat at every Meal-time.

Veget

NATIONAL BREAD

The "Daily Bread" of thousands of local families

BEN WORSLEY LTD., NORTH END BAKERY, DARWEN

ENGINEERING

Bill Navesey started an Agricultural Engineering business at Silk Hall in 1971, firstly with a mobile workshop repairing and maintaining machinery on site for the farming industry. He later opened a workshop in a barn opposite Silk Hall Manse. This building was recently renovated and evidence found that showed it had also been a dwelling as a fireplace was uncovered. There had been a barn and shippon attached to either side of the house. The building is thought to date from about 1612.

Bill has now diversified into general engineering due to the demise of farming in this area and fifteen years ago his son, Mark, joined him in the business which now caters for all aspects of engineering. The business has expanded and a modern Unit behind the barn now serves as the main workshop.

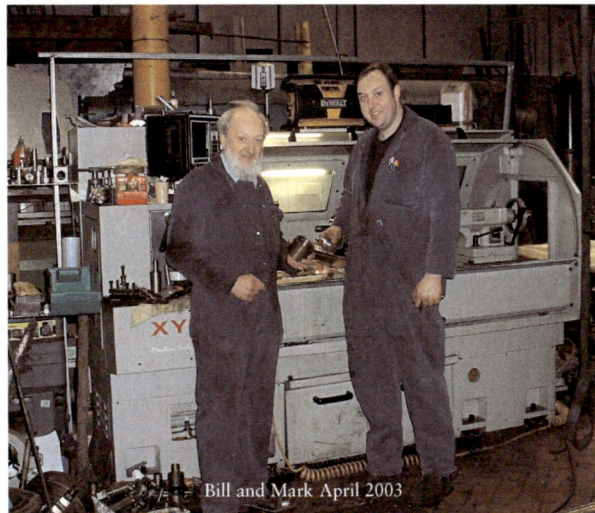

Bill and Mark April 2003

PUBLIC HOUSES

There are three pubs in the Village, The Rock, The Victoria and The Royal Arms. As well as public houses there have several 'beer sellers' recorded on the census returns and also a couple of beer shops, one at No. 10 Hollinshead Terrace called the Royal Oak and another at Quarryman's Farm, known as The Quarryman's Arms.

The Rock January 2003

The Rock Inn The date stone over the front door records a Roger and Ann Roscow 1791, but the Yates Map shows there was a building on this site in 1786. The original structure was only half its present size, and there was also a large barn that stood on what is now the car park, with several outbuildings in the field behind. The barn is referred to on the 1848 O.S. Map as the Smithy. Margaret Tapley described the Inn from a childhood memory of 1914/18 as being "a busy spot, – a residential public house. It looked gloomy, being built of local grey stone and topped with a slab roof. Funeral and wedding parties were held at the Rock, but no flowers grew up there. There was a kind of stone bench set in the wall and a large drinking trough for the horses".

The north side of the house was originally divided into farm outhouses, having a front doorway into one room and two other side doors. The rooms contained haylofts, with access via a ladder. This area is now the ladies toilet area and the doorways have been either filled in or made into windows. It is no longer the gloomy, grey building described above, but a creamy pebble dashed dwelling with superb views across the countryside to the coast. However, it is in a very exposed position and during a violent storm in the late 1980's the wind whipped off the whole of the west side roof, flipping it like a playing card over the east side onto the car park.

The Victoria Hotel is at the heart of the Top o' the' Low area and, as previously stated, appears on the Greenwood Map of 1818, but is thought to be considerably older. It is likely that it changed its name to The Victoria, in honour of the newly crowned Queen Victoria in 1837 or shortly afterwards.

Like Nook Cottage the bale hoist doorway can still be seen at first floor level and it is thought the upper portion of the building could have been a warehouse, and the ground floor a weaving or spinning shed. Two doorways are still clear visible at the front, signifying the top half of the building with the narrower door has been a dwelling and the other half was used as the business premises. The top gable has a large, arched window at the upper level, which suggests there was once a view up the hill, the view now obscured by the Old Post Office and cottages. An access pathway still exists between the Inn and the Old Post Office buildings and is thought to have been wider at one time, to allow passage for horses and carts to the rear of the Inn. Still visible, inside what is now the toilet area, is the old back door, a mirror image of the front door and equally as big. The car park area was once the site of three attached cottages, the nearest one being the Brewhouse with a well in the cellar. The property has been much changed over the years and was extended in the late 1970's.

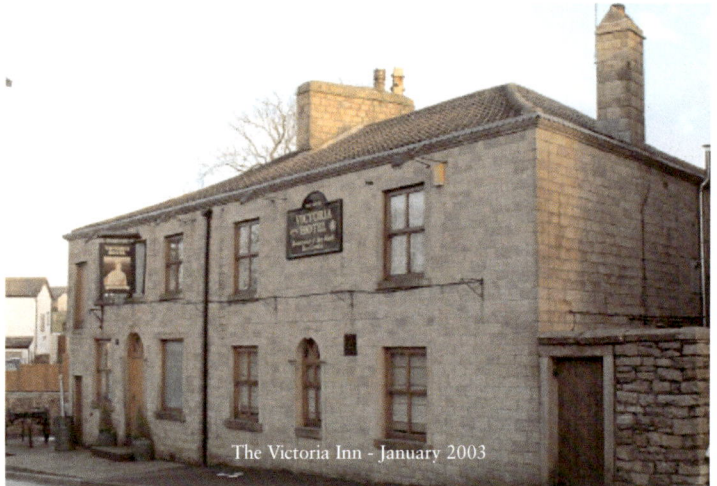

The Victoria Inn - January 2003

PUBLIC-HOUSE TO LET.

To be Let by Ticket,

And may be entered on immediately,

At the *Victoria* Public House, in Tockholes, on THURSDAY the 9th day of JANUARY, 1840, at Six o'clock in the Evening;

ALL that well-accustomed PUBLIC HOUSE known by the name of the "*Victoria*," situate at "The Law," in Tockholes, with Brewhouse, (near to which and within the premises is an excellent spring of Water). Stable, &c., now in the occupation of Mrs. PICKOP, to whom application for further particulars may be made.

The **Royal Arms** is situated at the southern end of the Village. This establishment was built in 1863 on land sold by Eccles Shorrock to Thomas Whipp, Farmer. It is first recorded on the Census of 1871 as Garstangs Pub and the landlord at that time was James Whipp, Quarryman/Publican, aged 26. In 1873 Thomas Whipp sold the land and buildings now called the Royal Arms to Thwaites Brewery, in whose possession it remained until quite recently. To the south of the Royal Arms is an extensive parking area on the site of the old Hollinshead Mill. In 1988 plans were drawn on behalf of North West Water Authority (now United Utilities), for the erection of a building as part of the West Pennine Moors project, to be used as an Information Centre for visitors and walkers to the area.

Popular walks from this area include the Roddlesworth Nature Trail and the westerly approach to Darwen Tower along the old Eccles Shorrock road built as access to his Mill at Hollinshead and mentioned in more detail in Chapter 5. In 2003 the Centre was closed solely as an information point and at the time of writing it is planned that the Centre will be soon be re-opened as a Tearoom, or similar, with information facilities provided.

The Royal Arms 2002

FARMING

Tilly Croft c. 1930

Last, but not least, farming has played a big part in the life of the inhabitants of Tockholes. In many cases, farmsteads passed from generation to generation for centuries and as farming was once a labour intensive industry it provided work for many family members and some of the local population

Agriculture underwent considerable changes during both the First and Second World Wars. Because of difficulties importing food Britain had to rely on home production and the government encouraged people to "dig for victory" by using every available area of land for growing vegetables and fruit. With many men away fighting, women formed a large part of the workforce and the 'Women's Land Army' was formed during WWII to replace the conscripted agricultural labourers. Later,

prisoners of war were also used as farmhands. Farmers were directed by the Government to convert grassland into arable land and, overall, arable land increased by 63% nationally. However, the only successful farm crop grown in the Tockholes area was turnip. Potatoes turned black before they matured and there was never enough sunshine to ripen the corn. Livestock numbers were also increased during WWII, despite the reduction of grassland. Shortly after the War tractors and other modern machinery became commonplace and transformed farming from its original labour intensive state, Tockholes being no exception to this modernisation.

Today, many of the farmhouses, farm cottages and most of the barns have been sold for development into dwellings and they no longer operate as working farms, but there are still several farmers who do pursue this occupation, keeping mainly sheep and cattle and supplying milk and eggs. There is only one farm operating as a milk producer compared with a dozen or more 20 years ago. Some farms have diversified due to the current state of British farming generally, and as a result planning authorities have looked sympathetically on the development of leisure activities in the countryside. Over the last few years the Planners have dealt with a number of applications in Tockholes concerning the provision of facilities such as stabling for horses and arenas for riders. The landscape is still very rural, new building having been kept to the renovation of old property and a handful of 'infill' properties.

Bill Croft (right) and farm labourers

Bill Croft harvesting
at Kiln Bank Farm c. 1930

CHAPTER 7

HOLLINSHEAD HALL

The exact date of when a Hall was first built on this site is unknown but in a Return of the tenants of the Duchy of Lancaster dated 1311 there occurs the following *"Richard son of John de Radcliffe holds the manor of Urdesale (Ordsall, near Manchester) ... a hundred acres in a place called Holinhed and in Tockhole ... from the King in Chief by Knight Service for 2s. per annum"*. This appears to be the first evidence that the Village had a definite existence almost eight hundred years ago. Over the next 300 years or so the Radcliffes are mentioned several times in documents as holding extensive lands in Tockholes and it is probably a member of this family who built the first Hall. In the latter half of the 18th century the estate had passed from a family called the Warrens of Cheshire into the hands of a John Hollinshead and it is thought that it was he who was responsible for rebuilding the Hall in 1776. This may have been when the house acquired the title of Hollinshead Hall. The Hollinshead name itself has been traced back to a Hugh Holynshead, or Holyns of Holyn's-head, as holding the lordship of Sutton in Chester in 1240 and five generations later a William Holynshead is mentioned as holding lands in Tockholes.

Nightingale quotes Rev. Gilmour Robinson as stating that *"There are some very large houses in Tockholes now subdivided, which make it appear it was once of more importance than at present. The principal house is Hollinshead Hall. This was long the residence of the Hollinsheads, who were lords of the manor, and now belongs to Eccles Shorrock, Esq. J.P. of Darwen. Lying a little to the right, on the road towards Belmont, it is completely hidden from view by a thickly wooded plantation. Some parts of it are very ancient, but in 1776 it was almost entirely taken down and remodelled. There is a small detached building in the garden, where is the 'Holy Spring.'* It is thought the Hall was only used occasionally for recreational purposes such as hunting parties, the main residence of the Hollinsheads being in Cheshire, but the Farm was tenanted and presumably the tenants also looked after the Hall. The estate eventually passed from the Hollinsheads to the Brocks through the female line. Two further generations then added the name of Hollinshead to that of Brock.

In 1838 Lawrence Brock Hollinshead sold the estate to Eccles Shorrock (now more famous for the building of India Mill and its fine Chimney in Darwen), but the Hall was only a small part of the manorial estate of Tockholes and Shorrock never lived there. Lawrence Brock Hollinshead died aged 60 on 25th July 1838. Eccles Shorrock died without issue on the 17th July 1853, aged 49 years, having made his nephew, Eccles Shorrock Ashton, his heir. On the death of his uncle Eccles Shorrock Ashton dropped the paternal surname of Ashton. In 1877 *Abram* writes *"Hollinshead Hall, the manor-house of Tockholes, is now untenanted and in a state of decay. A wing of the existing hall is of some age, but has no interesting feature. The other block was rebuilt in 1776. ... The Manor estate of 890 statute acres is now the property of Eccles Shorrock Esq. JP of Low Hill House, Darwen."* The Hall remained unoccupied and in a state of dereliction right up until its sale to the Liverpool Corporation as mentioned previously.

A little further information on the Hollinshead family is provided by the research of Mrs. Elspeth MacKay of Kelso, a descendant of the Brock Hollinsheads:

"The chronicler, Ralph Holynshed, so valuable to Shakespeare, was of the Cheshire family who owned Hollinshead Hall.

The last Hollinshead died in 1802 leaving his property to a cousin, William Brock of Stockport, who added Hollinshead to his name. William died in 1803 leaving his estate to his nephew Laurence, who married Margaretta Edwards of Wrexham. She died and afterwards Laurence married again, to Mary Potts of London. They had five children and the eldest, Henry, succeeded Laurence in 1838.

Henry was born in 1819 and became a Solicitor in the Blackburn firm of Neville, Ainsworth and Hollinshead. In 1849 he married Margaret, the eldest daughter of James Neville of Beardwood. Henry became Borough Treasurer of Blackburn in 1851 and was also the first Clerk to the Darwen Board of Health in 1854. He was well known in sporting circles. In 1840 Blackburn press carried an account of a race between one of his horses called 'De Clifford' and one nominated by W. H. Hornby called 'The Doctor'. The race was at Kersal and 'The Doctor' won by a length."

Over the years many articles have been written about the Hollinshead Hall estate by historians and newspaper reporters and the same information, or misinformation, has been repeated so often much of it appears to have become fact. Many theories have been put forward regarding the significance and meaning of the Holy Well or Wishing Well and the following is a collection of such information, gathered from various named sources, which will give readers chance to reach their own conclusion.

Darwen News 20th August 1932

HOLLINSHEAD HALL
An Historic Ruin

"A conjuring trick popular still with both old and young is the extraction of a rabbit out of what appears to be an empty hat. Something of the same kind of legerdemain is required of the historian who would write of Hollinshead Hall and its history. The material must be introduced surreptitiously before it can be produced from the inkpot alive and kicking.

Anyone who pursues his way up the Roddlesworth Valley will be able to understand why men should build their habitations there at an earlier period than in other parts of the district. To the east and west of the river were vast tracts of moorland, much of which is still uncultivated even in this twentieth century, but the flats along the river banks offered opportunities to the agriculturalist which must have been seized upon before the intake of patches of moor was even thought of. The place-name Tockholes is evidence of that. While it is not quite clear what the second part of the name may actually mean, it is certain the Toc is the name of a man. It has been ingeniously suggested the holes is the word howe, or burial mound, disguised in pronunciation. We should then get Toc, or Toki's

burial mound as the meaning of the name. About 1200 the name was written in the Chartulary of Cockersand Abbey as "de Tocholis", which seems to rule out the suggestion that holes is a mound. It is rather more likely, perhaps, that Tockholes stands for Tocca's hollow or valley. But whichever explanation is accepted the name is certainly old and Tocca may have been a Dane who got into this part of the country during the incursions of the Danes in the 9th Century and settled here.

At the southern end of the valley is the place whereon once stood Hollinshead Hall. Hollinshead is simply the hill on which the holly grows, a thing which every schoolboy in Lancashire knows, or if he doesn't his school teacher is at fault. The earliest record of the name in writing is in a Lancashire Court Roll of 1324, where it is spelt "Holynhevid". It is perhaps worth remarking that the word Roddlesworth also preserves a personal name, that of Hrodwulf, and his worth, of course, was his worp, his enclosure, homestead or farm. The name is written first, that is as far as we known, about 1160.

FIRST SETTLERS

The place names themselves tell of an early settlement hereabouts and it is to be observed that it is the settlement of a man, not of a tribe or a community. These first settlers would, of course, have their followers and their servants, but it is of the greatest significance that the names themselves, Tockholes and Roddlesworth, are each the name of a man, while Hollinshead is simply the name they would give to a hill that was covered in holly bushes.

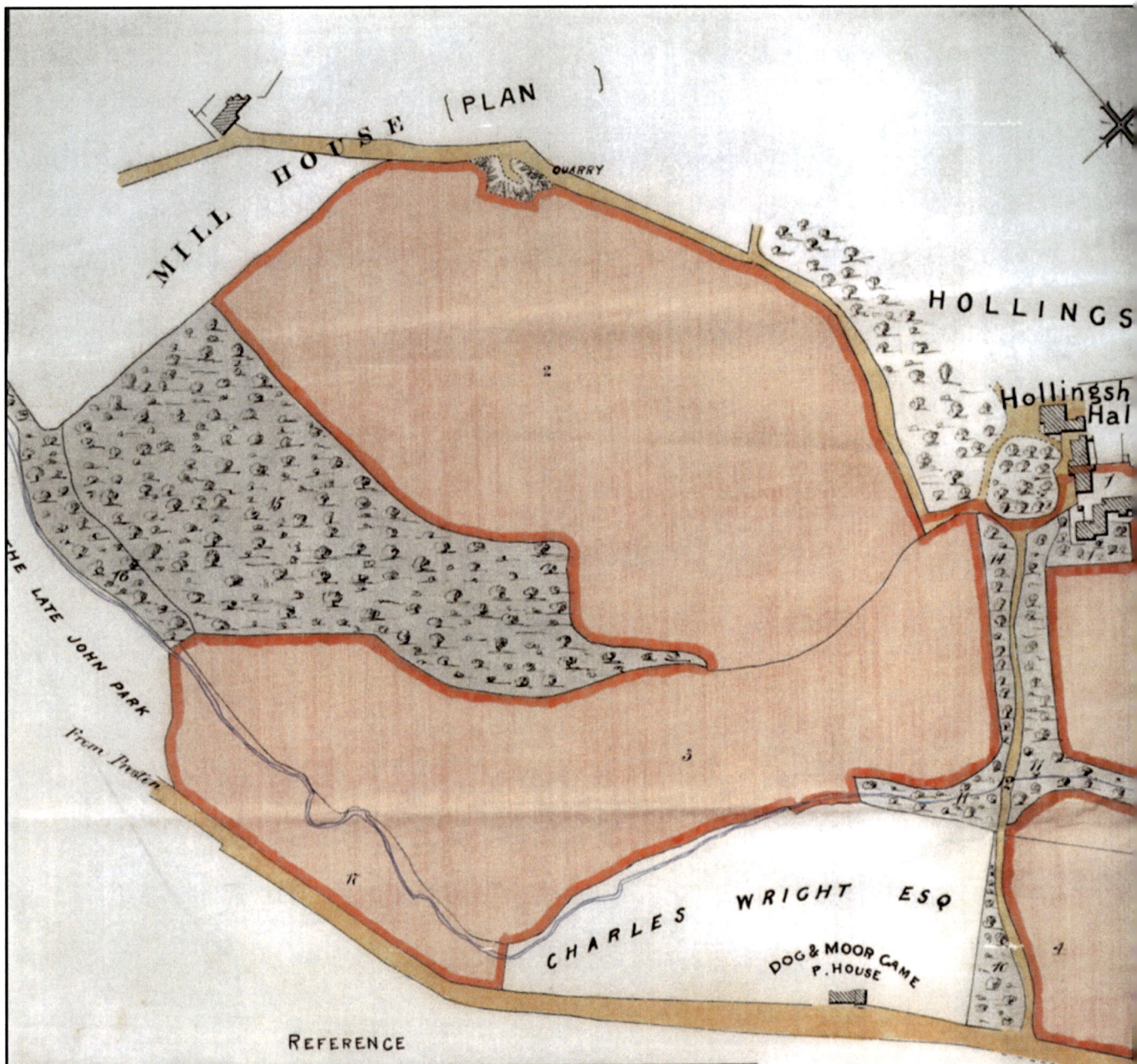

PLAN SHOWING THE LAY-OUT OF THE HOLLINSHEAD HALL COMPLEX TAKEN

Map labels: MILL HOUSE (PLAN) · QUARRY · HOLLINGS... · Hollingsh Hal · THE LATE JOHN PARK · From Proten · CHARLES WRIGHT ESQ · DOG & MOOR GAME P. HOUSE

REFERENCE

Nº in Plan	DESCRIPTION GEORGE CROFT (OCCUPIER)	A	R	P STATUTE	A	R	P	A	R	P CUST[E] YARDS	A	R	P TO THE PERCH
1	House Outbuildings Garden & Fold	.	2	3				.	1	6			
2	Slipper Law	17	1	23				9	1	17			
3	Slipper Law Meadow	11	3	8				6	1	16			
4	Part of Rough	1	3	36				1	6	10			
5	Potatoe Field	.	2	20				.	1	14			
6	Great Meadow	19	3	36				10	2	58			
7	Potatoe Field	1	0	20				.	2	16			
8	House Close and Rough	37	3	20				20	1	19	49	0	20
13	Cottage	.	.	3	91	1	14	.	.	4			
	IN HAND												
9	Plantation	2	3	28				1	2	12			
10	Dº	.	.	23				.	.	13			
11	Dº	1	0	3				.	2	7			
12	Road	.	1	6				.	.	26			
14	Plantation	1	1	6				.	2	31			
15	Dº	8	1	13				4	1	37			
16	Dº	7	0	14				.	2	13			
17	Dº	2	2	20	17	2	33	1	1	26	9	2	6

NOTE – The Fences
The Lines m...
was survey[ed]

PLAN OF
HOLLINGSHEAD HOUSE
IN THE TOWNSHIP OF
TOCKHOLES SHARPLES

COPY

D HALL (Plan

ingshead
ouse.

Eccles Shorrock Esq.
(IN HAND. PLAN

6

8

S

7

TOWNSHIP

OF

SHARPLES

TOWNSHIP BOUNDARY

10 CHAINS

to the adjoining Landowners are distinguished by a dotted Line on the Outside thus
h a Cross shew that the Fences which existed in 1855 when the Estate
en removed.

FROM DEED RELATING TO ECCLES SHORROCK'S ESTATES IN TOCKHOLES

Hollinshead Hall during demolition

The first thing we know about Tockholes is that in the first half of the 13th century (1200–1250) the Manor was in the possession of a family who bore the local name, and of the Pleasington family, each holding a half, the tenure being theynage (held by a thane or freeman), and the yearly service 2s.

About 1250 Joice de Tockholes released his tenement here to Elias de Pleasington, his lord, and early in the reign of Edward I, or earlier possibly, William de Livesey, as mesne tenant, granted the feudal rights and services due from Geoffrey de Sutton, who held Tockholes presumably in demesne, to Robert de Pleasington.

Adam de Tockholes held the other moiety in 1246 and he was followed by two more Adams, his son and grandson presumably. The interest in the Tockholes family then, passed to Roger de Ratcliffe, who acquired also the Pleasington moiety of the manor.

On the death of Roger, Robert, the bastard son of Richard de Ratcliffe, came into possession of the manor in accordance with the terms of a deed of settlement, and he having no issue, it passed in remainder at his death, in 1345, to his younger brother, John de Radcliffe, of Ordsall, Kt. The estate was afterwards seized by the Crown, probably on account of the debts due to the Crown which Robert had left unpaid as under-sheriff at his death. In 1362 Richard, son and heir of John de Radcliffe, petitioned the Crown and obtained restitution of lands in Livesey and Tockholes. In 1380 Richard was drowned in Rossendale, and ten weeks later John, his son, had livery of his estates including "Le Holynhed in Tockholes", which his father had held in chief by the yearly rent of 2s.

A DOVECOTE AND WATER-MILL

The manor remained in the possession of the Radcliffes until 1641. In 1613 we find Lady Anne Radcliffe, widow, and Sir John Radcliffe, Kt. (mother and son), as sole lords of the manor, claiming the wastes of Tockholes against Edward Osbaldeston, Lawrence Ainsworth and others, charterers there. It was ordered that the plaintiffs should retain possession of the wastes and improvements, while the defendants should enjoy pasturage, turbary (getting turves of fuel), stone and marl as heretofore, a most interesting gleam of light on the activities and the doings of the inhabitants of the early seventeenth century.

In 1641 Alexander Radcliffe, K.B. passed by fine to William Davenport and Thomas Gerard the manor of Tockholes, fifteen messuages, a water-mill, a dovecote and lands in Tockholes, Hollinshead, and Livesey, probably for sale. The water-mill and the dovecote should be noted. In 1662 Edward Warren was paying 2s. yearly to the bailiff of the honor of Clitheroe for the "Hollinshead." In 1761 George Warren, of Poynton, County Chester, Kt., passed this and other manors in Lancashire to trustees by whom Tockholes was sold to John Hollinshead, from whom it descended to his cousin, William Brock, who assumed the additional name of Hollinshead on succeeding to his cousin's estates. Mr. Brock-Hollinshead died in 1803.

There are evidences of great antiquity still to be seen at Hollinshead Hall itself. Hundreds of people visit the place every year with the foggiest of ideas about it, some of them as absurd as they are foggy. The old road from Darwen to Hollinshead still runs across Darwen Moor, and it provides the most convenient way of getting there for those who have not exchanged their legs for internal combustion engines. Where the old road over the moor runs down to the Tockholes-Belmont road, now tar macadamed, a few steps to his right will bring the walker to the end of the old road which leads directly to the Hall and apparently ends there. Rushes and bracken threaten to overgrow it now, but it continues down the hill until just through a gate into a stack garth one observes the outline of a built-up gateway with fragments of walls and stones scattered about, hardly one of them being left on the top of another. Rarely, indeed, is an old building found in such a complete state of ruin. Yet is seems to have been inhabited up to quite a recent period. By what bolt, one wonders has such complete destruction been wrought! (NB as previously mentioned, the building was dismantled on the orders of the Liverpool Corporation to prevent habitation, which in turn would cause pollution to the watershed around the reservoirs)

A DISCOVERY OF A DATE-STONE

The hall itself stood on the right of the track on the other side of the field gate. Our photograph shows it as a house with three gables, apparently late eighteenth century work, though the wing to the left of the photograph appears to be older. These inferences are borne out by what appears in print respecting the house. According to Abram, the historian, of Blackburn, whose history was published in 1877, the building was then untenanted and in a state of decay. "A wing of the existing hall", he says, "is of some age, but has no interest feature" – a statement we may be permitted to doubt. "The other block was rebuilt in 1776." It may be supposed that had Abram visited the place he would have written a more detailed description. There is no reference to any date-stone and yet among the ruins now, a date-stone is to be seen which will be referred to later. Abram, however, whilst being an excellent historian, had the faults of the writers of local history of his age. He is much more concerned with genealogies and descents and family connections than about the relics of past ages, and he and his fellows were concerned to pick up and preserve what might have been picked up and preserved at any time, while they neglected those evidences of man's activity which were visible to them but which now have disappeared."

The Victoria County History of Lancashire is not much more explicit. Here is what it says:-

"Hollinshead Hall stood at the foot of a wooded knoll among the moors at the southern extremity of the township, but it is now in ruins and a modern farmhouse erected about the forties on the last century not far from the old house, bears its name. The hall was of seventeenth century date, but one wing has been rebuilt in 1776. In the garden was a well, enclosing a spring of water of curative properties to which the name of Holy Well was formerly given."

Robert Dick, the baker of Thurso, said that the writing of books was the chopping of straw which had been chopped a thousand times already. It is fairly evident that these fragments of local history have been chopped so many times over that by this time they are nothing but a small heap of dust, to which the present writer hopes he may add a few hitherto unchopped straws.

WAS IT MOATED?

The first question which might be raised is whether the old hall – for a hall must have stood on the site for many centuries – was surrounded by a moat. There are, I think, definite indications that this was so, and that the fourteenth century house was so protected. At any rate it seems to have stood on a sort of platform, and must have been a very extensive building from the fragments of it that are left. Portions of the upstanding walls have still their plaster coverings, but these evidently belong to the eighteenth century house.

Among the ruins of the house is to be seen a date-stone which bears the letters and the date

H – B – H
1843

under an elaborately carved and undercut moulding. The letters are not incised into the stone, they have been carved in deep relief, and at the first glance the thing might be taken for an iron casting. Such elaborate work at the date bespeaks a building of some importance.

In its way this stone is a mystery. Both Abram and the Victoria County History inform us that William Brock-Hollinshead – whose connection with the manor is given above – died without issue in 1803, leaving the estate to Laurence Brock, his nephew. By him it was sold to Eccles Shorrock, of Darwen, who thus became the lord of the manor. But Lawrence Brock-Hollinshead died in 1838, so the sale must have been concluded before that date.

Lawrence, by his second wife, had a son, Henry Brock-Hollinshead, described as of Billinge Carr, Blackburn, who died in 1858. In 1843, the manor belonged to Eccles Shorrock. How comes it then that Henry Brock-Hollinshead – for it is impossible the initials are anybody's but his – in that year, either added to, or rebuilt part of the Hall! It would seem, on the face of it, that Henry Brock-Hollinshead retained the Hall after the estate had been purchased by Eccles Shorrock.

THE MYSTERY OF THE WELL

To the north of the site of the house, in what I presume was the courtyard, or possibly the gardens of the house, is – the Victoria County History's "was" in the wrong tense – the well, which is variously described as a wishing well or as a holy spring. In his monumental work on the "Crosses and Holy Wells of Lancashire," Henry Taylor makes no reference at all to it, an unaccountable omission.

However, the writer of an anonymous fly sheet, which bears no date, says:

"Here no less than five different springs of water, after uniting together and passing through a very old carved stone representing a lion's head, flow into a well. To this well pilgrimages were formerly made, and the water, which is of a peculiar quality, is remarkable as an efficacious remedy in ophthalmic complaints".

This is exactly what we should have expected. The water is believed to have a medical value, and because of that the well becomes to be regarded as being holy. Dr. Kuerden, writing two centuries and a half ago, about St. Helen's Well, near Brindle, says of it: "Over against Swansey House, a little towards the hill, standeth an ancient fabric, where hath been a chapel belonging to the same, and a little above it, a spring of clear water rushing straight upwards into the midst of a faire fountain, walled square about in stone and flagged in the bottom, very transparent to be seen, and a strong stream issuing out of the same."

Dr. Kuerdon goes on: "The fountain is called Saint Ellen's Well, to which place the vulgar neighbouring people of the Red letter do much resort, with pretended devotion, on each year upon St. Ellen's day, where and when out of a foolish ceremony they offer or throw in the well pins, which there being left may be seen a long time after by any visitor to that fountain."

A QUESTION ANSWERED

For the moment we may overlook the reference to pins being thrown into the well. The question we have to consider is whether the well at Hollinshead is a holy spring or a wishing well. That question the writer hopes to answer definitely and unmistakably. The people of the district declare emphatically that it is a wishing well, and on a recent etching it is described as such by the artist. On the other hand Abram says it was, in days of yore, given the name of "Holy Well", and he puts the words between quotation marks.

The answer to the question is to be found in a careful examination of the building in which the spring or well is contained. As a matter of fact there are two buildings. At one time, before any building was erected, the water issued from a cleft in the rock and made for itself a pool on the ground. Then, at some time during the 15th Century probably, a vaulted chamber was erected over it.

Now it must be obvious that mere wishing wells were not enclosed in vaulted chambers, however implicitly their virtues might be believed in. That would be to destroy the very reason of them. Indeed, the pins that were thrown into the water, and the scraps of cloth that were hung on the trees round about them were intended as votive offerings to the spirit of the water, for it was anciently believed that every stream, every spring, and every fountain had its own spirit. It is a pity this belief has not survived to our own days. We might then have continued to go on making offerings of pins and rags, instead of filling up the wells with empty salmon tins as is our present habit.

A PILGRIM'S REST

Then at a later date, possibly during the 17th Century, the existing building was erected over the stone vaulting. It is possibly the most interesting antiquity this district can exhibit. In front of the building, in a dilapidated condition, is an open vestibule, the walls of which are finished by two stone pillars surmounted by stone ball ornaments. Round the vestibule is a stone bench on which pilgrims to the well might sit while the necessary ceremonies were being performed.

The stone lintel on the doorway into the well house is supported on two delightful corbels, which are carved out of the solid. The roof is covered with stone slates, and a story is told that some lads, one day, determined to get into the well house, removed some of these slates,

Well House 1975

but of course they only found themselves on the top of the stone vault underneath.

The building is kept in excellent repair by the Corporation of Liverpool, which is now the owner of the estate, the windows are filled with opaque glass protected by iron gratings, and the door is kept securely locked. The building is cleaned out from time to time by workmen sent for the purpose, and I was informed that a very high value is placed upon it. (One wonders if the Catholics of Liverpool are responsible for this). Report has it that the Catholics of Darwen and of Blackburn have tried to buy the well, but how much truth there is in this I do not know.

The present writer has not been inside the well house, and therefore cannot describe it at first hand. However, from the photographs he has seen it is evident that the lion's head, with its supporting pillars and plinths, are 17th Century workmanship, that is, they are of the same date as the outside of the building itself. Over the lion's head is an inscription, but the only word in it to be made out is the word "Well". The pool is about nine inches deep.

SINGULAR COINCIDENCES

Tockholes had a chapel of ease dedicated to St. Michael, which is said to have been erected about 1450. There is also a tradition that pilgrims to this well found in St. Michael's Chapel a place of rest and refreshment by the way. There is nothing inherently unlikely in that. But the date is important. The year 1450 might well mark the time at which the stone vault was put over the spring, and significantly enough, the restored Chapel of St. Michael had over the east window the initials of Sir John Radcliffe and the date 1620, a date which would fit the Hollinshead well house and the lion's head.

But there is more to be seen. On the right hand as one looks at the well house – there can be little doubt, I think, that it is a chapel, and therefore consecrated – is a wall with, built into it, a defaced shield, which once bore the arms of the Radcliffes in all probability. Right under the shield is a stone runnel which goes through the wall to the other side projecting on either side of the wall for a couple of inches. The runnel has not been inserted there for no purpose at all, but what purpose it would serve it is quite impossible to say.

The writer hopes he has now adduced evidence enough to show that Hollinshead Well is a holy well and not a wishing well. But has still more surprising evidence to put into court.

Behind the above the Holy Well Chapel is the wishing well. It is some three feet deep, of an oval shape, being walled from the bottom to the top. It contains about three inches of water and several inches of sludge. It is to be wished that the Liverpool Corporation will have this cleaned out in order to discover whether the bottom is paved or not. Trees hang over it, giving it an air of mystery which is entirely befitting to its purpose. Here is the pin well, the wishing well, the well round which votive offerings might be hung, but why it has survived side by side with its christianised neighbour it is impossible to guess even. It is a matter for question whether such another example remains in the country.

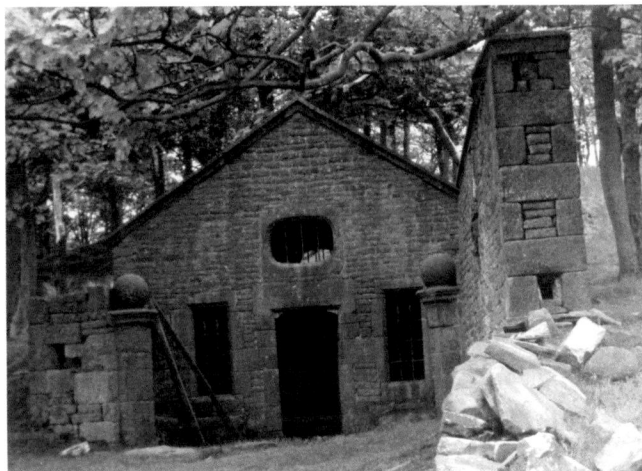

During restoration work West Elevation - 1975

DO WISHING WELLS WORK?

The subject of wishing wells is one much too long to go into now. There is one at Boston Spa, really at Thorp Arch across the Wharfe, near York, into which pins are still dropped by visitors and fragments of cloth hung on the overhanging trees. You form your wish and drop your offering into the water and your wish will come true if only you say nothing at all about it to anyone. When you have obtained your wish you make an offering of a strip of cloth by hanging it on the trees round about the well, as a thanksgiving. Of course, seeing the secrecy with which the wish, when it is once made, must be kept, it is quite impossible to say whether wishing wells work or not. To judge from the number of offerings made at the Thorpe Arch well, it evidently does.

How far back in history this wishing well takes us, who can say? Somebody at some time has thought it worth while to line it with stones and possibly to pave the bottom of it also. The Liverpool Corporation has planted the district round about it with trees, but doubtless there was a path down to the well from the road at the top. As I stood over it I was reminded I was looking into a long and very dim past back to the time when Tocca and Hrodwulf, bringing with them their religious beliefs which saw the whole of nature animated by gods and spirits, built their halls thereabouts.

It may only be hoped that this wishing well will not be filled up with refuse as so many others have been. At any rate it has survived to a good old age, possibly because it is in such a secluded spot.

The old stone pillars which once marked the entrance to the Hall are still to be seen built into the wall which runs along the Tockholes-Belmont road. I have been told that when Eccles Shorrock bought the estate he furnished the house intending it to be occupied by a member of the Ashton family, who, however, never went into it, for some reason or other. The remains of an old barn are to be seen, the upper chamber to which was approached by a flight of stone steps outside the building. One day a man named Fish went up those steps, fastened a rope to the building, the other end of which he fastened round his neck, and throwing himself down, succeeded in hanging himself. So that Hollinshead Hall is not without its tragedy after all."

R. H.

MORE ABOUT HOLLINSHEAD HALL
A CONSECRATED HOLY WELL
From Darwen News 17th September 1932 p.6

The articles which have been appearing in this journal on the old halls which are to be found in Darwen and the vicinity have attracted a considerable amount of attention, and some of the conclusions arrived at by the author, particularly with regard to Hollinshead Hall, have been questioned in some quarters, in a perfectly friendly spirit it may be added.

Mr. Sydney Ashton has called the writer's attention to a letter written by his brother, Mr. H. D. Ashton, and which appeared in these columns some years ago. In this letter Mr. H. D. Ashton says of the Holy Well in what was once the garden of the Hall:

"It is a Roman Catholic Baptistry Chapel and the two fonts of water are there, one to baptise men, and the other women. I well remember the late Father Vandenweghe coming to the office at Hope Mill one morning. The kindly old gentleman was in a state of great excitement. He had been over to Hollinshead the day before, to administer the last rites of his Church to a dying haymaker, and strolling into the garden had, to his intense surprise, seen the Holy Well. He said it was like many Baptistry Chapels in his native land of Belgium, and had come to ask my father by whom it had been built and why it was there. There is very little known about it, possibly the Brock-Hollinsheads may have erected it when they rebuilt the hall in 1776, for I believe they were a Roman Catholic family."

This goes a long way towards proving that the building is a consecrated one as the writer of our article suggested. The statement has been made that the building was originally intended as the buttery of the hall and it is surprising to find how many people have this idea. But Mr. Ashton gives additional proof. ...

"When I first knew the Holy Well," he says, "it was in perfect preservation and the windows were filled with stained glass." That settles the matter. It is very unlikely, to say the least of it, that the windows of a buttery would be filled with stained glass. Mr. Ashton goes on: "My own theory is that this is the side of the "Cell" of one of the first missionaries of Christianity, who may have come from Ireland or Iona, to preach the gospel to the heathen Saxons or Angles in what is now Tockholes. Here he built his little "Cell" and baptised his converts at the spring that still flows into the present building.

"The situation is just the one such a man would choose for his habitation and is like many similar ones in Cornwall and other parts of our country. There would be a considerable population to preach the new faith to, for it is thought that the name Anglesarke, given to the moor immediately to the West, suggests that here the Angles had an "Ark" or "Refuge" of some strength. Traces of the fortress can still be found on the moor, I am told, but I have never seen them myself.

"That the well has long been a place of sanctity is proved by the name of an adjoining farm called Halliwell Fold. Halliwell is obviously "Holy Well" and named after the Holy Well in Hollinshead garden. The buildings of this old farmstead have been removed in recent years by the Liverpool Corporation, but records of it go back as far as 1570, when Richard Halliwell was assessed to a "subsidy," and was a defendant in an action for trespass in 1811. The numerous families in Darwen and neighbourhood bearing this surname, undoubtedly trace their descent to this "Halliwell" or "Holywell Fold."

THE HOLY SPRING:
HOLLINSHEAD·HALL:
Nʳ WITHNELL; L'ANCS:
AS RESTORED

Part of a plan made in 1905 for the
proposed restoration work to the Well House

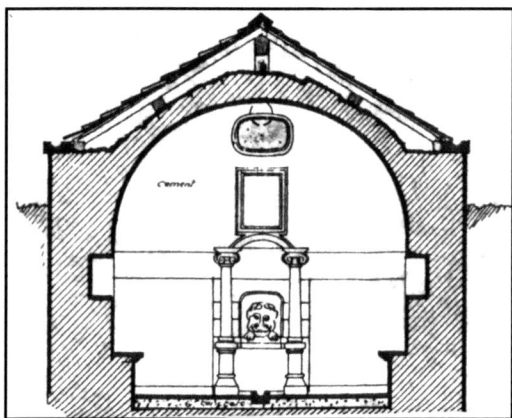

Cross section of well interior from 1905 plan

Thus the case is clinched. The suggestion that there was a cell of one of the first missionaries of Christianity, is of the first importance. It is thought that Paulinus was the first to preach the Christian Gospel in these parts, and there is every reason for thinking that from Whalley he might have come along the old road from Whalley to Haslingden and so on to the ford which crossed the Darwen herebabouts, baptising the people he converted by his preaching. It may have been one of his converts who established himself at Hollinshead near a spring of water which even then was regarded as having curative powers, in order that he might perform the office of baptism for those who required it. At any rate it must have been in some such manner that a knowledge of the Christian teaching was spread among the people who lived in these wild and scattered regions.

The place names of the district, if they do not provide any argument for these suggestions, at least do nothing to contradict them. "Halliwell Fold," of which the writer had never heard until he read Mr. Ashton's letter two days ago, is most suggestive, and the other names, Tockholes and Roddlesworth as was pointed out in the article on Hollinshead Hall, are evidences of very early settlements having been made there. I am very greatly obliged to Mr. Sydney Ashton for bringing this letter of his brother's to my notice. Had I seen it before, my task would have been made all the lighter.

That there is nothing very improbable about the theory which was advanced by Mr. H. D. Ashton as to this well having been used by an early convert to Christianity for baptising others is demonstrated by the existence of another well, known as the "Christening Well" at Plemstall in Cheshire. Here it was the Plegmund, who became Archbishop of Canterbury in 890, had a retreat after his old home at Canterbury had been sacked by the Danes, and here tradition affirms, he baptised converts. At any rate "Seint Pleymondes Well" figures in a deed of the beginning of the 14th century.

Darwen News 24th September 1932

HOLLINSHEAD HALL

To the Editor of the "Darwen News"

Sir,   With reference to your recent articles in the "Darwen News" on Hollinshead Hall, which have given me great pleasure and enlightenment, I have one or two suggestions to make. In my opinion the well, the well-house and the spout were all built at the same time,

High stone wall with trough and plaque

Close up detail of
trough and plaque

probably between 1830 and 1850. Evidence of this is the stone troughs on the well-house which were used at this period. (To my knowledge there is only one exception to stone troughs being used on buildings before about 1830. This is a barn at Lower Darwen, which has a date stone about 1780, but this appears to have been rebuilt). There are lead drain pipes going from the troughs to the well, which enter the well about 1ft down from the top. Also there is mortar between the stones of the well on the side nearest the well-house. This suggests that the well was built or part re-built when the well-

house was. There is nothing to show, as far as I could see, that the well-house was not all built at the same time, nor is there anything to suggest that the wall where the spout is was built at any other time.

The spout is about 1 foot to 18 inches below the level of the drain that feeds the well, and it is almost in line with the water-course. That brings the water from the fields above. A short stone drain connects to the water-course almost at right angles, and enters the well 18 inches from the top. It would seem that when the water in the well was above a certain height the surplus was taken by the spout. If the well-house was a chapel of ease it would point from west to east. Actually it points from south to north. I would suggest that it was used as a buttery for the farmhouse, and that the buttery and the spout wall formed part of a beautiful garden. (I hear that damsons used to be grown there.) In the middle of the nineteenth century Italian and Roman gardens were the fashion, and it may be that this is an imitation of some Roman garden.

I have looked for a pool under the spout, but I have not found traces of one yet, but I have found bits of broken red plant pot in the soil.

The shield above the spout has no inscription on it, and I wonder if a blank shield has any significance.

I have been told that the spout was used before the other well-house was built. It will be noticed that a great deal of earth has been taken away from one side of the spout wall, and it may well have been that this spout is in its original position, built in a new wall, because the older wall and well were undermined by the digging.

Yours truly,
J.S.E.
Darwen 22nd September 1932.

133

October 1st 1932
To the Editor of the "Darwen News"

Hollinshead Hall

Sir, Your correspondent, "J.S.E." is to be compli-mented on the observations he makes upon what he has found at Hollinshead Hall, even though the conclusions at which he arrives are rather difficult to understand. Personally I am unable to understand what he means by the "stone troughs on the well-house". There are some stone gutters on the well-house, but I don't known of any stone-troughs. I beg "J.S.E.'s" pardon; I understand now what he means by stone troughs, but I can hardly get accustomed to the Lancashire use of the word. This matter of stone troughing is of some importance in determining the date of the building.

When was this little building erected? "J.S.E" suggests at some time between 1830 and 1850. But to defend this suggestion he must explain a few other things. Hollinshead Hall was purchased by Eccles Shorrock soon after 1830, and it was never occupied again after that. Why, then should Eccles Shorrock build a "buttery" for a house he never used? Again, what is a "buttery", and what is its use? "J.S.E." might look this up. The buttery had a definite place in the plan of an old hall. It was always situated behind the screens of the hall and had a half-door over which the dishes could be handed out. Then "J.S.E." might tell us what significance the following statement by Abram, the historian of Blackburn, which was published in 1879 has on the question?

> *"Hollinshead Hall, the manor house of Tockholes, is now untenanted and in a state of decay. A wing of the existing hall is of some age, but has no interesting feature. The other block was rebuilt in 1776. (No reference to any building about 1830, be it noted). In the garden is an antique well enclosing a spring of water of curative properties to which of yore the name of Holy Well was given." (The words antique and of yore are of importance.)*

"If the well-house was a chapel of ease," says "J.S.E.", "it would point from west to east". But nobody, as far as I know, has ever suggested it as a chapel-of-ease. Why should there be one at Hollinshead when there was one at Tockholes? And "J.S.E." is certainly wrong when he suggests that Roman and Italian gardens were the fashion in the middle of the nineteenth century. He will have to go back at least a century and a half to find the fashionable Roman and Italian gardens.

"I have looked for a pool under the spout," your correspondent goes on, "but I have not found traces of one as yet." But the pool is there! "J.S.E." can take my word for it! He will find the pool inside the building which he calls a buttery. He will find inside the building, also, two troughs – Mr. Ashton suggests that one was used in the baptism of men and the other of women. And he will find, also, inside the building, a lion's head

set in the wall through which the spring of water runs, with an inscription about it in which the word WELL appears. These are rather curious things to find in a "nineteenth century buttery." I, for one, would be very glad to known what "J.S.E." thinks of these things.

Yours etc. R.H.

Our Correspondent's Full Investigation. New Light Thrown on Ancient Stone Structure
First Description of Well-House
From the Darwen News 22nd October 1932

Since the issue of which the second letter of J.S.E. appeared, I have had the opportunity of going over the ruins of Hollinshead Hall with Mr. Sydney Ashton, J.P. who remembers the building as it stood fifty years go, and of inspecting with him the building at the end of the garden in which the wishing well or holy well is contained.

In the first place then, I will endeavour to describe as clearly as possible what the building contains.

It is quite a small building some fourteen feet by ten or thereabouts, and has a vaulted roof which, on the outside, is covered with a thatch of stone slates., It is placed as nearly as may be, east and west, not quite directly east and west, but as nearly oriented to these points of the compass as the site will allow. In the front of the building is a vestibule which has a stone bench on either side of it, finished to the west with two stone pillars, on which are mounted stone ball ornaments of a large size. A third ball ornament once appeared on the finial of the gable end of the roof, but this has either been blown down or pulled down during recent years. There is no doubting the existence of this ornament, for it has been preserved in the building until recently.

The door is in the centre of the west front of the building, and on either side of it is a small window, both door and windows having stone lintels. Over the door is a nearly oval aperture, which is filled with iron netting. At the east end is a similar aperture, into which a number of upright iron bars have been fixed by the instructions of the Liverpool Corporation. The eaves of the stone slate roof feed into stone gutterings or trough-ings, which are placed on the top of the outside walls – which means that the roof does not overlap the outside walls. These gutterings drain into the ground at the east end through circular holes, which have no lead pipes attached to them nor do they appear to have had any such things.

The building, at the very latest, is eighteenth century work – 1680 would be a probable date – and the gutterings are part of the original building. There can be no question of that.

AN AMAZING BUILDING

It is the inside of the building, however, which is most amazing. It is dimly lighted, and it is only after one has been in it for some little time that its details become clear to the sight.

At the east end, between two short pillars with Ionic capitals, is a lion's head resting on its two front paws – a remarkable piece of sculpture – through the mouth of which, a stream of water pours into a stone trough beneath. This lion's head is deserving of the closest study. Quite evidently two coloured stones – I hesitate to say they were precious stones, though they may well have been such – were inserted in the eye sockets and the rims of these sockets have been tinted with white paint. There were a party of five persons of us altogether, and this was the first thing which struck our attention. The water runs clear out of the mouth of the head into the pool below.

Above the lion's head is an inscribed stone slab set in an old stone frame, the frame evidently being part of the original design. The slab is modern, and records the names of the members of the Liverpool Waterworks Committee when the estate was taken over by them in the year 1905. At the top are the words, THE WISHING WELL. What was in that frame before the present slab was placed in it, it is impossible to say. There was quite evidently something in it, but it is hard to think that if that something was a date-stone, that the Liverpool authorities would have covered it up.

The trough or stone tank which is beneath the head is fifteen inches deep and has stone bottom. It measures about three feet and a half by two feet. The water overflows from it into a stone drain or channel, which cuts across the stone-paved floor to the door and into a grate placed just within the threshold. This stone channel is older than the floor itself.

MYSTERY TANKS

On either side of this centre-piece is a stone tank, the front edges of which are in a line with the base of the lion's head. These tanks, one at each side, are excavated into the hillside behind the building and are covered with stone slabs which are set about four feet from the floor level. They thus form two alcoves. It is difficult to say how deep the stone tanks are, because they have evidently been filled up with loose stones, but I discovered in one of them about five inches of water. They again overflow into the stone drain which runs across the floor. The water with which they are now filled has evidently percolated through the roofs above.

In the walls at either side of these tanks – that is, in the north and south walls of the buildings, are aumbries or cupboards, the oak doors to which may be original. These cupboards go into the walls for about twelve inches and are at present used to keep cleaning materials in or anything of that kind. They are not the least interesting nor least important features of the building.

On either side is a stone bench similar to the stone benches in the vestibule outside. These are contemporary with the building itself.

The walls themselves are constructed of layers of thin stone, but the vault which covers them is composed of larger stones, as might be expected. (It is much easier to construct a vault of large stones than of small stones). The vault is half circular in form, and is a very handsome piece of work. Above, in its centre, is a stone boss, without any indications of decorations upon it. Why that boss has been set up there, is a mystery. It has not the slightest use as a keystone, and, indeed, must have called for some ingenuity in the fixing of it there. One may hazard the guess that it was intended to be sculptured after it had been placed in position.

WHAT IS A BUTTERY!

These are the contents of the building which "J.S.E." has convinced himself is a "buttery" – to use his own word – though he has quite evidently never consulted any dictionary of architecture to discover what a buttery is. To make the case complete against him I will quote from Atkinson's Glossary of English Architecture:-

> *"BUTTERY. A 'buttery,' a room at the lower end of a medieval hall in which victuals, and especially liquors, were kept. It opened into the screen's passage. The door was in two heights like a stable door, the lower part having a shelf on the top for convenience in service out provisions."*

Our readers must decide for themselves whether T. D. Atkinson, who is a distinguished architect, or "J.S.E." is the better authority.

But by "buttery" "J.S.E." evidently means dairy. "This room," he says, "is made that it will keep cool even in the hottest weather," and so on. There is no question but that this building at Hollinshead would answer that requirement. Then he says: "Now in many farmhouses, and that is what the halls about here were, there is a room with a well in it." Exactly! I have not seen one of them, but will take "J.S.E.'s" words for it. But what a bloomer he makes in thinking of Hollinshead Hall as a farmhouse. It was not a farmhouse; Hollinshead Hall was the hall of the Lord of the Manor of Tockholes, and, maybe, as some suggest, of

Interior of Well House

135

Over Darwen also. Hollinshead is in the same category as Smithills Hall or Hall i' th' Wood, neither of which are many miles away. When Eccles Shorrock bought Hollinshead Hall he became Lord of the Manor of Tockholes.

Hollinshead Farmhouse

A LORD'S MANOR HOUSE

But there was a farmhouse at Hollinshead; there was both a hall and a farmhouse, the one behind the other. And to imagine that Eccles Shorrock or anybody else built this well-house in order that "the gentry might not be disturbed by labourers and milkmaids coming into the house" is, to say the least of it, ridiculous, for to get from the farmhouse to this "buttery" the labourers and milkmaids would have to pass through the hall, in which case they would probably sit on the stone benches to wait until the butter was cool before they ventured back again. And that's that, as we say in Lancashire!

Eccles Shorrock acquired the Hollinshead property in 1838, and since that time Mr. Ashton is confident the hall has never been occupied, not even by a doctor from Withnell. The farmhouse has been occupied, but not the hall itself.

Again, "A tale told me by a Catholic," says "J.S.E.," "runs something like this: A priest is said to have stated that it was very like a building in Italy, and that it may have been used as a chapel of ease." A chapel of ease for what? But why is "J.S.E." so obtuse? An article which appeared in your paper on September 17th gave the name of the priest and what he had said the building was used for. Why should "J.S.E." go gossiping about when he can get the fact from the lion's head so to speak?

The first part of "J.S.E.'s" second letter may be quoted here in extenso, because he says it represents facts. Here it is:

When was the well-house erected? By the stone troughs and the arch shall ye know it. All the building and the walls were erected at the same time. There is no evidence otherwise. The stone troughs make the odds 100 to half-of-one that it is not older than 1830. The arch is nearly as definite.

To be arch-minded in those days was modern, just as air-mindedness is modern today. Large doors such as were needed for making mills could not well be made without the arch and so the arch was re-discovered. I imagine railway tunnels would be a great newspaper topic. I would be glad to know of any other arches on the Hollinshead estate that are older than 100 years.

STONE TROUGHINGS

Point one: Before there were any troughings at all used on buildings the eaves overlapped the walls and the water droppings just dripped down on the heads of any who might be underneath them. On some buildings gargoyles were fixed at the end of the gutters so that in rainy seasons the water simply poured out as through a spout. Then later the eaves of the roofs were finished into stone gutterings, which were placed on the tops of the outside walls. "J.S.E." may take my word for it, or not, just as he pleases, that stone gutterings were being used in England long before 1830-. Indeed, it is probable they were contemporary with stone roofs.

Point Two: Arches have been used in this country continuously since William the Conqueror landed here in 1066. "J.S.E." asks for another arch on the Hollinshead estate that is older than one hundred years. It is this question that convinces me he is trying to pull my leg. In return I will ask "J.S.E." to produce even another roof on the Hollinshead estate of any age whatever. But I will tell him where he will find a lovely arch in Darwen, which was built long before the days of railways, if that will meet his order. Under Arch-street! It is still there, though an unfeeling Council has had it filled up. "The arch was rediscovered!" What on earth is "J.S.E." talking about?

INTENDED FOR BAPTISM

There can be no doubt that the late Mr. H. D. Ashton was right, and that this building at Hollinshead was intended to be and was used as a baptistery. But it ought not to be implied that babies were baptised there. It was intended for the baptism of adult men and women, who were thereby received into the Christian faith. The cupboards in the walls were possible those in which the sacred oils were kept, for oil as well as water is used in the ceremonies of the Catholic Church. And, oddly enough, if "J.S.E." will feel at the tops of the pillars on either side of the lion's head in the building, he will find a cup-shaped depression in each of them. What were these depressions for? They were not made for the fun of making them. In all probability those depressions were intended to the holy oil into which the priest who was performing the ceremony might dip his finger and make on the forehead of the baptised, the sign of the cross. One of the troughs was used for men and the other for women, says Mr. Ashton, and he had the authority of a Catholic priest for making that statement, a priest whose name has been given in print.

"There is more to tell," says "J.S.E." I, too, have more to tell, but for this time I have occupied more than enough space.   R.H.

HOLLINSHEAD HALL
"J.S.E." AND "R.H." - A WRANGLE OVER SHROUDED DETAILS
Darwen October 28th 1932
TO THE EDITOR OF THE "DARWEN NEWS"

Sir, - I am glad, "R.H.," you have not disappointed me with your letter, and I appreciate it very much. I would have liked to have been with you on your visit to Hollinshead Hall, as you have made one or two obvious mistakes about it, to which I shall refer later.

The direction of the well lies almost dead North-East. I measured it to be 2 degrees East of North-East. The striking fact about it is that it is dead square with the farmhouse and the hall. It would just have been as easy to have made it dead East.

Now we come to one of your mistakes. You state that the stone troughs don't appear to have had lead pipes to them. The trough that is on the North-West of the building has a lead pipe coupled to it. This pipe is flanged over into a recess like the old stone slopstones and pipes are. It enters the outside well or settling tank, as I will now call it, as I have before described. The other trough has traces of lead in the hole, and the pipe is there under the ground. This again goes to the tank. When you estimate the age of buildings it will be instructive to us if you state why you are of your opinions.

Here is another of your mistakes. After stating that you estimate the age of the building to be about 1680, you go on to say: "The lion's head resting on its two front paws – a remarkable piece of sculpture, etc."

If you will look for sculpture, in Pears Cycolpaedia, you will find this statement: "Not until the 16th century did England produce any particularly striking sculpture," and in Jack's reference book you find "There was a revival in the 14th and 15th centuries followed by a second decline in the 17th. The modern revival dates from the end of the 18th century.

From what I have seen I think that pillars used for ornament alone are typical of the 1800-1860 period. The stone channel on the floor is very like the channelling used in shippons round here. The earliest date that they were used is about 1835. Why do you think that the channel is older than the floor itself? When you say paved, do you mean that the well-house was flagged?

The mystery tanks on each side of the lion will not have much mystery about them if you will compare them with other wells in the district. There is a drain in the settling tank which rather puzzles me. Did you see any likelihood of there being any connection with this tank and the mystery tanks? You are quite right in that. I have never consulted a dictionary of architecture about the word buttery. I will call it anything you like so long as you understand. Of course Hollinshead Hall was the Manor House of part of Tockholes. When I said halls round here I meant such places as Lord's Hall, Whitehall and Darwen Bank. Here is another of your mistakes. On the map in the reference library dated 1610, you will find Smithills Hall, Hall o'th' Wood, and Samlesbury Hall, but no Hollinshead Hall. It is thus not in the same category.

Will you please state, as clearly as you can what you mean by saying that there was both a hall and a farmhouse, the one behind the other? Was this farmhouse there before the one built in 1844? If so, what was its position?

And now the stone troughs. You admit they were placed there when the building was built. °We have now only to date them. You can't find me a building in Tockholes over 100 years old that has them on. I have looked in Darwen, Blackburn and districts, but I have not seen one yet. These buildings date continuously from 1590 onwards. There is one at Lower Darwen dated 1691, but this seems to have been rebuilt. I assure you I am not pulling your leg about arches. I will be glad to know of any arch over 100 years in the area from Sunnyhurst to Withnell and from Fernhurst in Blackburn to Hollinshead.

There is a well behind the kiosk in the Sunnyhurst Wood like the settling tank at Hollinshead. I have good reason for saying that it is less than 100 years old. Up to now this letter has been corrections and explanations, but to liven things up a bit, do you know of the ghost story of Hollinshead, and do you know that there is a beautiful ladies dress still in existence that was worn by a lady at Hollinshead 100 years ago? I may tell more about those some other time. I beg you to keep on with your interesting articles on old Darwen and district.

Yours truly, J.S.E.

Ruins of Hollinshead Hall 2002

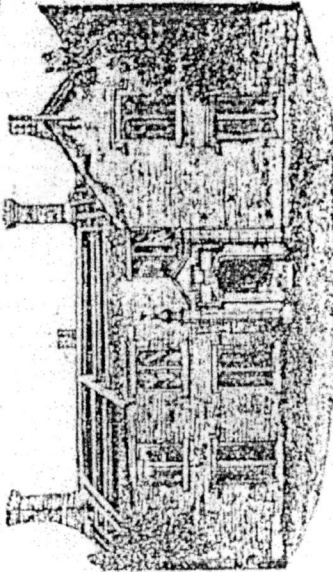

The hall during restoration in 1776.

Riddle of Hollinshead Hall

—and the solution

IN 1912-1913, while demolishing the last remaining portion of Hollinshead Hall, the ancient manor house of Tockholes, Mr R. Robinson, of Brinscall, noticed a corner of the old building had been rounded off and a number of slits, similar to archers' slits in old castles, had been made.

The purpose was obscure. The slits could not have been used by archers for they were six feet from the floor.

The stones taken out by Mr Robinson and Mr J. Paley were built into the dry-stone wall which runs along the top side of the road from where the old Tockholes cotton mill once stood to a point where the road joins the Bolton-Preston main road just above the hall.

But the mystery remained until, in 1913, Mr Robinson met the late Mr George Hull, the Lancashire poet and an old gentleman who turned out to be an historian. Here is the explanation he gave for the "mysterious" slits and the rounded corner.

WHEN Julius Cæsar formulated his calendar he measured the time it took for the sun to travel round the earth (yes, they believed that the sun travelled round the earth in those days) was 365¼ days, and he decreed that there should be a leap year every four years.

This calendar continued until the latter part of the 16th century. At that time there was a Pope named Gregory, a great astronomer. He had better instruments than Cæsar and found that Cæsar's reckoning was inaccurate.

About this time, Galileo discovered that the earth travelled round the sun. Pope Gregory, by careful reckoning found that the actual time it took the earth to travel round the sun was 365 days 5 hours,

49 minutes and 10 seconds. He computed that since the days of Cæsar the world was 10 days behind correct time. In 1582, the Gregorian calendar was adopted by almost all the countries on the Continent, and to bring the time up to date they "jumped" 10 days.

But England lagged behind because at that time Queen Elizabeth I., an ardent Protestant, was on the throne, and anything connected with the Pope or Rome was not allowed in England.

A hundred and fifty years passed. About the fifth decade of the 18th century Britain was doing a great amount of trade with Continental countries. The difference in dates caused great confusion and an agitation arose to adopt the Continental calendar. Foremost among those concerned was the head of the Hollinsheads of that period. He was asked to bring forward his proof that Britain's time was wrong.

He had that corner of the room rounded off and those "slits" made in the wall. In the room he installed a clock

which received its motive power from two large stones for weights. This clock was fixed so that the sun shone on its face through those "slits." It was set to keep accurate time by all the leading clocks in England.

By carefully watching the clock for six years, Hollinshead found that it had lost more than an hour by the sun. Here was his proof that Pope Gregory was right and Britain at last adopted the Gregorian calendar. But even then there was a dread of anything concerning Rome and for a time the new time was known as "the new style calendar."

This change was a little complicated, for by this time Britain had lost another day. To bring the time up to date, on September 2 at midnight they "jumped" 11 days, the next day being September 14, 1752.

There are no dates in British history between September 2 and 14 in that year. But this change did not take place without trouble, for people were superstitious in those days and they believed they were being robbed of 11 days of their lives. They paraded in large numbers in all our cities and towns crying "Give us back our 11 days.

Pope Gregory also found that a leap year every four years would not keep the time accurate, so it was decided that the year at the end of every century that will not divide by four without a remainder should not be a leap year. Thus 1700, 1800 and 1900 on the Continent, 1800 and 1900 in Britain, were not leap years, but the year 2000 will be.

The Shetland Islands and the Isle of Foula still adhere to the old Cæsarian calendar and are now 12 days behind the rest of the world. They celebrated their 1953 Christmas day on January 6 this year.

That was the old gentleman's story. Mr. Robinson again takes up the tale.—

Somewhere in that old dry-stone wall that stretches along the top side of the road from where the old Tockholes Mill used to stand to where it joins the main Preston—Bolton-road are many stones from Hollinshead Hall, some carved with hideous faces and some with inscriptions.

I remember a building in a stone about a foot square that had at one time had an iron ring let in with lead, but the ring was rusted away. I have no doubt that was one of the stones which Hollinshead used as a weight to operate his clock that brought Britain up to date with the continent. Where those stones are could not now say for certain, but some day when that old wall falls down some people will wonder where those strange stones came from.

<table>
<tr><td valign="top" width="50%">

To be Let
For a Term of a Year
At The Rock Inn, Tockholes
On Tues 27th March 1821
at 4 o'clock

Plot 1: Consisting of an excellent Dwelling House, barn with shipponing for 24 cows, and about 30 acres of highly improved meadow and pasture land situate at **Hollinshead Hall** within Tockholes

Plot 2: Consisting of an excellent Dwelling House, barn with shipponing for 8 cows and about 13 acres of highly improved meadow and pasture land at the same place

Plot 3: Consisting of a new Dwelling House and barn at **Halliwell Mill**, the Mill, Meadow and Pasture for 4 or 6 or more cows in Halliwell Fold Pasture

The Whole will be free of Tithes and of Poor and Highway Rates. Further particulars apply at Hollinshead Hall

Blackburn Mail 21st March 1821

</td><td valign="top" width="50%">

To be Let
By
PRIVATE TREATY
Hollinshead Hall with Tockholes

With sundry parcels of Meadow and Pasture Land called:-
The Slipper Law, The Calf Croft, The Great Meadow, The Old Meadow, The Kitchen Croft and The Thornley Bank

Containing about 40 customary acres of 7½ yds. The House six rooms upon a floor and is in complete repair and any further quantities of land will be added if desirable to the Tenant – or the premises will be divided and let in parcels if suitable offers are made.

Apply James Park on the premises

Blackburn Mail 24th January 1821

</td></tr>
</table>

HAY & FARMING STOCK
To be Sold by AUCTION
At Hollinshead Hall within Tockholes
On Friday 29th November 1822.

About 200 yds of Hay in Lots, 4 Cart Horses, a Brown Horse 7 yrs old by Aaron, Chestnut Mare 4 yrs old by Calliban, 2 Grey Fillies by Forester, a Short Horned Bull, several cows and young cattle, about 70 sheep in lots, 2 broad wheeled cars and different other husbandry utensils.

The Sale to begin at 1 o'clock.

May be viewed by application to James Park Hollinshead Hall

Blackburn Mail 27th November 1822

Blackburn Standard

(For God, the Queen, the Peers, and the People)

Wednesday 8th January 1845

3rd Week. – Quarter No. 321 VXL 5d per Quarter in Credit. 4/9 in advance

Printed & Published by James Walkden, 9 King William Street, Blackburn

Advertisement:

    To Be Let (and may be entered upon immediately) for a term of years

    In a very cheap and retired part of the country

    The Mansion called **Hollinshead Hall** situate in the township of Tockholes in the Parish of Blackburn.

The house contains Drawing Room, Dining Room, Library, Breakfast Room, Housekeeper's Room, Pantry, Kitchens, etc. on the ground floor. Five best Bedrooms, four Inferior Bedrooms, water closet etc., Coach House, Saddle Room, five stalled stable, and two stalled stable (if required), good gardens and pleasure grounds.

    The House has lately been painted and papered. Any part of the furniture may be taken at valuation.

    The above is well adapted for a Private Boarding School.

N.B. If the House be not let very shortly, the whole of the furniture will be disposed of by Public Auction.

For further particulars, and for tickets of admission to view the House and the Premises, apply to the Reverend Gilmour Robinson, Incumbent of Tockholes, or George Radcliffe, Agent, Blackburn.

To be Sold by Auction

By Mr. William Salisbury

On Wednesday, Thursday and Friday, the 27th, 28th days of February and 1st day of March 1845, at Hollinshead Hall, in the Township of Tockholes, in the County of Lancaster; by order of H. B. Hollinshead, Est., who is leaving the neighbourhood; sale to commence at 10 o'clock each morning:

The Entire of the Valuable Modern Household Furniture
Comprising in the

Dining, Breakfast, and Sittings Rooms, Library, etc.

A set of 12 very handsome Carved Oak Chairs with loose cushions, upholstered with Curled Hair, in Crimson Damask;

A beautiful Carved Oak Sofa, with loose cushion and pillows, upholstered with Curled Hair, in Crimson Damask

A set of 7 Antique Oak Chairs, with cane seats and loose Curled Hair cushions, in Drab Damask;

A set of 7 neat Oak Chairs with Hair seats, neat Oak Pembroke and Library tables';

Handsome Mahogany Sideboard, with Raised Back, Shelf and the usual conveniences;

Mahogany Dining Table upon Reeded Legs;

Sets of Mahogany Chairs with loose Hair Seatings; capital Carved Mahogany Couch with loose cushion and pillows, upholstered with Curled Hair in Hair Cloth;

Handsome Mahogany Lounging Chair, neatly upholstered with spring seat and back in Crimson Morocco Leather;

Recumbent Chair and loose Hair Cushions; very neat Mahogany Dumb What-Not;

Handsome bronzed and steel fenders with standards, and polished steel Fire Irons;

Very superior Brussels Carpets and Rugs

Elegant suits of Crimson and Drab Damask Window Curtains with cornices, tastefully finished;

Chimney glasses in gilt frames; Bronzed Lamp, upon a beautiful Ornamental Stand;

Splendid Spanish Mahogany Book-cases and shelves, with deep moulded cornices, mahogany and glazed doors, drawers, and the usual conveniences.

The Engravings

(Very Superior and Proof Impressions) are splendidly framed and glazed and include

The Queen receiving the sacrament at her Coronation;

The Duke of Wellington, as Chancellor of Oxford

Hawking in the Olden Time;

Dignity and Impudence;

Laying Down the Law;

Children of the Duke of Sutherland;

Her Majesty's Stag Hounds;

Melton Breakfast;

Highland Drovers;

Highland Whiskey Still;

Rape of Europa;

Trial of Lord William Russell;

The Cheshire Hunt

The Lady Jane Grey;

The Rev. James Slade;

Musicians;

Ambulars, and a few others

The Paintings

Are very fine in Ornamental Gilt Frames, and include

Life Guards at Waterloo;

Retreat of Napoleon;

Battle of Assaye;

Boy and Deer Hounds, etc.

The Prints, etc.

Dutch and English Girl;

Duke of Wellington;

Foresters in Search of Game;

Gamekeeper's Pony;

Down Charge (sic); (possibly 'Dawn')

Keeper going round his Traps;

Shooter's Companion;

The Lovely Sisters;

Little Red Riding Hood, in glass case;

The Three Graces, set;

Liverpool Steeple Chase;

Charles XII;

Cotherstone;

Attila, and a few others

In the Hall and Stairs

4 elegantly Carved Oak Hall Chairs, beautifully upholstered in the best Curled Hair, in a Crimson Silk Velvet Damask;

Antique Hall Table upon twisted legs;

2 Mahogany Hall Chairs;

2 very handsome Brackets

Barometer;

Bronzed Hat and Umbrella Stand;

Painted Oil Cloth;

Good stairs carpeting;

Brass Rods, etc.

The Lodging and Dressing Rooms

Are also furnished in a superior manner, and include handsome Carved Oak, Mahogany, etc. Post Bedsteads, with neat foot rails, and deep moulded cornices tastefully hung with Crimson, Drab, and Brown Damask Hangings, and Window Curtains to match with neat cornices;

French Bedsteads; sofa bedsteads furnished with Print Hangings, and window curtains to match.

Prime goose feather beds;

Curled Hair mattresses;

Good bedding;

Handsomely carved Oak Dressing Tables, Towel Rails, Chest of Drawers;

Night Commodes;

Capital Dressing Glasses in Mahogany frames;

Excellent carpeting, rugs, etc.

The Housekeeper's Room, Store Rooms, etc.

Comprise a good assortment of neat, useful furniture, excellent Dinner and Dessert sets, China, Tea and Breakfast Sets, handsome cut Spirit Bottles, Wine Decanters, Wine, Jelly, Custard and Tumbler Glasses, etc.

The Kitchen and Servants' Bedrooms

Comprise a variety of excellent articles adapted for general domestic use and include:

Clock and case; painted dressers; cupboards; wardrobes; tent and post bedsteads; bedding; tables; chairs etc.

Purchasers to pay the Auction Duty.

The whole may be viewed on Monday 24th February next from 11 o'clock in the morning until 3 o'clock in the afternoon. Catalogues will be ready 4 days prior to the day of the sale and may be had from the auctioneers as AUCTIONEERS at his office, Limbrick; or at the "Standard" Office, Blackburn, or on application will be sent by Post.

Additional items listed:-

After the Kitchen and Servants' Room entry, the following –

One valuable double plate Electrifying Machine; Electric Battery; and various jars – by Knight (in italics) of London

Various chemical apparatus

A valuable strong 7" Centre Lathe with Roze Engine; Eccentric Chuck, Drill, Motion, Cycloid Motion and gearing (etc.); a fine Telescope with stand in a Mahogany case; Capital Marble Chimney Pieces; Full Register Grates and Kitchen Fire Ranges.

CHAPTER 8

LEGENDS, CURIOSITIES & AMUSING TALES

OLD MARY FROM RIVINGTON

In the days of the Rev. James Grimshaw (1778-1782) an old lady called Mary, and her dog, used to come from Rivington, a distance of 8 miles or more, to worship each Sunday at the Chapel. A suitable place was provided in the pew for the dog during the service. One Sunday morning Mary was late. The minister had taken his text and got nearly through the introduction, when she walked in. He paused in his sermon and said, "Mary, your mind has been here long before your body this morning. I know you like to hear about Jesus Christ." Looking up in his face she replied "Aye, I do." Then for Mary's benefit he gave out his text afresh, and recommended his sermon. Another Sunday she was unable to come on account of sickness. The day was terribly wet, but the dog came alone; and some of the good people at the Chapel at once wrote down the text, tied it round the dog's neck and sent it home to comfort the good old woman. She was afterwards interred in the east doorway of the Chapel and one old lady to whom Mary was known, in entering the Chapel would never set foot upon the flag which marked her last resting place, but always stepped aside. It is said that the dog continued to come alone long after her death.

ANOTHER DOG STORY

It is said that a dog connected with Duck Hall, formerly the house occupied by one, Jeremiah Gregson (1802-1869), was a regular visitor to the Chapel. When the people rose to sing the dog put its front feet on the book board and joined in most energetically. The owner, on one occasion, thinking it an annoyance in the service, shut it up in the house, but it managed to escape through a window behind the house and howled at the Chapel doors until admitted.

THE USEFUL APPLE TREE

Writing in 1886 Nightingale quoted the following story: "Fifty years ago there lived in Tockholes one concerning whom the following particulars are curious and interesting. In her youth she set the pip of an apple, which had been roasted, and it grew. For some reason her leg had afterwards to be amputated and the tree which had grown out of her apple pip was cut down and made into a wooden leg for her. Moreover, it was always said that she had twice one and twenty children* of whom two were born on one day, two baptised on one day, two married on one day, two died on one day and two buried on one day. Four of her daughters afterwards married six brothers of another family. She was interred at the old chapel, February 7 1853 aged 69 years. *(NB the only burial recorded in the Chapel Register around this date is for an Agnes Brindle interred 6th February*

(The above stories were taken from Nightingale's 250 Years of Nonconformity)

1853, but the news report of the Blackburn Standard *1842 confirms this name)*

* A common expression about Tockholes. When a person had twenty one children, if one died and she had another, she was said to have had twice one and twenty.

RACING IN TOCKHOLES

Whit Tuesdays in Tockholes were celebrated by the Dissenters of the village with Services held in the Chapel and Ministers from all parts were accustomed to attending, especially students from Blackburn Academy. But the day was far from being a religious holiday. The road from The Rock Inn to Silk Hall was one mass of stalls, and *'sin and intemperance abounded'*. Closely associated with this event were the Tockholes Races. The races are thought to have been instituted by a member of the Brock Hollinshead family, *'a family much addicted to field sports'*. The course in 1843 was over several rough pastures, crossed at right angles by a deep old lane, covered with water to the depth of a foot and flanked on either side by rough stone walls. The competitors were the young farmers of the district, mounted on their own nags, all of whom completed the course without a fall. A foot race, open to all natives, concluded the sports which attracted numbers of idlers from Blackburn and Darwen, for whose provision also a sort of fair was held in the village.

TOCKHOLES RACES.—Thursday last was a day of rare fun at Tockholes, the farmers of the neighbourhood having assembled in goodly array for the purpose of trying the mettle of some of their nags over the stone walls which are rather numerous in that district. The place selected for the races could not have been more judiciously chosen, not the least admirable portion of it being a lane, which crossed the course at right angles, having on each side a rough stone wall and being covered with water to the depth of about a foot, into which the Nimrods of Tockholes plunged their steeds like "good uns," even at the risk of wet jackets. We are glad, however, to say that not even one rider had his courage cooled by a tumble into the liquid element, all getting across the lane in good style. The day, after a thunder shower or two had fallen, was truly a beautiful May day, and never did the sun shine brighter over the delightful scenery by which the race course was surrounded. After several spiritedly contested races (a foot race winding up the amusements) the merry throng separated highly gratified with their day's fun. Five horses, belonging respectively to Mr. H. Wortenworth, Mr. E. Kellet, Mr. Whalley, and Mr. Townley, started for the first race, which was won by Mr. H. Wortenworth's. For the second race four horses started.—Won by Mr. Whalley's b. g. Chance. The third race was for a sweepstakes of £2 each, and was won by Mr. Hollinshead's b. m. Vixen.

A FAMILY AFFAIR

From the Blackburn Standard 10th May 1843

One anecdote for a church baptism recalls that the child's father played the organ, his grandfather sat in the choir, his great grandfather sat as church warden and his great, great uncle would have been there but for illness - and he turned up the following week!

THE 'WISHING' WELL & HOLLINSHEAD AREA

It has been claimed that there is an air of mystery about the Well in the grounds of Hollinshead Hall and that it has a ghost. Indeed, there are several fanciful tales connected with the Hall and the Well told in the 1948 book *"The Wishing Well – A Story of the Withnell Moorlands" by A Moorland Lad (i.e. P. Robinson of Brinscall).* One such story concerns the doomed love affair between a Hollinshead son and a maid from a neighbouring hamlet. The affair was strongly disapproved of and forbidden by the lad's father and on discovering that the pair were still meeting, the father locked the lad in the Well house overnight as a punishment, but in the morning the young man was totally deranged and incoherent. In such a state he galloped through the Valley and was shot at and injured by the maid's father. He lived to tell the tale but the maid and her child died in childbirth.

A similar tale of unrequited love concerns a young woman whose father forbade the relationship and in his despondency the young man hung himself on a tree close to the place where the lovers usually met.

Yet another tale concerns the two builders who were dismantling the Hall in January 1912. They were forced to stay overnight in the Well house due to a severe snowstorm and allegedly one of them saw many ghosts during the night. All knelt at the Well to pray and gave the sign of the Cross. The first was a girl of about 18 praying for the safety of her lover who had sailed to a far off western land; the second was a man dressed as a cavalier at the time of Charles I and he prayed for success in forthcoming battles; the third was another woman of about 25 dressed in C18th costume and speaking in a Scottish accent praying that the "troubled times" would soon pass. The fourth and fifth were a young bridal couple praying for long lasting happiness; next came a very old man praying to be able to look upon the face of his love one more time and lo and behold – who should appear but his long lost love. Finally two boys appeared swearing eternal friendship and devotion to each other. One of the boys had apparently appeared to the builders whilst they were working earlier that day. The writer then linked the first three mentioned 'ghosts' firstly to the lover having sailed for America on the Mayflower; secondly to the Civil War Battles of Marston Moor and Naseby; and thirdly the possibility of the young woman being Flora MacDonald praying for the safety of Bonnie Prince Charlie. Quite a dream! So whose ghost is it that allegedly still appears?

MOLE HILLS

Several years ago there lived in the Village a delightful, elderly man with a very sweet and trusting nature. He was a keen gardener and was horrified to discover that moles were destroying his beloved allotment. He discussed the problem in the pub with his friends and was given advice on how to get rid of the moles and was also given the loan of a mole trap. A week later he had had no success, so back to the pub he went, bemoaning the fact that the moles were still wreaking havoc. Later that night two well known local jokers decided they would 'help' out, so they acquired a dead mole from one of their own traps and 'planted' it the empty one and awaited the reaction next day. Needless to say our gardener was delighted when he thought he had finally caught the culprit, and even more so when he found another the next day and yet another the day after! He still did not suspect anything when on the fourth day he discovered two moles, nose to nose in the same trap! He never did find out about the joke played on him, but he never had any more mole trouble.

HOW TO GET TO HEAVEN?

Nearly 30 years ago a local granddad was looking after his three year old grandson for a while and decided that he would take the child with him when he went to see how his son was progressing with the digging of a new grave in the churchyard. There were endless questions from the grandson about what the grave was for and what happened at a funeral etc, so granddad explained fully telling the child that after someone died there was a service, then they were buried and their spirit went to heaven, but he was rather taken aback when asked "Do they skin 'em first?" Having been brought up on a farm the boy obviously thought this process was normal procedure, much to granddad's amusement.

When about the same age the same grandson was caught furiously stirring the water in the farmyard well into which he had popped some very young pups. When asked what he was doing he replied "I'm teaching 'em to swim, Granddad". The pups were all retrieved safe and sound.

LYONS DEN

About 1700 a man called John Lyons made his home on the moors south of Tockholes. Legend says that he never came into any local village and acquired such a mysterious reputation that eventually three local men, William Shorrock, Andrew Duxbury and Ralph Almond

Ruins of Lyon's Den 2002

143

went to see what they could find out about him. When they located his dwelling they found it was a sod hut, and at their shouts Lyon came crawling out on all fours. This gave rise to the name 'Lyon's Den'

Lyon, it seems, was an immensely strong man with a 'mane' of thick red hair.

Originally from Westhoughton, he was rarely seen locally because he preferred to buy his needs in Preston, reputedly carrying 100lb sacks of grain home on his back. Later he sold his farm to Henry Shuttleworth and moved on to what came to be known as Old Lyons Farm, eventually selling this, too, and moving to Walton-le-Dale, where he died, leaving a daughter. In due course, Old Lyons was purchased by James Grime, once the owner of Bobbin Hall, where he made wooden rollers for Hilton's Paper Mill.

OLD AGGIE'S

This property is just within the Darwen boundary, but as it is so near Tockholes and of such interest it was considered fitting to include it.

The legend of 'Old Aggie's' taken from the *"Blackburn Times"* of Friday 14th October 1949:

"Old Aggie's, a cottage on Darwen moors, was the scene of a murder. It was here, the story goes, that one night "Old Aggie" was killed and robbed of her money and belongings after a party of men had burst in through her door.

The men 'celebrated' the success of their crime at an inn in the locality where their free-spending aroused suspicion and finally brought them to justice.

The cottage is also known as "Step Back" and it is believed to have derived this name from a phrase – "Step back. Go no further." – attributed to Cromwell.

Once a refreshment house and a favourite rendezvous for picknickers, "Old Aggie's" is now an empty desolate-looking building on the slope of a gorge and lies wide of Victoria Jubilee Tower on the way to the upper reaches of Tockholes."

The remains of the cottage, built against the steep banking of the gorge, can still be seen at Stepback Clough on the walk towards Darwen Tower via the path leading from Hollinshead Terrace. All that remains is the outline of the house, one corner of the building which still stands about 4 feet high, and heaps of stones that once formed the house. Aggie's ghost is still said to walk there – or so the legend goes.

The Census Return of 1841 shows a brother and sister, Evan and Agnes Marsden, aged 44 and 46 respectively, both unmarried, living at Step Back at that time. With them lived three nephews and two nieces between the ages of 13 and 26. The eldest, James, was a Gamekeeper, Evan was a Farmer of 15 acres and the remaining members of the household were listed as Cotton Weavers. By 1851 only one nephew, George, and one niece, Mary, remained living with their Aunt and Uncle, all still in their same occupations except George who was now described as 'Servant'. Evan and Agnes stated their place of birth as Blackburn. There is no

Lyon's Den - Date Unknown

Ruins of Old Aggie's – (Route of New Gas Pipe Line can be cleary seen in background)

The Late Daring Burglary at Over Darwen

At the South Lancashire Assizes before Mr. Justice Keating, John Doran, 20, Thomas Atkinson, 22 and John Warden[9], 23, were charged with burglariously entering the house of John Singleton on the 5th of November last. The prosecutor and his wife were very old people and kept a small farm near Over Darwen. On the night referred to, they made up their house and went to bed as usual. After they had been a short time asleep, they were awoke by a noise in the lower part of the house. When the old man lighted a candle, three men entered their room, one having a gun and another a hammer with which they threatened to kill the old couple unless they delivered up the money that was in the house. They (the prisoners) told the old lady that they would allow her five minutes to pray before they murdered her. She became very much alarmed and directed them to a box in which was deposited a five-pound note, which they took as well as a small bottle of whisky. The old man, being also terrified, gave up his purse containing 17s 6d. The prisoners, who were known to be poor, were seen after the robbery to have money in considerable sums. The prosecution called a number of witnesses to prove the case as alleged. Mr. Kaye prosecuted and Messrs. Pope and Torr defended Atkinson and Warden; Doran had no counsel. It was strongly urged by Mr. Torr that the candle lighted by the prosecutor and the candle of the thieves having been both extinguished during the confusion which ensued on the entrance of the prisoners, there seemed not to be a sufficient identification. Mr. Pope urged that the £5 note found upon one of the prisoners, not being proved to be the note stolen, was no evidence of the prisoners' connection with the robbery and that, though 17s. 6d was the sole amount of money stolen, the prisoners, when drinking together afterwards, were seen not only in possession of the note but of two sovereigns. All the prisoners were found guilty. Doran and Atkinson were each sentenced to 20 years penal servitude and Warden to 10 years similar punishment.

mention of the property being licensed premises or Refreshments Rooms. Could this Agnes be the lady around whom the legend began.

The next Census of 1861 shows new occupants at Step Back, one of them being another Agnes. This time Agness* (*sic) Singleton and her husband, John, both aged 66 years and both born in Over Darwen. He is described as a Farmer of 4 acres and she, as Farmer's wife. Again, there is no mention of licensed premises or refreshment rooms, but the following accounts from the *Blackburn Standard* certainly give credence to the legend of an attack on an 'Old Aggie', although not a murder.

Wednesday 14th November 1860
Burglary at Darwen

*At the Darwen Petty Sessions on Monday, before J. Shorrock Esq., Revs. E.C. Montriou and P. Graham, John Doran, *John Steudney and Thomas Atkinson were charged with burglariously entering the house of John Singleton of Step Back, on the 5th of November; and, after searching the house and committing assaults upon the persons of Mr. & Mrs. Singleton, left. They were apprehended by the police and taken before the justices and remanded till Monday, when they were fully committed to take their trial at the next Liverpool Assizes. The court was crowded during the hearing of the case.*

---

[9] *There appears to have been some confusion over the name of the third man accused. Perhaps he initially gave a false name to the Police, or it was later discovered to have been another man.*

Old Aggie's – date unknown

Some 50 years after the attack on the Singletons a newspaper article appeared in the local press about a "Chair with a History" and showing a picture of the chair in question. It was reputed *"to have been in the possession of the Marsden family for over 800 years and was associated with "Old Aggy" of Stepback, for in it she died, her death probably being hastened by the savage assault made on her in 1860 by two men, who received long terms of imprisonment. Many offers have been made for it, but the present owner, Mr. George K. Marsden of Hope-street, Darwen, declines them all, saying it must be handed down from one generation to another."*

Several months after this article, Mr. George Marsden's obituary appeared in the *Darwen News* and by this time the ancient chair was now only 200 years old:

The *Darwen News* of Saturday 31st August 1912:

The Late Mr. *J. K. Marsden (*sic)

The funeral took place on Wednesday at the Darwen Cemetery of Mr. George Kay Marsden, of Hope Street, who was well known locally. Deceased gentleman was 76 years of age and he died in Blackburn Infirmary from an internal complaint on Saturday morning last. In his younger days, Mr. Marsden was connected with the Ancient Order of Shepherds and was treasurer of the organisation for 25 years. He passed through all the offices and received a certificate of merit. Deceased was a nephew of "Old Haggie" of "Stepback" and has left in the possession of the family an old carved chair, quite 200 years old, which formerly belonged to "Old Haggie" and was kept in her cottage.

A further Darwen News report of Saturday 12th October 1929 recorded the funeral of an *"Old Darwen Native – Mrs. Saward & Her Recollections"* as follows:

The funeral took place at the Cemetery on Wednesday of Mrs. Nancy Saward, an old Darwen resident, who lived at 2 Church-terrace up to the time she went to reside at Honister-avenue, Blackpool. She was 88 years of age and was the widow of Mr. Robert Townsend Saward, a well-known officer in the Volunteers at one time, who died 25 years ago. Mrs. Saward was born in 1841 in a house which stood in Bentley's woodyard, the site of which is now covered by the Market Buildings. The river ran by the house and she could remember seeing the furniture, chairs, tables and even cradles carried past on the flood of water which came from the Bold Venture reservoir when it burst (on 3rd August 1848). One of her early recollections was when she was required to give evidence at Liverpool Assizes. A woman known as "Old Aggie" was robbed and Mrs. Saward, whose parents at that time kept the Greenway Arms, served the thieves with beer on the evening before the robbery, and they had no money to pay for it. The next morning they had money and the evidence she gave at their trial was to this effect. The deceased lady left Darwen to become matron of the Whitechapel Workhouse (London) and later moved to a similar position at Gayton Workhouse, near Sandringham, and could remember seeing the late King Edward, when he was Prince of Wales, on many occasions. The funeral service was conducted by the Rev. F. G. Hurst, vicar of St. Cuthbert's. The body was brought from Blackpool for interment here. She left no family."

146

The 1851 Census confirms that a John Bentley resided at The Greenway Arms in Duckworth Street, Darwen, with his family, including a daughter Nancy aged 9 years.

So which Agnes is it around which the legend revolves – or is she one and the same person – both women being the same age? Perhaps Miss Agnes Marsden married John Singleton late in life, but not if the places of birth stated on the Census Returns are to be believed. Maybe the place should best be remembered as at one time being a Mecca to many local people seeking fresh air and relaxation on the moors, who called for teas and refreshments well into the 1950's. Certainly a Mr. Potter, writing to the Darwen News from Bristol in 1898, recalled the many happy hours he spent there in his younger days when he composed the following poem:

"Old Aggie's Cottage still I view

With brightly sanded floor,

And rosy maids with laughing free

Come peeping at the door

The ample table laid for tea

For many a happy pair,

And dried oatcake and buttermilk,

And sweet Elysian fare.

And then we join the merry dance,

And merry games we play:

Stands the old cottage where it did,

On the rough moorland now?"

Above information from the Darwen Reference Library

147

CHAPTER 9

VARIOUS NEWS REPORTS

Blackburn Mail 26th June 1802

Coal Mines in Tockholes and Sharples to be sold or let. In the estate of John Hollinshead, worked by Messrs. Heys & Co.

Blackburn Mail 1803

Hollinshead Hall for sale. In occupation of Edmund Charnley. Apply Lawrence Brock-Hollinshead of Chorley.

Blackburn Mail 1805

Collections were made after the Battle of Trafalgar for 'Patriotic Fund'. Tockholes collected £18.10s.0d. and Darwen Chapel £17.8s.0d.

Blackburn Mail 24th June 1816

SALE AT TOCKHOLES, Lot 2. A valuable estate called **WHITBANK** in the occupation of **THOMAS LEIGH**, Farmhouse & buildings, garden, orchard and 7 closes of Rich Land within a ring 8a 1r 8p

Blackburn Mail 1825

FOR SALE at Tockholes **CHAPELS FARM** with Warehouse suitable for manufacture. Milk and butter may be disposed of in the neighbourhood.

Blackburn Gazette 1832

Lawrence Brock-Hollinshead made a J.P. He was about to move into this area from Cheshire

Blackburn Gazette 2nd November 1837

Sale of furniture at Pickering Fold. *(Wm. Pickering of Pickering Fold, and donor of the land upon which the present church stands, had died October 21st 1837 aged 85 years)*

Blackburn Standard 4th November 1840

PRIZE FIGHT - One of those exhibitions which seem to be coming to greater vogue than that in which they have been in the last few years, viz a prize fight, took place last Monday morning at an early hour, in the township of Tockholes, between two young men of this town, named respectively Mills and Grundy. The stake was £5, £2.10s.0d. a-side. We believe the parties fought nearly an hour at the end of which period Mills had contrived to mill his adversary.

Blackburn Standard 11th November 1840

Letter to the Editor: Sir – You will oblige me by correcting a misstatement which appeared in your last week's journal, relative to a prize fight which is said to have "taken place on Monday morning last in the township of Tockholes" and at an "early hour". No such brutal exhibition took place therein. The fighters, I believe, never made their appearance. The very respectable landlord of the Rock Inn having given information to the constable of the township, by his activity the fight was stopped in Tockholes, but I am given to understand it took place afterwards in the township of Lower Darwen.

Yours obediently,

T.C.

Tockholes Nov. 7 1840

> **"TO BE SOLD BY AUCTION,
> SILK HALL in TOCKHOLES** near
> Blackburn, on Thursday the 8th of **MAY**
> next
> A Quantity of **MACHINERY,** consisting of
> Carding Engines, Roving Billies, Mules, Spinning
> Jennies and a Devit
> Also a Parcel of Carpenters' Tools, Stoves etc. etc.
> Further Particulars may be had by applying to James
> Walkden in Darwen-street, Blackburn, Auctioneer."
>
> **Blackburn Mail 30th April 1794**

Blackburn Standard 1841

FARM known as **LION'S DEN, TOCKHOLES, FOR SALE**: 7 tons prime hay, 50 tons lime and soil, brown mare, cart and household furniture. Property of William Hodson.

Blackburn Standard 1842

AGNES BRINDLE of Tockholes, reported as having had twenty children, ten boys and ten girls. There were some strange coincidences as two were born on the same day, two christened on the same day, two married on the same day, and two buried on the same day. During her lifetime Agnes had a leg amputated and the wooden leg she used was made from an apple tree she had planted at the time of her marriage.

Blackburn Standard 1842

2000 people were present at Tockholes Whit Monday sports. Steeplechases for sovereigns given by Brock Hollinshead. (Brock-Hollinshead was a considerable rider himself, often winning races in the area)

Blackburn Standard 1843

Blackburn Steeplechase, run in the area of the Bonny Inn, Salesbury. 25,000 spectators. Four Races. Brock-Hollinshead won one, came 2nd in another in spite of turning a complete somersault. It was hoped this steeplechase would be a regular event.

Blackburn Standard 15th March 1846

James Mason of Bury Fold, Darwen, was killed whilst walking over Tockholes Moor when he fell into a badly covered coal-pit.

Blackburn Standard March 25th 1846

On Thursday last, J. Hargreaves Esq. held an Inquest at the Rock public house, Tockholes, on view of the body of **Richard Crook**, aged two years, who was burned to death in consequence of having been carelessly left by his mother in a room with a fire in it. A verdict of "Accidental Death" was returned.

Blackburn Standard 14th May 1851

John Horsfield of Tockholes, aged 1 year 2 weeks, died when accidentally dropped by his brother, aged 10.

Blackburn Standard 9th November 1851

A 14 year old was found at Tockholes with illicit spirit. He was not far from the coal pit where he worked. He had no father or mother and was fined £25, withdrawn if he said whose liquor it was.

Blackburn Standard 1856

HIGHER HILL ESTATE FOR SALE. Farm in occupation of Richard Catterall. Three dwellinghouses at Lower Hill, with weaving shops. One house and weaving shop at the Bottoms. A house and weaving shop at Higher Hill.

Blackburn Standard 1857

FINE PETER'S HOUSE and Orchard for sale. Cottage, warehouse, barn, shippon etc. Pickering Fields, Greenhill, Howcroft. Factory on land. Lodges, gasometer etc. Good for coal.

Blackburn Standard 1859

Partnership of Nicholas Fish Snr. And Nicholas Fish Jnr. in **Old Lion's Colliery**, dissolved. Son dropped out.

Blackburn Times 1867

Elizabeth Marsden, Halliwell Farm, Tockholes, threw her illegitimate child into the lodge on the farm. Her father and Thomas Leigh and John Waring rushed to help, but were too late. She had tried before. Elizabeth was unable to tell the time or count money.

Blackburn Times 1868

Procession of 350, with banner, at St. Stephen's Church. Drum and fife band. The field for sports was lent by Mr. Coar of Yew Tree Farm, Livesey, who also gave 100 quarts of milk for the children. Thomas Ratcliffe of Livesey took the chair and there was tea, followed by glees from the choir. The vicar, Rev. Charles Hughes, spoke.

Blackburn Times March 1872

Victoria Mill Tockholes for sale. East side of road to Bolton. Power Looms and four cottages.

Darwen News 1892

TO LET MILL HOUSE or **SLIPPER LOWE FARM, TOCKHOLES** – about 34 acres. Apply W. T. Ashton

Darwen News 1892

CROW TREES FARM, TOCKHOLES on Friday next 11th November 1892 at 1 o'clock. **SALE by AUCTION** as above of farm stock, implements, furniture, hay etc. for Mr. Andrew Knowles. Eli Smith, Auctioneers, Feniscowles.

Darwen News 1895

UNDER Deed of Assignment **GORSE FARM** adjoining the Church, Tockholes, Nr. Darwen. On Monday next 29th April 1895 at 2 o'clock prompt **WILLIAM SMITH** will sell by **AUCTION** as above, entirely without reserve, farming implements, dairy utensils, household furniture, ground mow of capital hay, etc. Auctioneer, Feniscowles, Blackburn.

Darwen News 19th September 1908

TO LET GREENTHORNE FARM. 17 acres. Mr. J. H. Lofthouse is declining farming. Talbot, Richmond Terrace, Blackburn

Darwen News 1915

Robert Brownlow died. For many years he had leased Lion's Den Colliery, then took to farming. The colliery was reached by a road from the 'Finger Post'.

MATTERS BEFORE THE COURTS

June 1810

James Barker of Tockholes was committed for trial accused of stealing 13 pieces of white calico, the property of Greenway & Potter of Over Darwen.

From Blackburn Mail December 15th 1824

ESCAPED from the hulks at Woolwich THOMAS BARON late of Tockholes in the County of Lancaster who was convicted of Felony at the Quarter Sessions holden at Preston in April last and ordered to be transported for 7 years. He was born at Withnell and is by trade a weaver, is 26 years of age and in height 5' 4½". Hair dark, eyes black, complexion dark. All constable and peace officers are requested to use their best endeavours to discover and apprehend the said Thomas Baron and to lodge him in any of his majesties gaols or prisons and to give information thereof to me. All reasonable expenses will be paid.

J. Gorst, Deputy Clerk of the Peace, Preston. 5th December 1824.

Blackburn Mail 1826

CASE FROM THE MOUNTAINS OF TOCKHOLES

'Partook of the unordered character of the inhabitants of those parts'

Two men, Bamford and Turner, were fighting in the nude, near the Rock on December 26th. Another man called Hawkins intervened so they set on him. All drunk. Case dismissed.

Blackburn Standard 1841

Henry Cottam of Over Darwen held a Temperance Meeting at Tockholes. It was interrupted by a gang who burst in with blackened faces and carrying scythes, spades and bludgeons. A blow was aimed at Cottam with the scythe. As a result James Morrell, John Aspden, John Aspinall, Thomas Kershaw, William Hargreaves and James Nightingale of Tockholes were fined £5 each, with alternative of two months in gaol.

Blackburn Standard August 1846

A group of some 50 Darwen Pitmen set off for Tockholes in search of 'Bobby Bloom'. His real name was Robert Aspden, so that the nickname suggests some effeminacy. They reached the Blackburn Bull, where they drank heavily and danced, having, it seems, forgotten why they had set out. They created so much disturbance that it was necessary for P.C. 73 to turn them out. They vowed the destruction of the police and pelted him with stones. Several were later ordered to give sureties for their good behaviour.

Blackburn Standard 1848

James Smith, a Tockholes Publican, was fined for allowing men to play cards in his Inn.

Blackburn Standard 1851

Nancy Warburton of Tockholes fined £5 for altering her child's birth certificate to allow her to obtain work in a mill. The factory inspector asked the magistrates to forego the fine as she had a sick husband and four other children and was extremely poor. The bench agreed.

Blackburn Standard 1853

Assault on Police Constable at Rock Inn. P.C. Greaves was attacked by Thomas Walsh, Henry Aspden, James Brindle and William Bradley. The charge was dismissed with costs, as Superintendent Sheppard of the County Constabulary said Tockholes was the best conducted township in his area.

Blackburn Standard 1856

William Farnworth of Tockholes stole mint from the garden of John Duxbury, Knowle Fold, Darwen (The Duke of Darren). He was not prosecuted but always thereafter known as 'Mint Billy'. He was later transported for another offence, to Bermuda. Some years later was reported back living in Edgeworth.

Blackburn Times September 1873

James Marsden set a sheep dog on the three Misses Bradshaw, in Tockholes. Marsden and two others were *'about to take hold of one sister'* when Miss Bradshaw the eldest said she would call the police. Hence the dog was released. Miss Bradshaw's tunic was ruined. The owner of the dog, one of James Marsden's companions, was fined 40 shillings.

Blackburn Times 23rd May 1874

Residents near the Royal were fined for polluting the stream to the Reservoir. The fine was One Shilling plus 20 shillings per day until the pollution stopped

Blackburn Standard August 1877

Failure of Eccles Shorrock, Bro. & Co. in business at Over Darwen and Tockholes. Liabilities £110,000

Blackburn Standard 2nd July 1892

BREACH of the FACTORY ACT at TOCKHOLES:

On Thursday, at Darwen County Police Court, the Hollins Head Mill Company, Limited, Tockholes, were summoned for a breach of the Factory and Workshops Act, committed on May 27th. Mr. J. Birtwistle, H.M. Inspector, said on the date named he visited the mill and found that the engine was not stopped until 5.38 p.m., eight minutes after the recognised stopping time. There were ten summonses against the defendants, who pleased guilty, and said the clock was wrong. In one case a fine of 20s. and costs was imposed, and, in the nine other case the defendants were ordered to pay costs.

Blackburn Standard 2nd July 1892

OFFENCES AGAINST THE GAME LAWS AT TOCKHOLES

John Longworth, 31 Gillibrand-street, and Alfred Lightbown, Argyle-street, were summoned before the Darwen County Magistrates for having committed a breach of the Game Laws at Tockholes on the 14th inst. The evidence showed that on the date named, P.C. Fenwick saw the two defendants on land belonging to the Marquess de Rothwell, which is preserved. He afterwards followed them and found a live rabbit in their possession. The defendants, who said the offence was not committed intentionally, were each fined 1s. and costs.

Blackburn Standard 22nd October 1892

BREACHES OF THE FACTORY ACT AT TOCKHOLES

At Darwen on Thursday the Hollins Head Mill

Company, Tockholes, were summoned for having committed breaches of the Factory and Workshops' Act (1878). Mr. Birtwistle, H.M. Inspector, conducted the prosecution. In one case the defendants were summoned for employing a child without having obtained from the school teacher a certificate as to the child's attendance. Since the summons was issued the school attendance had been proved and Mr. Birtwistle only asked for costs. In three other cases the defendants were summoned for employing children who had not passed the doctor. The defendants' manager pleaded guilty, and the Bench imposed finds of 20s. and costs in two cases and costs in the other two.

Blackburn Standard 20th January 1894

ALLEGED BAD MEAT AT TOCKHOLES

SERIOUS CHARGE AGAINST A BEERHOUSE KEEPER

At Darwen County Police Court on Thursday, John Aspin, landlord of the Quarrymen's Arms, Tockholes, was summoned for having, on the 13th inst, had on his premises in preparation for sale a quantity of diseased beef, and also for having on the same date sold 18lbs of diseased beef. Mr. R. C. Radcliffe conducted the prosecution on behalf of the Rural Sanitary Authority and the police. The defendant was represented by Mr. Broadbent. Mr. Radcliffe stated that on January 10th, John Samuel Taylor, a farmer of Tockholes, had a cow about 2½ years old which had been ailing for some time. In consequence of something which was said to him by his son, he had the cow turned into the yard, when he found that it was in such a state that he shot it. Shortly afterwards, when Taylor was on his way to the knacker's yard at Blackburn he met the defendant. He told Aspin that he had shot a cow which had gone wrong, and the defendant asked him what he would take for it. Taylor replied "10s. or 12s." Aspin then said that

IF THE ANIMAL WERE IN FAIR CONDITION

he would give him 10s. for it. Taylor accepted the offer, and did not proceed to Blackburn. The carcase was removed from the farm the same day, and on the 13th it was discovered that the defendant had dressed it and had it prepared for human food. On that day police officers found eleven pieces of the carcase in the defendant's house and Dr. Armitage, who had examined the meat, said that it was unfit for food. The defendant had sold some of the meat at 5½d. and 6d. per lb. Ellen Wearing, a married woman, said that she purchased 4 lbs of flat ribs from the defendant, for which she paid 6½d. per lb. Shortly after they had partaken of the meat both she and her husband complained of being ill. When they ate it their tongues became swollen. James Clough, a weaver, said that he purchased 7 lbs of meat at 6d. per lb from the defendant. He ate some of it. Mr. Radcliffe: "What were the effects?". Witness "I cannot tell. They may come yet." Margaret Thomas, widow, of Ryal's Farm, said that she

PURCHASED 6LBS OF THE BEEF

at 5d. per lb. The defendant told her that he had killed the cow in his madness. John Aspin, who purchased 3¾lbs of beef for 1s. 10½d. said he ate a small portion, which he considered good meat. Mark Turner, butcher, of Livesey, spoke to having dressed the carcase on the 10th inst. for the defendant. He might have told Aspin that the meat was fit to eat. P.C. Nevison stated that he visited the Quarrymen's Arms at 11.15 on Saturday night and asked Aspin whether he had anything left of the carcase he had purchased from Taylor. Aspin replied, "What beef I have in the house I intend to destroy with my own hands." Witness then searched the house and in the parlour found a small piece of beef wrapped in paper. In a boiler in the kitchen he also found 11 pieces of meat. P.C. Fenwick, by whom Nevison was accompanied to the Quarrymen's Arms, stated that Aspin said in answer to a question, "The meat is good, and I ate some myself." Inspector Whittaker gave formal evidence as to a magistrate having ordered the meat to be destroyed. Dr. Armitage, Medical Officer of Health for the borough, said that he had examined the meat which was found in the defendant's house and also four pieces which had been sold by the defendant. The whole of the meat was thoroughly diseased. It was dark in colour

SOFT, FLABBY AND SLIMY.

On the piece which had been purchase by Mrs. Wearing there were two tubercles of moderate size, which proved conclusively that the cow had suffered from tuberculosis. Mr. Broadbent, for the defence, raised a technical objection. He contended that the meat ought to be examined by a medical officer or nuisance inspector at the place where it was deposited or exposed, and that it could be seized after such examination. As this had not been done in this case the summons ought to be dismissed. The magistrates retired to consider the objection and not feeling justified in giving a decision that day adjourned the case for a week.

Blackburn Standard 27th January 1894

THE TOCKHOLES DISEASED MEAT PROSECUTION

Collapse of the Case

On Thursday at the Darwen County Police Court, the case of the Police v. Aspin was again before the Magistrates (Messrs. C. Shorrock and R. H. Eccles). A week ago James Aspin who is the Landlord at the Quarryman's Arms, Tockholes, was summonsed for having diseased beef on his premises in preparation for the sale and also for having sold 18lbs of diseased beef. At the conclusion of the case for the Prosecution, Mr. Broadbent took a preliminary objection that inasmuch as the meat was not examined either by the Medical Officer or Nuisance Inspector at the place where it was deposited or exposed (the defendant's house) the Prosecution must fail. The Magistrates adjourned the case for a week in order that the point might be considered and this morning Mr. R. C. Radcliffe who concluded the prosecution on behalf of the Police and the Rural Sanitary Authority, stated that he had considered the effect of the case quoted by Mr. Broadbent and he now asked the Bench to allow the summonses to be withdrawn, but at the same time he felt that his Authority and the public were indebted to the Police for the course they had taken. Mr. Broadbent objected to these general remarks, and a little later Mr. Radcliffe stated that upon the facts of the case there could be no dispute whatever. Mr. Broadbent:- "I must protest against this. I had a strong and complete defence on the merits. I do not want to say any more." The magistrates said they would allow the Summonses to be withdrawn.

Darwen Post 27th April 1899

TOCKHOLES LANDLADY FINED

The Bona-Fide Traveller Question

At the County Police Court, on Thursday, before Mr. J. Dimmock (chairman) and Mr. L. H. Wraith, Ellen Haydock, who keeps the Victoria Inn, Tockholes, was charged with selling during prohibited hours; and James McKenna, John Durkin, both labourers, of Clarence Street, Darwen and John Durkin (sic) of 12 Penny Street, Blackburn, were charged with unlawfully being on licensed premises. Mr. Broadbent defended Mrs. Haydock. P.C. Bailey stated that he, in company with P.C. Hoole, visited the house about noon on Sunday, the 8th inst. The defendant's son let them in and he asked him if they had any travellers in the house. He replied that they had three in the bar parlour from Moulden Hall, near Feniscowles. They went into the room and found the men, each with a pint pot containing beer in front of him. On asking them where they came from McKenna said from 96 Clayton Street, Bolton Road, Darwen and John Durkin gave the name of John Larkin, saying that he resided at the same place. William Durkin said "same place." McKenna afterwards said "we might as well tell the truth." They then gave their correct names and addresses. He called Haydock's attention to the men, and said all of the men told him that they came from Moulden Hall. McKenna replied that they said they came from Bolton-road. Cross-examined by Mr. Broadbent, the witness said when the landlady's son began to question them, after they had asked to be admitted, as to where they came from, they told him they were police officers, and he at once admitted them. That was neither his nor P.C. Hoole's beat, but they knew the district. Mrs. Haydock was evidently much troubled about the affair, and he believed he gave her to understand that he thought the men had tried to deceive her. Superintendent Myers said Mrs. Haydock had taken no steps to summon the men for deceiving her. P.C. Hoole corroborated the last witness's statement. Mr. W. Stubbs, borough surveyor, said that he had measured the distance from the Victoria Inn, Tockholes to Clarence Street and to Moulden Hall. To Clarence Street the distance was one mile 1240 yards, and to Moulden Hall two miles 1323 yards. Mr. Broadbent for the defence said there was an exception in the Act of Parliament protecting licensed victuallers in cases of this kind, which was contained in the 10th section of the Licensing Act, under which the defendant was summoned. It was to the effect that if in the course of hearing the information it appeared to the satisfaction of the magistrates that the licensed victualler truly believed that the person whom he served was in fact a bona-fide traveller within the meaning of the Act, the person charged was entitled to an acquittal. He thought it was clear beyond all question that these men were not bona-fide travellers, whether they had come from Moulden Hall or Clarence Street, but that did not affect the case in relation to Mrs. Haydock, who at the time she served them believed they had come three miles and were entitled to be served with refreshments. Mrs. Haydock had kept the house over seven years in an irreproachable manner, and he did not think there was a better conducted house in the district. Mr. Jas. W. Haydock, a gas inspector in the employ of the Blackburn Corporation, gave evidence similar to that of the constables, but said he believed that Moulden Hall, Feniscowles, was three miles away from the house. Mrs. Haydock also gave evidence. All the defendants pleaded guilty. The Chairman said with reference to Mrs. Haydock the case was not a serious one, but still they thought it was within the power of the landlady to have ascertained the distance to Moulden Hall. She must have frequent applications from people to be served and ought to know whether people who came from Moulden Hall would be bona-fide travellers. She would be fined 2s. and 6d. and costs, and each of the other defendants would be mulcted in a similar penalty.

OBITUARIES

Blackburn Standard August 1838

DEATH OF L. B. HOLLINSHEAD, ESQ – We regret to announce the sudden death of Lawrence Brock Hollinshead, Esq., of Pendlebury, which took place about two o'clock on Wednesday morning. Mr. Hollinshead was an active and highly respected magistrate for this county, and we believe he was also on the commission for the adjoining county of Chester. On Tuesday he was on the bench at the New Bailey, and heard most of the misdemeanour cases in the new court, while Mr. Maude took the felonies in the old court. On his return home he was attacked with a violent fit of gout to which he was at times subject, and before any relief could be afforded to him the disorder reached his stomach and caused his death. His loss will be severely felt at the New Bailey, where he was a very regular attendant, and where he rendered most valuable assistance to the police magistrate by holding a second court whenever the number of prisoners rendered it necessary. In private life Mr. Hollinshead was highly esteemed by a large circle of friends, and to his family the sudden bereavement will be a source of inexpressible grief. – *Manchester Chronicle*

Blackburn Standard Wednesday March 17, 1858

DEATH OF HENRY BROCK-HOLLINESHEAD ESQ

Death has been again at work in our midst, and has made his desolating presence felt by the sudden cutting down, in the prime of life, of one who was universally esteemed – of one who was as much and deeply beloved by all who had the honour and pleasure of his acquaintance, as he was highly respected by the community at large. We refer to the mournful announcement in our obituary today of the death of Henry Brock-Hollinshead, Esq. of Billinge Scarr, which took place at a little after six o'clock on Sunday morning.

Mr. Hollinshead had been complaining for some weeks of cold and influenza, but so trifling did his ailment appear to himself and his family, that on Sunday week he was in his accustomed place in Trinity Church, accompanied by his children, and enjoying the ministrations of the respected incumbent, whose labours he ever seconded with a liberality which was at times profuse. His cold got worse on Sunday afternoon, and during the week following he was confined to the house, sometimes to his room. It was only on Saturday that dangerous symptoms manifested themselves. On Saturday forenoon he was regarded as really ill; but he rallied in the afternoon and evening, and was much better, when his wife took leave of him about ten o'clock at night. About five o'clock on Sunday morning the nurse by whom he was tended perceived a great change for the worse, and immediately aroused Mrs. Hollinshead, who was instantly at his bedside. He was then insensible, and continued so till he expired at a little after six o'clock.

The suddenness with which the painful event came upon the family prevented their securing the attendance of Mr. Morley, the family surgeon, or the presence of Dr. Robinson, their pastor, whose Christian conversation during the last hours of an ebbing life would have been so consoling to the dying and so comforting to the surviving. Dr. Robinson, however, was apprised of the death early in the morning, and he at once proceeded to Billinge Scarr, which he found to be indeed a house of mourning, and administered those consolations which only religion can impart.

Mr. Hollinshead, who was descended from a very ancient family, was a partner in the firm of Ainsworth, Hollinshead and Kay, solicitors of this town. When the borough was incorporated in 1851, he accepted the office of borough treasurer, the duties of which he discharged till about 12 months ago. He was one of the clerks to the county justices, and he also held the office of clerk to the Darwen Local Board of Health. He was a warden of Holy Trinity Church, in the prosperity of which he always took the greatest interest. In every scheme of benevolence in connection with that church he was foremost with his subscription; and the Sunday scholars will miss the pleasant Whit-Monday treats to which he invited them – frequently having on his meadows at Billinge Scarr as many as a thousand children, in whose sports he joined with a juvenile heartiness, and for whom he generously provided a very highly appreciated feast of coffee and buns. When Dr. Robinson communicated on Sunday last to his Sunday school the mournful tidings that their friend was gone, the loss was instinctively felt to be a grievous one, and many of the scholars sobbed outright. When the parsonage at Trinity Church, which was so much needed, was projected, Mr. Hollinshead became one of the most generous contributors to the fund.

In addition, also, to his uniform liberality in support of the church, he presented at a considerable cost, the handsome reredos which now adorns the communion. By the congregation worshipping in Trinity Church his death will be felt to be a severe loss. The announcement made from the pulpit on Sunday caused a sadness and gloom to over-shadow many countenances.

The poor in the neighbourhood of Billinge Scar found Mr. Hollinshead to be a generous neighbour. In every season of distress his hand was open to supply their wants, and he manifested the greatest interest in everything that tended to their moral and social welfare. He was a liberal supporter of Billinge school, and hundreds will yet remember, and will now recall to mind, the pleasant new year meetings to the hilarity of which the presence of Mr. Hollinshead so much contributed. The deceased was a member of the mystic fraternity, and amongst the brethren held high office, and was much esteemed. In private life he was very much respected. He was a kind and devoted husband; an affectionate father; and a firm and generous friend. He leaves behind him to mourn his loss, a wife and seven children, the youngest of whom is but three weeks old, and a large circle of friends, amongst whom his widow and orphan children will find abundance of the sympathy due to their bereaved condition. The funeral of the deceased takes place on Friday.

Blackburn Standard 7th March 1903

JOHN PICKOP, ESQ.

It is with profound regret that we announce the death of Mr. John Pickop, J.P., which occurred at his residence, "Winston", East Park Road, Blackburn, on Wednesday morning. Mr. Pickop enjoyed considerable popularity amongst all classes of the local community, hence the news of his demise, upon becoming generally known, occasioned universal sorrow and regret. Blackburnians were also surprised to learn of his sudden end, for though it was known to a few that the deceased gentleman had not been well for about a week, anything in the nature of a serious result was never anticipated. Nor apparently did Mr. Pickop himself regard his indisposition as cause for anxiety, for he refused to allow a doctor to be summoned. When Dr. Martin was called in, he found that Mr. Pickop had been dead some hours, probably from heart failure. The flag flying at half-mast over the Town Hall was the first intimation of the sorrowful event, and very shortly afterwards the flags of the two Conservative and the Literary Clubs and the Free Library betokened the passing away of one who was a loyal and worthy citizen.

Although Mr. Pickop belonged to an old Tockholes family (his father was in his day lord of the manor of that district), he spent practically the whole of his life in Blackburn. It was in the year 1840 that his parents came to reside in Montague Street, and when their son had completed his scholastic duties, he was articled to Messrs. Robinson and Purfitt (now Messrs. Robinson and Sons), of King Street, thus entering the legal profession. Upon passing his final examination, Mr. Pickop commenced practice on his own account in Library Street, where he soon prospered, securing for himself a large private connection, and also winning his spurs as an advocate. Indeed, he early won for himself a high opinion in legal circles, and there is no doubt that had he remained in practice he would have attained a lofty position in his profession. But, fortune smiling upon him in another direction, he did not find it necessary to pursue his duties as a solicitor for any great length of time. Benefiting largely under the will of a Miss Hargreaves, of Mellor, he began to make land purchases, which, as years went by, greatly increased in value, until he became possessed of considerable wealth. He retired from practice about thirty years ago, and built himself a residence in East Park Road, where he has since resided.

He was placed on the Commission of the Peace for the Borough on October 28th 1875, and for a great number of years was to be seen occupying his seat on the Bench with unfailing regularity. In his capacity of magistrate Mr. Pickop displayed wonderful tact, ability, and astuteness, and was wont to be regarded especially in his latter years, as an ideal substitute for a stipendiary. The working classes, as well as other sections of the public, held this opinion, and doubtless he would have filled such a position with credit to himself and complete satisfaction to those who would have come under his ruling. He had, so to speak, the law at his finger ends, and often enough his decisions on intricate points were very timely, and their accuracy universally accepted. His whole attitude in the magisterial chair betokened his business-like habits and efficient acquaintance of the numerous matters calling for attention and his judgments were rarely called in question, either by litigants or the members of the legal profession. His generous nature was frequently brought into play when he sat on the Bench, as many a poor prisoner and defendant could testify were such testimony necessary. He was not slow, moreover, to put a stop to the "windy" statements of solicitors or witnesses where he found them detailing something irrelevant to the questions under trial, with the result that only the essential evidence was allowed to be given.

Not only was Mr. Pickop a successful solicitor and magistrate, but he also at one time occupied a conspicuous place in the government of the town. He first entered the Council on October 21st 1873 when he was returned as the Conservative representative for St., John's Ward in the place of the then Mayor, Mr. John Thompson, who had been promoted to the aldermanic bench. Twelve months later – on the 9th November 1874, to be precise – Mr. Pickop was also made an alderman, an office which he continued to hold until November 1880 when he was re-elected, but declined to again fill the position. His refusal necessitated the holding of a special meeting of the Council on the 24th of the same month to elect a successor. Whilst a member of the Local Council the deceased gentleman displayed considerable activity in municipal affairs, and as chairman of the Waterworks Committee wrought much good work. Mr. Pickop further attained to the dignity of mayor of the borough, being elected Chief Magistrate

on the 10th of November 1873, and holding the office for one year.

His appointment was hailed with general satisfaction, and he fulfilled the duties connected with the mayoralty with gratifying success. During his occupancy of the chair the present Free Library and Museum were opened, the ceremony being performed by Mr. Pickop himself. It was fitting that the honour should have devolved upon him, irrespective of his being mayor at the time, for it was through his generosity that the site of the institution was forthcoming. He bore an excellent reputation as a public speaker, and his speeches were always enjoyed by his hearers. Perhaps one of his most noted utterances was at the opening of the Free Library and Museum above referred to, when he spoke on literary topics in a highly interesting and intelligent manner. Upon leaving the Council Mr. Pickop practically went into retirement, for, excepting that he continued to sit on the Bench, he took little part in the management of local affairs. Though a staunch Conservative he never dabbled in politics and had little to do with the active forwarding of his party's cause. He was always ready with his purse, however, as more than one Tory club in the town has realised to its benefit in the years gone by.

At the time of his demise, Mr. Pickop was president of the Junior Conservative Club, and three years ago occupied a similar position at the Central Conservative, and took a great interest in both organisations. His sporting instincts led him to offer cups and like prizes for billiard and other handicaps, the competition for which always evoked considerable enthusiasm among the members, and, naturally, the winners always prized the "Pickop" trophies. Other clubs and sporting organisations of the town also elected him as their president or as one of their vice-presidents, and received the benefit of his generous offers of cups, etc., for competition. Included amongst the number was the Literary Club, of which he was president at the time of his demise, having occupied the position for many years. He displayed a keen interest in its affairs, frequently attending its meetings and lectures, and helping it forward in every possible way. He was also for many years chairman of the Infirmary Board of Management, in which capacity he proved a good friend to the institution, and for which he has ever had a warm corner in his heart. More than once, also, he was called upon to act as arbitrator in labour disputes, his noble character and fairmindedness being fully recognised by both employers and employed.

As we have already observed, Mr. Pickop was very fond of all forms of sport, but was especially devoted to bowls and shooting. He was a member of the Gentlemen's Subscription Bowling Club, Shear Brow, where he was frequently to be seen plying the woods, whilst at other times he could be discerned following his favourite pastime on the green of the East Lancashire Cricket and Bowling Club, of which he had long been an ardent member. He had also a fondness for music, which he oftentimes demonstrated by his pecuniary support of musical undertakings and sympathetic interest in all such ventures.

A loyal and devoted citizen, Mr. Pickop was also a

154

loyal Englishmen. He proved this in a very practical way during the late South African war. It will be remembered that when an appeal was made to the volunteers of the country to take up arms on behalf of England, the men of the 1st V.B.E.L. Regiment readily responded, Mr. Pickop came forward with an offer to defray the entire cost of equipping an active service company of the battalion, an offer which was gratefully accepted by Colonel Robinson, commanding the regiment. Besides equipping the company in a handsome and liberal manner he presented each man with pipes, tobacco, and other comforts, and displayed the greatest interest in the departure and home-coming of the men. When a second contingent was ordered Mr. Pickop repeated his offer, with the result that like their comrades, the second Active Service Company went to South Africa fully equipped, and possessed of those comforts which are so prized by the fighting Tommy. In their return he evinced no less interest than before and the volunteers of the 1st V.B.E.L. Regiment will long revere – as they have good occasion to – the name of John Pickop. He was the recipient of ringing cheers from every volunteer who returned from the front, for he was the admiration of them all. He was himself an old volunteer. He joined the 5th Lancashire Artillery Volunteer Corps (now the 3rd Lancashire Royal Garrison Artillery Volunteers) as a captain on the 12th May 1871 and resigned in March 1874. Mr. Pickop, whose purse was always open to all charitable institutions and undertakings, was a bachelor. His death means another great loss to Blackburn.

CHAPTER 10

MISCELLANY

TOCKHOLES-CUM-LIVESEY OR TOCKHOLES <u>AND</u> LIVESEY?

14th July 1668

Upon a full rehearing of the differences betwixt the inhabitants of Tockholes and the inhitants of Livesay concerneing the poor within the villages and townes aforsd wherein the inhitants of Tockholes alledge themselves to be a distinct town from Livesay and therefore ought to releeve their poor separately according to the late act of parliamt which the said inhitants of Livesay deny them to be a distinct town or village and alledge they ought to conjoyne with them in releef of their said poor and upon a full and long debate of the matter and upon hearing of several proofs on both sides this court doth unanimously declare their opinion that the sd townes or villages are two severall and distinct villages and the overseeing of the poor within the sd townes ought severally to releeve and maintaine their poor according to the sd late act of parliamt.

On adjudication at Preston Quarter Sessions 16th July 1668 that Livesey and Tockholes are two separate townships, the Court declared that they are "*....two severall and distinct villages and the overseers of the poor within the said townes ought severally to relieve and maintain their poor according to the said late act of Parliament.*"

'REMOVAL' NOTICE

In 1662 the Act of Settlement and Removal was introduced which restricted a person's movement to only within the boundaries of his/her Parish of birth or settlement. Various amendments were made over the next two centuries, but people were not expected to become a burden on the parish rates if they moved to a new area and if they did they could be forcibly removed. Overseers were appointed to deal with transgressors and 'Removal Notices' were issued to send people back to the Parishes of their Birth if they did not meet the criteria of the time. One such notice relates to a Mary Barker of Tockholes and is as follows:

"Middlesex: To the Constables of St. Lenard Shoreditch in the said County or any of them: And to all Constables Headboroughs and other Ma'ies. Officers whom this may Concerne

Fforasmuch as Mary Barker the wife of Richard Barker was this day taken wandering in the said parish of St. Leonard Shoreditch and for such her vagrancy hath bene punished according to law;

and whereas it appeareth unto me one of her Ma'ies Justices of the peace for the sd County of Midx. upon oath that about five years agoe her said husband Richard Barker came from out of the parish of Blackbone the County of Lancaster and there he was borne and always lives until within the said space of five years; and hath gained noe other place of legall settlement since, and that her said husband is gone away and left her and shee verily believes is now in the sd parish of Blackborne, these are thearfore in her Ma'ies name to require you on sight hearof to pass remove convey the sd Mary Barker from and out of the sd parish of St. Leonard Shorditch and through the sd County of Mid. and deliver her to one of the Constables of the Town of Barnet in the County of Hertford, the same beinge in the direct to the parish of Blackborne afforesd in the order to be conveyed according to the direction of a Lait act of parliment in the case made and provided and this is the warrant given under my hand and seal this 20th day of September Ano Domi. 1704 Anog, Regi Regine Anne Anglic Tertio:

Signed John Caborne & John Hawkins – Church Wardens, and Robert Ashworth, Constable."

REBELLION & 'SKREAMING' IN TOCKHOLES

At one time it was normal practice for the bishop, as the ecclesiastical authority, to send his representatives into each parish to deal with offenders against ecclesiastical law. Such offenders were 'presented' by the churchwardens. Records were kept in visitation call books, and some of these are kept at Chester. Amongst the usual complaints about adultery etc. there is a letter from John Hadwen, curate of Tockholes written in September 1765.

After polite preliminaries, he writes that he *'humbly presents the persons whose names are under written to be taught their duty (all other means proving ineffectual to reduce them to order and obedience) in time of divine service. When I admonish and endeavour to reduce them to order and uniformity, they give out that I have no business with the chapel or the government of it, also that (notwithstanding anything to the contrary) they will pursue their own resolutions.'*

Indignantly the curate continues that his clerk is a sober man, and has a promising group of scholars in his care, but *'when he gives out one psalm and appoints tunes, they (the offenders of the congregation) oppose everything he orders. He orders one tune and they boldly and obstinately take a contrary one, so that two* tunes are 'skreamed' at the same time, which creates a shameful dissonancy.'

Not only this but the miscreants have introduced a musical instrument during worship, 'I think they call it a bassoon.' Consequently the curate is forced to dismiss the congregation.

The trouble makers are named as William Ward, Peter Ward, Thomas Hogg, James Bainford, John Cuerden and Richard Cuerden. '*I desire thee to return their names amongst the other criminals of the visitation*' concludes the curate. Other church members are cited as witnesses - George Morris, John Rawstone and Bannister Pickop.

The outcome is added to the document in other writing. The culprits were seen and confessed, but denied introducing the bassoon. They were admonished and ordered not to take instruments into church, or to go to public houses on Sunday.

KILL FIELD

Preston Guardian 6th May 1905:

"... *During the campaign of 1643 Sir Thomas Fairfax, the distinguished parliamentarian general, despatched Sir John Seaton at the head of a considerable body of men against Preston. His route lay through Bolton, Tockholes and Blackburn and from "Cartridge Hill" which is supposed to take its name from the circumstance he is said to have stormed Hollinshead Hall .... (he entered Preston on 9th February 1643)*". The article also makes mention of one mill "*being rapidly raised to the ground*" but this would not relate to the cotton mills in the Village as they were not built until the 19th Century. However it does lend credence to the belief that a skirmish occurred in the field known as Kill Field, not far from Chapels Farm.

"The historian, *Baines*, records that various relics of a battle were disclosed in a field on Mr. Parker's farm in Tockholes. "*Forty horses' heads, bones, cannon-balls and clubs were, in 1826, dug out of a field in this township called 'Kill Field', in which a battle is believed to have taken place in 1642.*" *Abram*, writing in 1877, disputes both dates and upon making his own enquiries from local residents wrote "*I ascertained that it was in the year 1833 the remains mentioned by Baines were discovered. The pit in which they were found is situated at the upper end of a field that slopes towards the dingle below Crowtrees Farm. The spot is about a quarter of a mile to the West of Tockholes Church. According to the statements of elderly persons in the neighbourhood who saw the remains that were brought up in the cleansing of the pit, the exact number of skulls of horses found in the muddy bottom was 38 and there were also several horses' feet and leg-bones. One informant mentions that some large metal buttons were turned up. The bones were removed to the farmyard by the farmer and what became of any other relics is not remembered.*

The field in which the pit lies is marked "Pit Field" on the Ordnance map. At the time of the discovery there was a similar pit in another part of the same field, which, it was conjectured, might have been the

receptacle of other bones, but this pit was filled up without being cleaned out. There is no mention of any battle implements having been found with the bones, but several cannon-balls have been picked up in other parts of the township within the last 40 years. One of these ancient missiles was found in a field called "The Green" just above the Bethesda Chapel. Another was found on Cartridge Hill, a lofty fell a mile or so further to the south. Some musket bullets, also, were once gathered in a small field behind the Old Independent Chapel a short distance from the pit where the bones were found. These are all the traces of the fight in this vicinity of which information can now be gleaned*".

Abram goes on to speculate that any human casualties of the battle would have been removed from the field for burial in the Churchyard, but, as yet, no written evidence to this effect has been found in the Church records. Whilst excavating the foundations for the Old School Gilmour Robinson recorded that a cannon ball was discovered in the churchyard. This is thought to be the one which for many years was displayed on a pedestal in the Church. It was removed for safe keeping in 1964 during the demolition of the 1833 church, but has since disappeared. As well as the cannon balls found on The Green and Cartridge Hill, more recently one was discovered during the building of the house on the corner of Weasel Lane and that is now in Blackburn Museum.

Cannon Ball displayed in
Church for many years

OLD PARISH POUND OR PINFOLD

Pinfolds are now very rare and were once used to house stray cattle and sheep until the farmer claimed them and paid for their keep. Situated at the bottom of Old School Lane this ancient Pinfold was in danger of being lost because the roots of a sycamore tree had caused one of the four enclosing walls to collapse. In 1984 the Parish Council wanted to preserve the pinfold and approached the British Trust for Conservation to see if they could help save this piece of history. They sent along a young lady, Liz Davies, to teach one of our Villagers how to build a dry stone wall. That Villager, Mr. Jack Grimshaw, had been Parish Clerk for many years and he worked alongside Liz and completed the renovation. A small door into the pinfold was renewed and a plaque affixed noting the historic site. The O.S. Map of 1848 shows a ruin on this site and the present perimeter walls include some large stone blocks, probably from the ruin.

LINKS WITH BYGONE DAYS

Old Parish Pound and Memorial Chapel

PARISH POUND, TOCKHOLES.   Photo: J. O. Haslam.

Proteus: Nay; in that you are a'stray: 'twere best pound you.
Speed: Nay, sir; less than a pound shall serve me for carrying your letter.
Proteus: You mistake; I mean the pound, a pinfold.
(Shakespeare.)

Some time ago a notice appeared in the Press that the National Trust had acquired the village pound at West Wycombe, Bucks., and the comment was added that it was believed to be "the only remaining pound in the country." This notice initiated an interesting series of letters in one of the leading morning dailies, which revealed that there are still a number of these interesting relics of bygone days in existence, and a general wish was expressed that the National Trust should take them over.

There is at Tockholes, near Darwen, a perfectly-preserved specimen, as illustrated in the accompanying photograph. The enclosure is the property of the local Parish Council, and it is let to a nearby cottager, who uses it as a poultry run. When I was a member of the local rating authority I tried to find out something of the history of the old pound; but the oldest inhabitants were unable to recollect it having served the purpose for which it was originally founded. There are no documents relating to it, the Parish Council having a possessionary title only. The explanation of its being so well preserved is, no doubt, that the tenants have protected it from destruction at the hands of the thoughtless—as has happened to so many relics of olden times in towns and villages.

Situate at a point almost in the centre of the township, at the junction of four old roads, many must have been the scenes—angry, pathetic and humorous—when straying horses, cattle, sheep, etc., were impounded, or the property of debtors placed within the four walls until a settlement was reached. Maine, in "Early History of Institutions," states: "There is no more ancient institution in the country than the village pound. It is far older than the King's Bench and probably older than the Kingdom."

The entrance to the Tockholes pound is situated on a length of one of the oldest highways in this district—the ancient packhorse road, which dates back to Saxon times. The late Mr. John Cotterell, who was for many years a well-known second-hand bookseller in Blackburn, once informed me that he spent a considerable time in tracing this old roadway from the Rossendale district to Crowtrees Farm in Tockholes, where the track is lost. The road crossed the Darwen Valley from east to west and skirted Whitehall and the edge of Darwen Moor to Sunnyhurst, entering Tockholes at Dean-lane. The Darwen pinfold adjoined this road, as did many of the old manor houses, such as Whitehall, Holker House, Fine Peter's, Higher Hill and Lower Hill. The late Mr. James Cooper, who lived at Whitehall, Darwen, was an acknowledged authority on this old artery for trade of former days. Along this disused road—sunken several feet by the mere trampling of horses and men—now quiet enough, might have been seen strings of packhorses laden with goods journeying to and fro.

It would be interesting to know if there still remains any other parish pound in this part of Lancashire, which, with the village stocks, were agencies for parochial justice in the olden times.

The small building shown amongst the trees in the photograph is a mortuary chapel erected in 1900 by the late Mr. John Pickop, J.P., of Winston Hall, Blackburn, on the site of a former chapel. In 1803 some differences arose between the minister of the Old Independent Meeting House and a number of his congregation—representatives of some of the prominent families in the district, viz., the Cockers, Richardsons, Leighs, Brindles, Smiths and Nightingales (as the original Trust Deed shows)—who erected Bethesda Chapel and joined the Countess of Huntingdon's Connexion. The original structure was large and oblong in shape, as was then common for Nonconformist places of worship, and had three pulpits. The cause does not appear to have prospered, and in the year 1851, when the Rev. Robert Abram (father of the Blackburn historian) was minister at the Old Chapel, Bethesda had been closed for a number of years. Mr. Abram appears to have had a liking for it, and persuaded his flock to occasionally hold services there on a Sunday evening and at anniversary times, and use it as a Sunday School. It was as a school that it served a very useful purpose for many years. The late Dr. B. Nightingale started his Christian work there. The Sunday School was afterwards transferred to Silk Hall.

In the spacious graveyard the ancestors of many well-known families are interred, and when my father (the late Rev. D. Critchley) proposed to build a new Sunday School, two prominent gentlemen offered £100 each if he would build at Bethesda. But he refused owing to the inaccessability of the site, and persuaded the farmer members of his congregation to cart the stone and other materials from the old building to the new site on the highway. This they did gratis. Mr. Pickop, out of respect to his ancestors, afterwards defrayed the cost of the present mortuary chapel, and the "silent acre" is kept in a state of respectability by the Tockholes Chapel Trustees.   J. CRITCHLEY.

Blackburn Times 20 April 1935

158

Back to school to save bit of history

Villager learns dying art . . . .

A PIECE of history is being preserved in Tockholes thanks to the efforts of the Parish Council and a pretty 24-years-old girl who is teaching former Parish Council Clerk, Mr Jack Grimshaw, the dying art of dry stone walling.

Mr Grimshaw needs to know how to build a dry stone wall so that he can keep intact a 300-years-old pinfold near to his home in Victoria Terrace.

Pinfolds, once used to house stray cattle and sheep until the farmer claimed them and paid for their keep, are now very rare.

And Tockholes was in danger of losing its pinfold because the roots of a sycamore tree had caused one of the four enclosing walls to collapse.

"The wall fell down about two years ago," Mr Grimshaw explained this week. "The Parish Council wanted to preserve the pinfold and got in touch with the British Trust for Conservation to see if they could help."

Twenty-four-years old Liz Davies does voluntary work for the Trust and she came along to show Mr Grimshaw how to build the wall.

Mr Grimshaw, 69, said: "I'll not say I'm an expert at dry stone walling yet but I certainly know a lot more about it than I did a few days' ago before Liz came along."

Mr Grimshaw and the occupiers of the other cottages in Victoria Terrace have pledged to keep the Pinfold in good order.

He is going to show them how to build a dry stone wall so that the art will not die out in the village.

A small door in the pinfold has to be renewed and the enclosed land will eventually be lawned.

The Parish Council has bought a plaque for the pinfold so that people will know what it is.

● Left, Mr Grimshaw displays the plaque while Liz builds up the wall. (AR1278).

Darwen Advertiser 23 May 1984

159

1977. Cllr. Harry Whittle outside the
Old Village Institute just prior to demolition

VILLAGE INSTITUTE

The old Village Institute stood on the site of the present children's playground, near The Rock Inn. The first building, erected in 1935, was the gift of Mr. J. Woods, of Bog

1976 The Opening Ceremony at the Current Village Hall
Clifford Singleton (Town Hall); Janet Ward (Church Harvest Queen);
Cllr. Harry Whittle (Chairman P.C.); Judith Knowles (Chapel Rose Queen);
Mayor & Mayoress of Blackburn;
John Hebden (Chairman of the Village Hall Committee)

Height Road and had previously been a Methodist Chapel at Dolphinholme. This building was burnt to the ground in December 1937 and was subsequently replaced by a corrugated iron structure with an asbestos roof. The opening ceremony was performed by Mr. Richard Thistlethwaite in March 1938 and was followed by a concert. The building served as a Village Hall until 1975 when, because of its dilapidated condition, it was pulled down. It was also considered by many to be too small for use as a hall as the billiard table took up most of the room.

Prior to the demolition of the second Institute building, negotiations had been taking place between the Parish Council and the local Borough Council in an attempt to obtain funding for the erection of a new, purpose built village hall, but this was considered too expensive an undertaking and a compromise was eventually reached whereby the Borough Council would rent the old Sunday School on the top road from the United Reformed Church authorities and be responsible for its refurbishment and subsequent upkeep. This arrangement was gratefully accepted and has worked well ever since. The hall is still used by the United Reformed Church for their special occasions and also by various other organizations including the Parish Council and its off-shoot the Village Hall Committee which organises dances, concerts, parties and the Annual Village Gala.

The Borough Council also took over the site of the old Institute and now provides and maintains a Children's Playground.

Interior of Old Village Institute c. 1940. Vicar - Mr. Wm. Hodgkin

Seated L to R: Alice Turner; Bill Farran; Isabel Farran; Harry Whittle; Mary Whittle; Jack Grimshaw; Mildred Fleming; Mrs. Butterworth;
Ada Weir; Mrs. Jepson; Alice Kellett; Mrs. Burras;
2nd Row: Mrs. Wagg; Mrs. Jepson; Percy Green; Mrs. Hanson; Frances Kitchen; Mrs. Everin; Nellie Holden; Betsy Gibson; Alice Walmsley; Norman Walmsley;
Gladys Entwistle; ?; Mrs. Sharples; Mrs. Bob Parker; Mrs. Ainsworth; Bob Parker. On the stage: Mr. Aspden; Judith Jacklin; Mrs. Aspden; Hilda Cleary; Eileen Shannon; Mary
Allen (Mayoress); Carole Salthouse; Rendall Allen (Mayor); Edna Grimshaw; ?; Alban Coughlin; Mrs. Barling; ?; Albert Entwistle

CLUBS AND OTHER ORGANISATIONS

Over the years several Clubs and organisations have been formed in the Village. The **Women's Institute** was formed in 1955 and flourished for many years. Initially it met in the Village Institute then the Village Hall and eventually closed about 1980. This group was instrumental in starting the Nature Trail in Roddlesworth Woods which opened in 1974. Under the chairmanship of Mrs. Edna Grimshaw they organised working parties of local volunteers, supported by Darwen Scout groups and members of the Blackburn Naturalists Field Club, to clear and improve paths and build bridges. A booklet was produced showing the route and explaining the points of interest and describing the plant and wild life of the area. This was put on sale at The Royal Arms Hotel, from where the trail began. Since then the route has been greatly extended and further improved by the Water Authorities who have taken over the responsibility for its upkeep.

Edna Grimshaw on the Nature Trail

WI 21st Birthday Party. Marlene Jump with cake. Front Ladies left to right: Molly Smith; Elizabeth Navesey; Edna Grimshaw; Nellie Holden; Alice Cross; Gladys Entwistle; Joyce Bentley and Mildred Fleming

ALADDIN: Standing left to right: Molly Smith; Unknown; Amy Kennedy; Irene Mercer; Edna Grimshaw; Mildred Fleming; Annie ? Seated: Frances Crompton; Joan Porter; June Ward; Unknown

In 1880 the **Druids** were celebrating their 24th Anniversary with a dinner at the Victoria Hotel, presumably where they also held their meetings. This was a mutual benefit society (sick and burial society) founded in London in 1781.

On Saturday 30th January 1892 Lord Cranborne opened a new **Conservative Club** at Tockholes and delivered an address on political matters at a meeting presided over by the Rev. A. T. Corfield. The Conservative Club House was later divided into two dwellings and stands on the brow of Old School Lane.

In June 1910 Blackburn Times reported on the opening by Mr. F. G. Hindle, M.P. of a new **Liberal Club** in the Silk Hall premises which had not been in use for some years. The Rev. David Critchley was elected president of the club, Vice president - Mr. W. Richardson, treasurer - Mr. T. Whipp, Secretary - Mr. J. Edmondson, assistant secretary - Mr. David Critchley Jnr. and Librarian Mr. James Critchley. The hall had been well furnished and a library of books had been given by Mr. Ralph Yates, J.P. and Dr. Ballantyne J.P. The library was

opened for the benefit of all villagers. The Deacons and Committee of the Chapel had held a special meeting in April of that year to approve the use of the Silk Hall Meeting Room as a Liberal Club and had given their permission on condition that 2/6d per annum be paid for the privilege, the premises would not open on Sundays, there would be no gambling and that no intoxicating drinks be sold or used on the premises.

The Club Houses – January 2003

Rear View Silk Hall showing access to
Old Meeting Room and Liberal Club

In its heyday the Club had an excellent reputation for billiards and attracted players from outside the Village as well as many local men. Due to complaints in 1920 various new stipulations were imposed. The Club must close at 9.30 p.m. each weekday evening and 10 p.m. on Saturdays, and, due to the serious danger of fire, the use of matches in the building and smoking were prohibited. The ban on gambling had to be rigidly enforced and as from the 1st January 1920 the rent was raised to One Shilling per week for the use of the room. It was also requested "that the Club be maintained as orderly and quietly as possible in consideration for the Tenants who occupied the rooms below." But by September 1931 the use of the 'Clubroom' was raised by the Minister who reported that "the primary cause of his leaving was that the Manse was not fit to live in. The nuisance of noise to the tenant underneath the Clubroom had always been a source of trouble – even when the room was used as a Schoolroom". After close consideration of the matter and in view of the Manse again being empty, the Trustees, also mindful of their liabilities in case of damage to the property of any tenant underneath, resolved that the Liberal Club be given 6 months notice to vacate.

Tockholes Football Team - Late 1950's
Back Row L to R: Derek Crane; Jim Turner; Derek Smith; 2 Unknown
Front Row: David Mayoh; Stephen Corran; Frank Worthington;
Geoff Smith; Unknown

FOOTBALL, CRICKET & BOWLING: There have been at least two attempts at forming a local football team as shown by the photographs, and also a cricket team, but sadly no photograph has come to light showing the cricketers. However, the Cricket Club account book for the 1880's was deposited at Lancashire Records Office along with various other papers and documents relating to the Church and School. The Village has also had bowling teams and at one time possessed two bowling greens, one behind the Café, now the site of Inglenook, a house built in 1990 and the second on land at the side of the Rock Inn, now overgrown.

Tockholes Football Team 1929/30 - all unknown

WAR COMMITTEES

In 1938 the Parish Council began preparations for War. After an address by the Authorities at an open meeting, several volunteers enrolled in different sections of the Air Raid Precautions Committee such as First Aid; Repair of Roads; Decontamination and Fire Brigade. The first meeting of the A.R.P. decided a Census of the population of Tockholes be made and the results were Girls 39, Boys 41, Women 167, Men 161, and 4 under 12 months old. By October 1942 a 'Salvage Committee' was also appointed, made up of representatives from the various areas of the Village and in November the same year a Ministry of Information film was shown in connection with the National Salvage Scheme. After the film show the main topic of conversation was the withdrawal of the Tockholes Sunday Bus Service and a deputation was appointed to meet with representatives of the Corporation's Transport Committee. The Parish Council records do not contain any minutes regarding the work carried out by the A.R.P. or indeed, any mention of the War at all, other than the suggestion of a party to welcome home the returning soldiers in 1946.

Mr Robert Leach – Home Guard

A Home Guard was also created and its "headquarters" were in a wooden hut on the site of the bungalow next to Golden Soney Farm. The Rev. J. Noel Smith, in his article written for the Chapel's Ter-Centenary booklet in 1962, described his brief time spent in Tockholes from September 1940 and mentioned his 'twice weekly stints with the Home Guard in a hut near the School for all-night watch, *(perhaps he meant the Sunday School, now the Village Hall)* but the only events were watching the raids on Manchester, except that one afternoon a lone German plane came over and dropped bombs on Darwen."

W.R.V.S. The Women's Royal Voluntary Service was formed in 1938 to help with the war effort, but the date of the formation of the Tockholes branch is unknown. Nationally work began by helping with the preparation for civilian care - assisting with evacuation, emergency feeding and clothing etc. By 1939 the organisation became known as the W.V.S. for Civil Defence and membership was drawn from groups who could not join the forces or do essential war work i.e. the elderly, the young and the housebound. Thrift became an absolute necessity and economy drives were started when jam jars, paper, string and food, among other things, were hoarded. Socks and other comforts were knitted from old sweaters etc. for the troops and others in need. In 1940 as refugees began to pour into the country the WVS were called on to provide not only clothing but food and the first mobile canteen was built to cater for the thousands of refugees placed at Alexandra Palace in London. In many cities rest centres were set up to cope with those made homeless after bombing raids, staffed by W.V.S. members, and incident inquiry points were also set up to give information about the dead and injured. Members also assisted with non-nursing duties in hospitals, jobs in libraries, general welfare work, schools and nurseries, foster homes, escort duties and many other necessary war time tasks involving the Red Cross, St. John Ambulance Brigade and many other organisations. Just how involved the Tockholes team became is not recorded, but it is understood the village knitting needles never stopped.

Tockholes A.R.P. 1939-1945
Frederick Counsel; Arthur Mickle; Hilda Kenyon; Mrs Dawson; Frederick Baron;
Victor Catterall; Mr. Baron (Lived at The Royal)
Front Row: Harold Smith; ?;?;?; 'Andy' Shuttleworth

Tockholes Women's Royal Voluntary Service - 1940. Photographed on Leach's Lawn (The Bowling Green).
Back L to R: Mrs Cooper (Post Mistress); Gladys Entwistle (nee Catterall); Elsie Berry (nee Fletcher);
Mary Whitle (nee Rossall). Middle Row: Mrs Mayoh?; Mrs Ada Leach; Miss Bessie Edwards (Café/Village Shop);
Alice Shuttleworth; Mrs Leach. Front Row: Isabel Farran (nee Rossall); Margaret Worthington (nee Rossall)

SCOUTS, CUBS, GUIDES & BROWNIES, YOUTH CLUBS AND PLAYGROUP

Over the years several Scout & Guide Troops, and Cubs & Brownie Groups flourished but, sadly, none of these organisations remains today. In the 1950's a very active and well supported Church Youth Club thrived and its activities included indoor and outdoor games, competitions between members in sports from football to draughts, regular speakers, and fund raising events such as Jumble Sales and Beetle Drives. During the meetings refreshments were served by the girls and the boys took it in turns to wash up and fetch the water! Day trips to places such as Blackpool and Morecambe were all part of the fun and all activities were reported in the monthly Church magazine. A further group was formed in the 1980's, but again, no longer exists.

The Playgroup was formed in 1972 by a group of young mothers in the Village as a way of bringing together pre-school age children. Various fund raising efforts were held to obtain money for equipment and toys and the mothers themselves supervised the group under the umbrella of the Pre-School Play Group Association. Originally, meetings were held in the top room at Silk Hall Farm twice per week, then for a short while at the Vicarage, but eventually they moved to the Village Hall as numbers increased. Once nursery school education was introduced in the late 1990's numbers fell to such an extent the organisation was disbanded.

1948-49 Tockholes Congregational Girl Guides 10th Darwen
Back Row: L to R Kitty Harrison; ?; Kathleen Jepson; Joyce Bainbridge; Ada Parkinson?; Beryl Miller; Mary Edwards; Barbara Tomlinson; Kathleen Burke; ?; Marion Edwards; Middle Row: First four unknown; Joyce Croft; Bessie Edwards; Lily Turner; four unknown; Mary Smith; Front Row: First six unknown; Louie Entwistle; Anne Smith; ?

Church Parade Remembrance Sunday November 1978
Vicar: Robin Foster. Cllr Harry Whittle (with wreath)
Scout Leader: John Cookson (in beret)
Guide Leader (centre back) Mrs. Elaine Watson

Play School Christmas 1993
Leader Alice Cookson standing next to Santa

PARISH COUNCIL

The Parish Council was formed under the Rules laid down by the Local Government Act 1894 and held its inaugural meeting in December 1894 in the Silk Hall Lecture Room. Present at the Meeting was Rev. Ashley T. Corfield, Clerk in Holy Orders; Rev. David Critchley, Independent Minister, Horsfield Horsfield, Farmer, Caleb Kennelly, Gentleman and William Martin, Mill Manager. The Chairman of the Meeting was William J. Gregory who became the Clerk at the first meeting proper. Also present was Mr. John Whipp who was nominated as District Councillor. Rev. Corfield was elected Chairman, Rev. Critchley, Vice Chairman and Caleb Kennelly, Treasurer. At the second meeting the Clerk's Salary was fixed at £1 per annum and the rest of the meeting set the scene for countless meetings in the future concerning the state of the roads with a view to getting the District Council to take them over.

The Parish Council consists of five elected members and a Clerk. Its powers are very limited and today it is mainly used by the Local Authority as a 'sounding board' for obtaining local opinion and to make representations to the authorities on behalf of local people

In its early days it had a much greater say in the events of the area and originally administered the 'Township of Tockholes'. Although it was still ultimately answerable to the District Council and Poor Law Union it was responsible for the raising and collection of the rates and dealing with the administration of the poor rate. It appointed both an Overseer and Assistant Overseer and Collector of Rates. These positions were of great importance and responsibility. In June 1899 the Assistant Overseer, who was also the Clerk to the Council, received the following rate of pay:

For Collecting and keeping Account of Poor Rate	£18 p.a.
For Collecting and Keeping Account of Sanitary Rate	£3 p.a.
Services as Clerk to the Council	£2 p.a.

Horsfield Horsfield was the Overseer and had overall responsibility for the collection of the Rates which were then paid over to the Poor Law Union and District Council. The serious nature of this position is highlighted in the Annual Meeting held 5th March 1902 when Horsfield was told by the Clerk to the Poor Law Union that the Parish should sue for non-payment of rates because if the correct amount was not paid over to the Union and the District council *he would have to fetch some of Mr. Horsfield's cows*

As previously mentioned, the inaugural meeting was held in the Lecture Room at Silk Hall, but by March 1897 the Minutes were recording that meetings were being held in Tockholes School in Rock Lane. Meetings moved to the Congregational School (now the Village Hall) in April 1924 where they have remained every since. Many of the responsibilities of the Parish Council were stripped from the Parish in 1925 when the Rating and Valuation Bill was introduced. This removed the collection of rates to the Local Authority and abolished the Poor Law Union areas and assessment committees. The Parish Council petitioned against the introduction of the new law, but in vain.

The majority of matters dealt with by the Parish Council have related to the repair of roads and footpaths, often by approaching the land owners requesting that they make good any defects; dealing with numerous attempts to close footpaths – not always successfully; the installation of electricity; sewerage matters; the installation of piped water (dealt with in more detail next); bus services and postal and telephone services. The Council has also organised many of the national Celebrations held to commemorate such events as the Peace celebrations in 1919 and Coronations and various Royal Jubilees.

The first celebration they were called upon to organise was for the Coronation of Edward VII. This was completed with the assistance of two delegates from St. Stephen's School and two from the Independent's School. A procession was formed near the Rock Inn at 2 pm headed by the Darwen Borough Brass Band. After the band came the Parish Councillors, followed by the Day and Sunday School scholars under the age of 14 years, females over 14 years and lastly males over 14 years. They proceeded along the highway to Fine Peters Farm and, en route, massed at Top O'th Low where the National Anthem was sung. They returned to two fields off Rock Lane, kindly lent by Mrs. Ellen Brindle, of The Rock Inn, and Mr. H. Horsfield, Farmer, who owned the adjoining field, where the Rev. A.T. Corfield addressed the inhabitants and expressed sympathy with the Queen on the serious illness of the King, and hoped for a speedy recovery, exhorting the people to be loyal subjects of the King and worthy citizens of this great empire.

Three cheers were afterwards given for the King and then three cheers for the Queen. Three cheers were also given for John Pickop Esq., who had generously given the medals distributed to all the school children of Tockholes. And finally three cheers were given for the Rev. A. T. Corfield (and his wife), Vicar of Tockholes and chairman of the Parish Council.

Pies, buns and coffee were served to all, and the remainder of the day was spent in an enjoyable manner. Races were indulged in by old and young alike, whilst the Darwen Band entertained.

The following provisions were bought for the occasion:- 550 pies @ 2d each, 550 buns at 1d each, 8lbs of coffee and 30 lbs of lump sugar from Blakey Moor Cooperative Society, Blackburn. Mr. Whipp & Mr. Horsfield supplied 40 quarts of milk, and 200 suitable pots were also purchased which were used on the field and afterwards given to each child under 14 years of age.

The headmaster, Mr. Tillotson, was given the task of hiring the Band and he and Councillor Kennelly were also asked to buy bats and balls etc, the sum not to exceed £1. 10s. 0d, to be used for entertainment on the field. Several marshalls were also appointed to ensure safety along the route of the procession and the Councillors and Schools delegates managed the affairs in the field, including overseeing the sports and games. The whole of the expenses were defrayed out of Parish Council funds:

C. Bullock – Coronation Pots	1	18	3
F. Frazer – bats, balls etc	1	10	0
Blakey Moor Co-op. Soc. provisions	8	4	6
Darwen Borough Band - band for coronation	3	10	0
Grimshaw – 1 qt methylated spirit		1	0
TOTAL	£15	3	9

The event was recorded in the Council Minutes as being *"most satisfactory and one of the best days ever enjoyed by the inhabitants of Tockholes"*.

The Coronation of George V was celebrated with a Gala on Saturday 24th June 1911. This time the 2nd Volunteer Battalion East Lancashire Regiment Band from Ramsbottom was engaged to lead the procession and to play in the field afterwards, but unfortunately the day was a very wet one, with heavy rain falling from early morning, making the field Gala entirely out of the question. The intended procession was to have been from Top O'th' Low to Back O'th Low and then to return along the main road to Tithebarn and back to the field, but because of the weather the Band played from Top O'th Low to the School and all the provisions were moved into the School. Once again the fare was of meat pies, buns & coffee. Races were run in the school and the school yard and the older people enjoyed themselves by dancing. During the week preceding the 24th, gill mugs were distributed to the homes of the inhabitants for all under 16 years of age, and beaker pots for all inhabitants over 16. The mugs and beakers bore beautiful coloured portraits of the King and Queen, and on the back *"Tockholes Parish Council, Coronation June 22nd 1911"*.

Expenses were as follows:

Reg't Band	5	10	0
Blackburn Ind. Co-op Society – Provisions	10	0	10
R. Crossley - Balls, Kites, skipping ropes	1	0	0
Moses Catterall - Posting bills		3	0
A. Crook & W. Whalley - assisting to deliver pots		6	4
Hy. Hunt - Pony & Trap (for delivery of pots)		7	0
John Forbes - Badges for M.C's		1	2
Hy. Hunt - Pony & Trap - 21st July		2	3
Grimshaw Park Co-op Society - Coronation Pots	6	7	0
John Crompton - refreshments for band		6	3
Total Expenses for the Occasion	£24	3	10

On the afternoon of Friday the 3rd May 1935 a tea party was held for the children of St. Stephen's School, Tockholes, to celebrate the Silver Jubilee of King George V. The children were entertained to a cup of tea and a cake by the Vicar, Mr. Hodgkins and members of the Parish Council, and later each child was presented with a memento - girls a Jubilee Brooch and boys a Jubilee Medal.

The main celebration for the Silver Jubilee was held the following Monday, 6th May, again on Rock Lane Field. The Vicar and Chairman of the Council, Mr T. H. Harrison, opened the proceedings with the singing of the National Anthem and the Congregational Minister, Mr. Dawson, then offered a prayer. After further suitable remarks were made regarding the occasion, sports, games and races took place. Once again the food offered was similar to that of the two previously mentioned celebrations.

Expenses:

J. Wardley & Son-printing of Badges for Sports Committee		6	3
Nevilles - Prizes for gala		4 6	0
2 Gross Cups - H. Walton	1	1	0
J. Hartley 500 pies & 500 Buns	6	16	9
Mrs. Cooper (Village Store) 3/4 lb Tea, 4 lbs Lump Sugar, 20 lbs Sugar, 8 lbs Coffee	1	1	11
Fred Baron Brewing Coffee 7/6d, Salt 2d, Milk 5/-		12	8
H. Crompton Brewing Coffee 7/6d, Milk 3/-		10	6
Gift of 1/- to all Old age pensioners 17/- spent at Coopers, 6/- spent at Café	1	3	0
TOTAL	£15	18	1

Gala for the Coronation of George VI 12th May 1937

Preparations began in February 1937 with a call for £18 to fund the celebrations and suggestions that the event be run along the lines of that of the Jubilee two years earlier. In case of bad weather, contingency plans were made to use both the St. Stephen's School and the Congregational School and invitations were to be issued to all members of both Church & Chapel, regardless of whether they lived in the Village or not. Orders for the refreshments were placed, this time with Hartley's Café, for 500 pies & 500 buns, also Coffee etc. Six male members each from the Church and the Chapel were recruited to help with the festivities and four ladies were asked to help with the younger children. The event was held in Rock Meadow and duly opened with speeches and prayers by the Vicar, Rev. Hodgkin, and the Congregational Minister, Rev. A. E. Dawson. The weather on the day was rather cold, but nevertheless a large crowd assembled to enjoy the sports, games and entertainment. The races held catered for every age starting with children up to 4, followed by girls 5-6, boys 5-6; girls 7-9, boys 7-9 etc. up to 16-20. Then came the turn of the adults – Ladies over 20, Men over 20, Ladies over 60 and Men over 60! Games included Tug of War for men, Tug of War for women; Balloon Blowing for Ladies; 3-legged races; novelty races such as women blowing up a balloon whilst running and men threading a needle during a race; sack races; hoop races where the hoop had to be knocked with a pencil; egg & spoon races; skipping rope races and potato & string races. Ward's of Darwen were allowed on the field to sell ice-cream and the Village shops and the Village Institute had stalls.

Expenses:

	£	s	d
J. Heatley (Sweets etc)	1	3	0
J. J .S. Cooper (15 Vouchers – gifts to all Villagers over 70)	1	2	6
Rev. A. E. Dawson - Printing		5	0
J. Hartley - Refreshments	7	18	5
H. Crompton - Brewing Coffee		7	6
F. Baron - Brewing Coffee		7	6
T. H. Harrison-Flags, tickets, string, spoons & clearing field		12	9
J. Harrison - Bunting & Milk		17	0
H. Boyes - Entertainer		15	0
TOTAL	£12	18	8

Expenses paid out before the event were H. Stott – £2. 15. 9d for Caps and Prizes; Nevilles – £3. 12. 2d. For Prizes; and Wm. Harrison 18/- for badges, making the final total £20. 4. 7d.

Sadly, the preparations for the Coronation of our present Queen were not fully recorded in the Parish Council Minutes. It was resolved that a separate Coronation Committee be formed embracing all organisations in the Parish and that the produce of a Penny Rate be earmarked for the festivities. A payment of £7 was eventually made to the Coronation Committee by the Parish Council, but undoubtedly the event would have cost much more.

Similarly, the Queen's Silver Jubilee in 1977 was also a Village event organised by the joint efforts of all Village organisations. It was celebrated in the Field above the bungalow in Long Lane on a much smaller scale than the previous royal celebrations, but nevertheless was a very enjoyable day. Each school child received a Silver Jubilee medal and the stalls were organised by each organisation to supplement their own funds. Races and games took place for both children and adults. This event is now regarded as the forerunner to the present annual Gala.

Children's Sack Race - Cumbria, Long Lane 1977 Silver Jubilee

Presentation of Prizes Silver Jubilee 1977. Catherine Cank, John Hebden, (Chairman); Jack Grimshaw (Parish Clerk) Cllr. Harry Whittle

Men's Sack Race Silver Jubilee 1977. First: John Hebden; Second: Alban Coughlin (Chairman & Vice-Chairman Village Hall Committee

Start of the First Fell Race to Darwen Tower - Gala 1978

Start of the Pram Race - Gala 1978

Fun and Games at one of the early Galas

Pram Race 'Babies' - 1978 Gala
Left to Right: Billy Rhodes, John Turner, John Smith

Water and Sewage Disposal

Well within living memory is the arrival of piped water to the Village. Prior to that everyone obtained their water from one of the many wells in the area, and it has become legend that the water acquired from the well behind what was the Café made the best cup of tea ever.

Outside closets were the norm until the late 1960's and a Parish Council Minute for November 1948 reports a visit by the Sanitary Inspector who gave information to the Council regarding *"the system and times of the emptying and disposing of the Pail closets of the Parish"*. This practice was referred to as 'scavenging'. Many of these out-buildings can still be seen around the Village, now used as coal sheds or garden sheds. The "Gentlemen's" toilet in the churchyard is still in a good state of repair and even has a two-hole wooden seat! The "Ladies", built to the West of the Church building had to be demolished in the 1980's as the site on which it stood became very unsafe, the land gradually collapsing into the stream below.

There have been several 'scares' over the years and the occasional outbreak of typhoid due to unsanitary conditions. In November 1881 a "Government Inquiry as to the Duty of Providing Sewerage" was held in the Free Library, Darwen, to investigate a complaint made to the Local Government Board by the Corporation of Darwen, that the Sanitary Authority of the Rural Sanitary District of the Blackburn Union had made default in providing the township of Tockholes with sufficient sewers. Present at the Inquiry were a Local Government Officer from London, and for the Borough the Town Clerk, the Mayor, the Borough Engineer and several Aldermen and Councillors. Representing the Union were two guardians, the Clerk of the Union, the Medical Officer of Health to the Rural Sanitary Authority and the Surveyor & Valuer to the Union. The complaint arose from the fact that, due to discharge of effluent from about 20 houses in the Ryal area into a feeder stream leading to the Dean Reservoirs, a serious outbreak of typhoid fever had been caused to the townspeople of Darwen in the Autumn of 1874 and because of this the owners of the properties had been pressurised to correct the situation, which they agreed to pay for if the Council would carry out the work.

This work was duly completed at a cost of £37.16s. 8d., but some five years later, when Liverpool Corporation discovered that the sewers had been diverted away from Darwen and into their watershed, they demanded the situation be reversed and on receiving no satisfaction they took it upon themselves to cut the connection of that branch sewer and so put the problem back to where it had been five years previously. Darwen Corporation then built a stone sough which drained into a tank to deal with the collection of sewerage, but this was only as a temporary measure until the proper local authority did what was necessary. The Corporation called upon the Sanitary Authority for Tockholes to make sufficient sewers for the district and because they could not come to an agreement as to whose legal responsibility it was to provide such sewers, and because of the alarm caused by another outbreak of typhoid, this time at a house in Tockholes, the eventual outcome was the Government Inquiry. A full report of the Inquiry appeared in *The Blackburn Standard*, but did not report what conclusion was reached or the outcome.

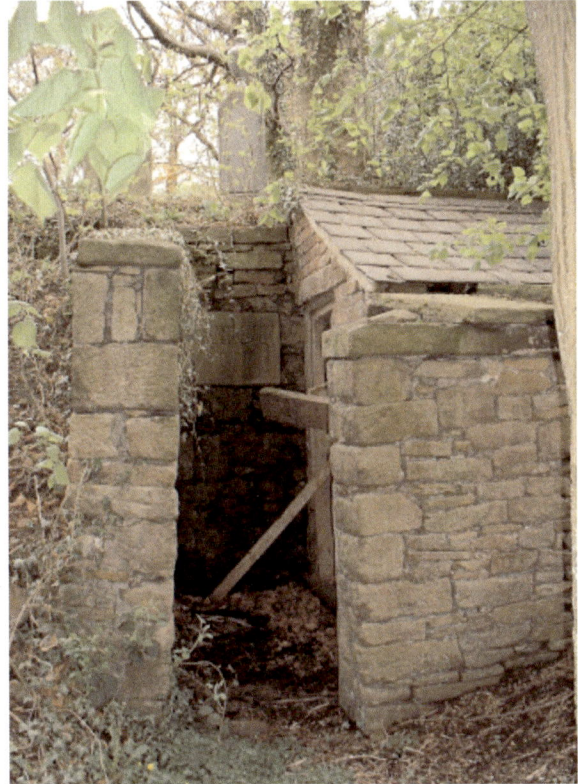

The old 'Gents' in the Churchyard

Parish Council minutes reveal the continued attempts to get piped water to the Village, especially in 1955 after receiving a complaint from a Villager that he and his wife had been very ill presumed to be through drinking contaminated water. By March 1958 the Blackburn R.D.C. had proposed a scheme for the provision of a piped supply of well water, using stand pipes at various points in the Village. This was not considered ambitious enough and that only a supply of Town Water taken directly into the homes of the Ratepayers would satisfy the Community as a whole. The R.D.C declined to go ahead with this suggestion and said nothing could be done until the new Water Authority had been formed.

By November 1960 the Fylde Water Board had been formed and so once again the Parish Council started their pursuit of a piped water supply. In the Summer of 1961 Fylde supplied an estimate to the Blackburn R.D.C., who would be required to act as guarantors for the project, and subsequently Blackburn R.D.C. sub-mitted the estimate to the Parish Council for its approval. The scheme was to cost approximately £22,000 and would serve 176 properties. The offer was accepted, but had still not been installed by March 1964. The next Minute regarding water is dated January 1966 where someone was complaining about the lack of water pressure and the inconvenience caused by lack of notification when the water was to be turned off. The last residents to acquire piped water were the residents of Lower Hill who did not receive their supply until 1968.

The next battle was to obtain a mains sewerage system and correspondence began almost immediately after the first water pipes were laid. This took several more years to achieve but by the early 1970's most of the Village properties were connected to the mains.

In the reservoirs—387,000,000 gallons. For the parish school—three gallons. 'Fantastic,' thinks the vicar

INTO the village of Tockholes today drove a school meals van from Darwen bringing the usual dinners for the children of St. Stephen's Church of England School—and three gallons of fresh water.

This has happened every school day since Blackburn Rural Council's Health department decided a month ago that the school's normal water supply—a well in an adjoining field—was polluted.

In the opinion of many people in Tockholes, this is the last straw. For in this village, which has within its boundaries three reservoirs, containing 387,000,000 gallons of water, there is no piped water supply.

"We know that Liverpool Corporation, which owns the reservoirs, is in no way responsible, not being the water authority for this area, but it is none the less a fantastic situation," says the vicar of St. Stephen's, the Rev. A. K. Bis brown.

Open gully

"Our school has always had to depend for its water on a well fed by a drainage pipe from Winter Hill. At one point the water passes through an open gully in farmland and it is not surprising that it has become polluted.

"When the pollution was reported, we were asked by the education authorities at Darwen to do something about it. But what can we do? We cannot purify the water because we have no control over it until it reaches the well. Our only hope is Blackburn Rural Council."

When, at Saturday's meeting of the Council, the subject was raised by the Tockholes representative, Mr John Cross, it was by no means for the first time.

"This subject is a hardy annual," said the chairman, Mr Harold Ryden. And Mr

THE LAST STRAW, SAYS TOCKHOLES

The school's normal water supply—a well now declared to be polluted. It still supplies water for washing-up and cleaning.

Cross agrees, but adds: "As far as I am concerned, it will continue to be a hardy annual until something is done.

No piped supply

"We are the only parish in the Council's area with no piped supply. As ratepayers, we are paying for a supply which we do not get. We want a full investigation into the possibilities of bringing water

here and into the cost of the undertaking. When we know what obstacles are in the way, we will see what can be done about removing them.

"The Council has agreed to receive a deputation from the village and we are hoping that this will be the first step towards ending what we feel is a very genuine grievance."

In the meantime the school will continue to receive its daily supply from Darwen.

Says the headmistress, Miss M. V. Simcock: "We keep it just for drinking purposes. I have never heard of anyone dying from drinking the well water, but we always took the precaution of boiling it before allowing it to be drunk in the school. We still use it for washing up and cleaning."

Northern Daily Telegraph 26 Nov. 1953

And here's the supply for St. Stephen's C.E. School— three gallons from Darwen

170

THE REV. BENJAMIN NIGHTINGALE

Author of *"Two Centuries and a Half of Nonconformity in Tockholes"* – a book which tells us more about our Village than any other. Nightingale was born in Tockholes in 7th January 1854 and was the son of Benjamin and Agnes {nee Brindle} Nightingale, whose family had been connected with the Congregational Chapel at Tockholes for several generations. He attended the Nottingham Institute and after two years he was sent on to the Lancashire Independent College. On completing a course of training there, he settled at Tomfield Congregational Church, Oldham in 1879 with his wife Anne, the daughter of Mr. William Sumner, who was also a representative of an old Tockholes family. Four years later he moved to Farnworth where he spent the next five years and then to Preston in 1888 where he worked very actively in Congregational work and the town's affairs. He became secretary to the local auxiliary of the London Missionary Society and also secretary of the Congregational Church Aid Society. He was secretary of the Nonconformist Council and afterwards the Free Church Council and was also President of the Congregational Council and the local Sunday School Union. He was also a member of the Harris Orphanage Council.

As well as the history of Tockholes, Nightingale wrote the history of Walker Street Sunday School, Preston, to commemorate its Jubilee Celebrations, but his chief work was the "History of Lancashire Nonconformity" the research of which took up most of his leisure time for several years. He was partly encouraged to take up writing by Mr. W.A. Abram, editor of the "Blackburn Times" and author of "A History of Blackburn Town & Parish" and whose father had been Minister at Tockholes Congregational Chapel from 1849-52. The following extract is taken from the Preston Guardian of the 18th February 1928.

AUTOBIOGRAPHICAL PAPERS BY LATE DR. NIGHTINGALE

BIRTH AND EARLY LIFE

I was born on January 7th 1854 in the little village of Tockholes, which lies some three miles from Blackburn on the old Bolton and Blackburn road. I am a little uncertain about the house. We lived for some time at Lower Hill, in a simple cottage with a somewhat tall chimney, which was once seriously damaged by lightening and from this place we removed to Silk Hall Fold, the top house near the main road, and I have always understood that this was the place of my birth.

My father's name was Benjamin, and the Nightingale family to which he belonged in all probability came from about Rivington near the middle of the 18th century. He was one of a numerous family, his father being William Nightingale, who was brought up at Lyons Den, a wild and desolate place on Darwen Moor looking down the Tockholes valley. He died after much suffering on January 26th 1865, at the early age of 45, when I was just 11 years old. My mother's name was Agnes Brindle, daughter of John and Agnes Brindle who lived at Lower Wenshead. The Brindles, like the Nightingales, were an old Tockholes family and very numerous about Darwen and Blackburn in later years, as well as Tockholes. My mother died in April 1881, and was interred in the graveyard of Tockholes Congregational Church. She made no profession of religion, but she was a good woman and most devoted to her children. Unless something absolutely prevented, she was never absent from the services on Sunday afternoon.

My early life was exceedingly simple and primitive, for in those days the village was very far removed from the town and weeks and months might pass without a fresh face appearing in it. Darwen and Blackburn Fairs were red-letter days in the year, when occasionally one had the privilege of going and, with a sixpence in one's pocket, one felt rich beyond compare and able to buy nearly all in the fair.

THE DAY SCHOOL

The day school that I attended was as primitive as all else. It was a simple structure at the back of the Bethesda Chapel, in a somewhat dilapidated condition, which was said to have been the manse when that place had its own minister. There were two rooms below, the one behind being unflagged, as was the case with many cottages, and called "The Shop," because there the handloom weaving was done.

The teacher was Thomas Nightingale, who was one of the great men of the village, being a deacon and choirmaster of the church, and, indeed, general leader of the place, who invariably conducted the week-night service when there was no minister and frequently occupied the pulpit. The three R's only were taught there, and those only in the very elementary stage.

Quite a number of "half-timers" came from Hollinshead Mill, then belonging to the Shorrocks' of Darwen, and in the village it needed little education to mark out a boy or girl as remarkably clever. The people would say with astonishment, "He con read th' Bable an' t' newspapper.' After a time the school was given up, and, being then a half-timer at the mill, for a short time I attended the one belonging to St. Stephen's Church, whose teacher was Mr. George Slater, who lived in Blackburn during his retirement.

I have a very vivid memory of the Cotton Famine in 1862, though I was only eight years old. Lancashire was never more hardly hit and the suffering of the people was very great. Many, indeed, who had moved in spheres of comparative comfort, were utterly reduced, and some carried to the grave burdens of debt then contracted. Tockholes, which was largely dependent upon its two mills, suffered as did many other places, and soup kitchens and food stores were opened. The vicar, the Rev. C. Hughes B.A., and the Congregational minister, Rev. Richard Crookall, worked heartily together in the endeavour to relieve the distress of the people.

THE COTTON FAMINE

Young as I was, I well remember spending days in travelling with my elder brother, William, in search of work to no purpose, and the rejoicing was great when the famine ended and the people again got to work. It was thought at one time, with a view to finding employment for the people, that an attempt would be made to level the Morris Brow, which has always been a serious difficulty for vehicular traffic between Blackburn and Tockholes, but the idea was abandoned as much too costly for the authorities to face.

There were several curious characters in the village, one of whom went by the name of "Owd Kester o'th cloise." He was of great age and was a Waterloo veteran. He was accustomed to go round the village selling small articles, and very few dared to refuse to buy. He was regarded by the people as the centre of much mystery, as he told strange stories of his doings when he was in the army.

When I was quite young, not more than 10 years of age, I began to go to the mill. There were two cotton mills in Tockholes. One, which went by the name of "Redmayne's Mill", was built about 1838 by the Redmayne brothers who had connections in both Blackburn and Preston. This subsequently passed into the hands of Henry Ward, of Blackburn, and in my young days it was at its best. The other was built by Eccles Shorrock of Darwen, in 1858, being known as "Hollinshead Mill." It was here that my elder brother and I worked, and in those days working hours were much longer than they now are, and the conditions much less favourable. This mill later passed into the hands of Messrs. George and Ephraim Hindle, of Blackburn. Both buildings have now disappeared, but in those days some two or three hundred people were employed in them, and they were a great boon to the village.

HANDLOOM WEAVING

About this time also there was a considerable amount of handloom weaving in the place, the looms being in that part of the house which has already been referred to as "the shop", and often far into the night and even into the early morning the candlelights might be seen twinkling in the windows, the weavers being anxious to finish their pieces so that they could take them on the Saturday to Blackburn to those who employed them. Not infrequently the weavers kept time with the shuttle by singing some well-known hymn, and it is said that a certain Darwen minister, who late in life gave himself to handloom weaving, used to sing "Oh what heavenly work this is, hands, feet and arms singing praise to the Lord."

Shut in within themselves and having so little contact with the larger world outside, it is no wonder that superstition lingered long in these villages, and Tockholes was no exception to this. Linked with almost every house of any age was some ghost story which was seriously believed by the people. There was at least one family also that had the highest veneration and reverence for the cricket. It was known that there was a considerable colony in the house, for the chirpings could be heard in the road some distance away.

Along with some of my school fellows, I had been most anxious to get a sight of this mysterious creature, as to whose strange powers many stories were in circulation. One day therefore, we went to the house and preferred our request. We were informed that we might see the crickets on solemnly promising not to injure one of them, the person adding that for some years ill-luck had attended the family in the way of sickness and death because some time ago one of the crickets had been killed.

The promise was, of course, given, and we were admitted to the house. The hearthstone was carefully lifted, and under it must have been hundreds of them, which were as carefully protected as if they had been so many guardian angels. Doubtless this was an exceptional case, for I cannot recall any other at all corresponding to it.

Nearly all the people were on the same social level, farmers and artisans, simple in their habits and plain of speech, which almost without exception was the Lancashire dialect.

I was always fond of reading, but in those days books were expensive, and for a country lad money was not plentiful, consequently my library was very small. My favourites however, were Robinson Crusoe, Captain Cook and Robert the Bruce. My heroes indeed were Bruce and Wallace, and it may not sound very patriotic when I say that I rejoiced exceedingly when I read of the defeat of the English at Bannockburn by my great hero. Bunyan's "Pilgrims' Progress" was my daily companion. I read it over and over again, told the story to my companions as we went together to our daily work, and often wished it had been literally true instead of allegorical, so that I might take a similar journey. So my young life went on happily in the little place which was not much longer to be my home.

AND FINALLY...

LAST MINUTE FINDS

United Utilities, Warrington, hold the title deeds to much of the land in the southern half of the Village and the following items are extracts from four such deeds.

Description of property known as Whitbank Estate taken from a deed dated 19th October 1875.

ALL THAT messuage farm or tenement with all and every the land and hereditaments and appurtenances thereunto belonging situate lying and being in Tockholes in the Parish of Blackburn in the said County of Lancaster containing the several closes closures fields and parcels of land hereinafter particularly mentioned that is to say the Great Whitbank with the stag lying to the lower end thereof The Croft lying on the back side of the lower barn commonly called The Barn Croft and two fields lying between the said Croft and the River the Intack the two Worthington Crofts the Roughs or Mosses commonly called the Pitts The Great Green Hill the Little Green Hill and The Moss lying to the north side of the Great Green Hill or by what other name or names soever the closes fields pastures or parcels of land meadow or pasture or any of them now are or heretofore

have been called or known or which said messuages lands and premises comprise a farm called Whitbank and were formerly said to contain by estimation 27 acres 3 roods and 1 perch of land or ground after the sale of 7 yards to the pole or perch or thereabouts but by a recent admeasurement have been found to contain 48 acres 2 roods and 24 perches in statute measure or thereabouts be the same more or less and are now in the occupation of James Smith as tenant thereof **AND ALSO** all and every the tithes and tenths of corn and hay oblations obventions privy tithes and all other tithes whatsoever coming growing or arising in from or out of the said messuage farm or tenement lands and hereditaments hereinbefore described and in from or out of a proportionate part of all common and waste grounds to the said messuage farm or tenement land and hereditaments to appendant appurtenant or belonging (save and except the Easter offerings and the surplice fees due and payable to the Vicar of Blackburn aforesaid or his curate or curates for the time being or the curates or ministers officiating at the several Chapels within the said parish or any of them for the time being) together with all houses outhouses edifices buildings yards gardens common trees fences hedges ditches ways water courses liberties privileges easements and appurtenances whatsoever to the said hereditaments and premises belonging or in anywise appertaining or usually held or occupied therewith or reputed to belong or be appurtenant thereto.

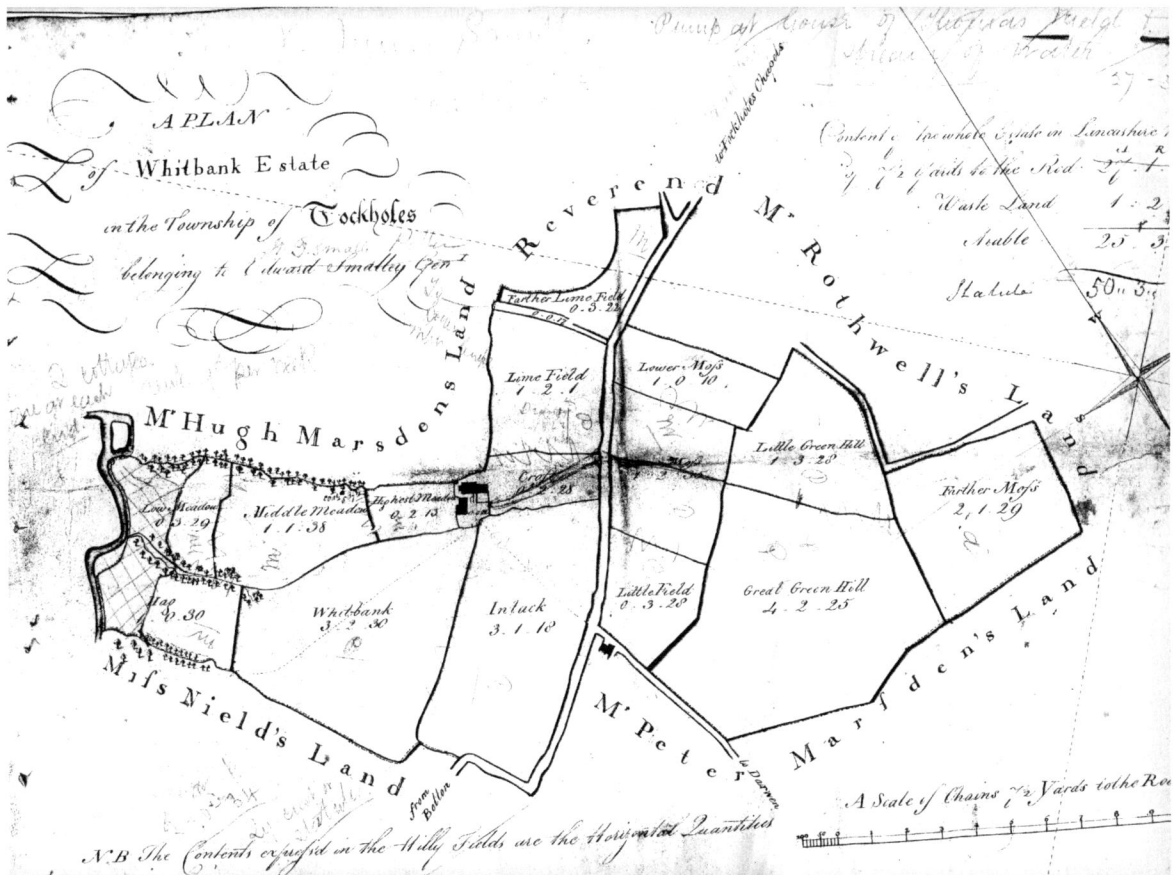

Last Proviso of John Walsh's Will dated 30th December 1891. John Walsh was the owner of the Whitbank Estate referred to above:

I lastly declare it to be my wish and desire that I may be interred at Christ Church near Colne and I hereby empower my Trustees to expend the sum of £500 in purchasing a Vault and erecting a memorial at a sub place and I desire the same and my Vault in the burial ground of the old Congregational Chapel at Tockholes and my grave in the Darwen Cemetery shall always be kept in good and proper state of repair and I hereby empower my Trustees during the minority of any person beneficially interested under the trusts of this my Will to retain out the income arising from my residuary trust funds or such parts thereof as shall for the time being be held by my Trustees upon the trusts aforesaid or any of them at a yearly sum not exceeding £7 which shall be applied to them in keeping the said Vault and grave in good repair.

* * * * * * * * * * * * *

Schedule dated 30th August 1883 attached to a Lease between Alexander Eccles Esq and Messrs. E & G. Hindle – Lease of a piece of freehold land, Mill machinery etc. situate in Darwen in the County of Lancaster i.e. Ryal Mill

Tape Room – Two Tape Sizing Machines complete with Kenyons pans attached also cylinder covers, sucking boxes for size box, fans, pipes etc. for carry away the steam. Two iron beam slings four iron beam clips four solid iron rods and 3 pipe rods for pressing beams · 13 sheeting rods for tapes · 3 striking combs for tapes · 1 three dasher size beck with pump · overflow valve and attached · 1 two dasher (1 dasher broken) size beck with pump · overflow valve and attached quantity of iron steam pipes and copper size pipes · fixed 64 weavers beams and flanges · 2 iron stands for extra beam · 3 twist guides 2 dozen spare change and other wheels

Size Mixing Place - 1 two dasher clay beck on landing stage · 1 six dasher steeping beck with pump and attached · 1 four dasher mixing beck with pump and etc. attached · 1 single purchase crab with snatch block · long rope and buckling chain · 5 old wooden looming frames · 1 large wooden water cistern fixed on the principals · 1 old beck over mixing beck · 2 step ladders

Winding Room – 4 Singletons "patent warping mills" with front and back expanding combs V shaped creel · hair pins and creel pegs complete · 51 warpers beams and flanges · 3 iron beam racks for flanges · 38 weavers beams and flanges · 1–300 spindle winding machine, very old, with cop boards brushes and spring cop skewers complete · 1–300 spindle winding machine nearly new with cop boards brushes and spring cop skewers complete · 2 wooden looming frames · 1 long sweeping brush · 1 pan clamps for cleaning shafting · 1 hook for heals

Weaving Shed - 318 steam powered looms complete in every way with one beam and pair of flanges to each also 2 loom weights · long check strap · short and long buffer straps · 2 buffers · 2 peckers · heald roller straps and spring straps to each loom · 506 extra loom weights besides allowing two to each loom · 4 tacklers benches and cupboards · 3 tacklers vices

Warehouse - 1 cloth plaiting machine by Hacking & Co nearly new · 1 power driven cloth press · 1 very long cloth counter · 2 small cloth tables

Boiler House – 1 set of firemans rods · 1 box key · 3 screw keys · Smiths hearth and bellows · upright drill with speed pulleys complete · 1 back geared lathe and bed complete · 1 face plate for ditto · 18½ " diameter 1 hand vice with 6" jaws 24 drills various sizes · 1 plank · 1 slake tub · 1 pair steps and 8 risers · 1 ladder with 11 staves · 15 screw keys various sizes for engines · 2 sledge hammers · 1 hand hammer · 8 box keys for engines · quantity of lifting rings and clamps with one large pair of gallopers for engines · 6 large spare bolts for engines

* * * * * * * * * * * * *

INDENTURE 1st May 1861 – between JOHN ECCLES of Leyland in the County of Lancaster Esq. RICHARD ECCLES of Lower Darwen in the said County Spinner and EDWARD ECCLES late of the same place but now of Liverpool Gentleman of the first part and ECCLES SHORROCK of Over Darwen of the second part and THOMAS JEPSON of Over Darwen in the said County Contractor of the third part

WHEREBY Thomas Jepson bought a plot of land on which to build some houses at **Hollinshead Terrace** together with 6 cottages which he had already built and to pay to the Eccles' and their heirs the annual sum or yearly rent charge due on 1st May and 1st November in every year the sum of £2.17.8d the first half yearly payment due on 1st May 1861

The yearly letting value thereafter was to be £6 per year for each house

Thomas Jepson was also responsible for paving with good smooth flags the pavements and also for creating and keeping in good repair the new intended street

* * * * * * * * * * * * *

The newspaper article "**A Quaint Tockholes Relic**" printed in Chapter 3 refers to music having played an important part in the religious life of the district and that in the Chapel graveyard, chiselled on the monument of a former local musician, was a hymn tune which he had composed. Fortunately the monument still exists and is in good condition and is shown in the photographs.

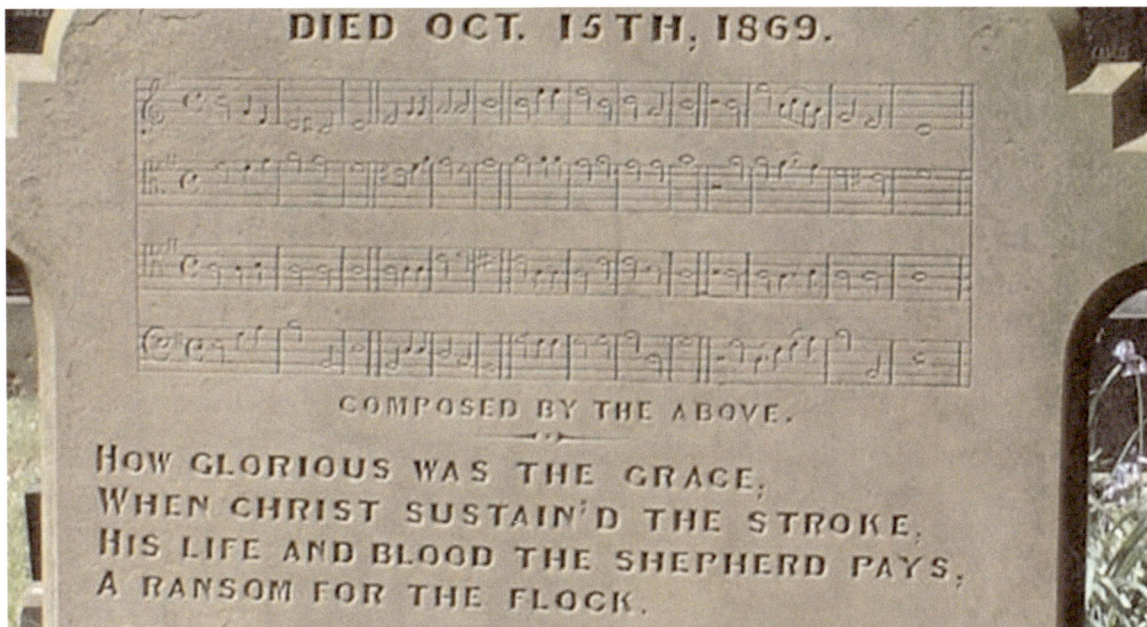

Entertainment country-style! Circa. 1980 outside the Victoria Inn.

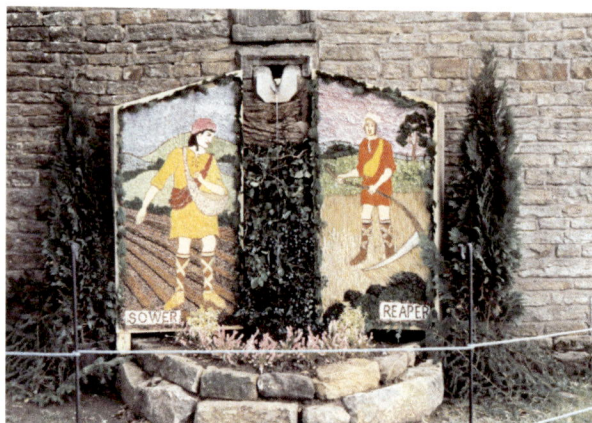

'The Sower and The Reaper'

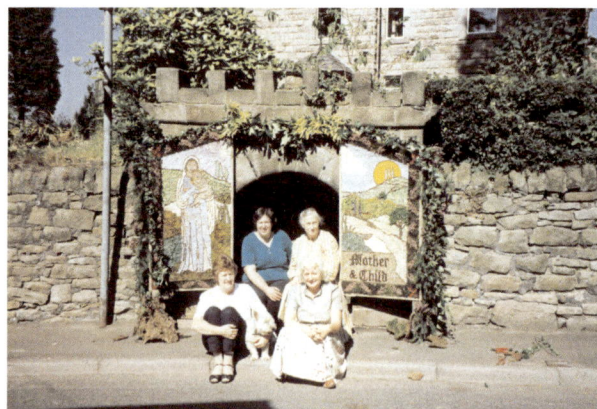

Well in Rock Lane. Back L to R: Anne Smith & Mrs. Sleightholme.
Front L to R: Judith Jacklin & Lyn Robinson

Well dressing was introduced to the Village in 1980 as the culmination to the excavation and renovation work which had been carried out at the Hollinshead Hall site. The "Sower and the Reaper" was the first panel produced and the Rev. W. Nuttall conducted a service of blessing of the waters on completion of the project .

The pictures were produced by preparing clay beds within wooden frames, then outlining the design with small pieces of twig and filling each section with flower petals, leaves and various other vegetation, thereby creating a colourful tableau. The preparation time was two weeks and involved many villagers who helped with 'puddling' the clay, marking out the design, collecting materials, and pressing individual petals and leaves into the clay. The finished panels were then erected around the well and blessed during the Harvest Festival Service. Because of inaccessibility to the Hollinshead site all the following ceremonies were held at the Well in Rock Lane. The last one was in 2000.

Top Road c. 1940

Lower Hill c. 1920

Dean Reservoir c. 1935
(Kiln Bank Farm top right and Dean Lane centre)

178

BIBLIOGRAPHY

Two Centuries and a Half of Nonconformity in Tockholes.
B. Nightingale
Published byJohn Heywood, Deansgage & Ridgefield, Manchester 1886

A History of Blackburn Town and Parish.
W. A. Abram
First Edition 1877. Limited Second Edition Reprint by T.H.C.L. Books, Blackburn,
1990

Darwen & Its People.
J. G. Shaw
First Edition published by J. and G. Toulmin, Printers, "The Times" Office,
Blackburn. 1889. Limited second Edition Reprint T.H.C.L. Books, Blackburn 1991

Riot! The Story of the East Lancashire Loom-Breakers in 1826
by Wm. Turner
Published by Lancashire County Books 1992.

Handloom Weavers Cottages in Central Lancashire
by J. G. Timmins
Centre for North-West Regional Studies, University of Lancaster. Occasional Paper
No.3 1977. Printed by W.S. Maney & Sons Ltd. Leeds.

The Wishing Well – A Story of the Withnell Moorlands
by A Moorland Lad. George Robinson. 1948

A Tockholes Child in the First World War.
Margaret Tapley
Printed and published by Nelson Brothers Printers Limited, Chorley (undated)

Darwen's Old School Tie
by Miss Annie Proctor. Published by Miss A. Proctor, 16 Belgrave Road, Darwen.
Printed by Wardleys of Darwen, Lancashire. (Undated, but thought to be c. 1970)

News reports
from – Darwen News, Blackburn Mail, Blackburn Gazette, Blackburn Alfred,
Blackburn Standard, Blackburn Times, Lancashire Evening Telegraph

Information from Blackburn and Darwen Libraries

Hollinshead Mill information and Maps courtesy United Utilities, Warrington.

Permission from Ordnance Survey for re-production of parts of their maps.

NOTES